IF RAIN DOESN'T COME

PUBLICATIONS OF THE SYDNEY ASSOCIATION FOR STUDIES IN SOCIETY AND CULTURE

No. 1 *Words and Worlds. Studies in the Social Role of Verbal Culture*, ed. Stephen Knight and S. N. Mukherjee, 1983.

No. 2 *Feudalism: Comparative Studies*, ed. Edmund Leach, S. N. Mukherjee and J. O. Ward, 1985.

No. 3 *Semiotics, Ideology, Language*, ed. Terry Threadgold, E.A. Groze, Gunther Kress and M. A. K. Halliday, 1986.

No. 4 *The Cultural Construction of Race*, ed. Marie de Lepervanche and Gillian Bottomley, 1988.

No. 5 *Revolution as History*, ed. S. N. Mukherjee and J.O. Ward, 1989.

No. 6 *Words and Wordsmiths, a volume for H.L. Rogers*, ed. Geraldine Barnes, John Gunn, Sonya Jensen and Lee Jobling, 1989.

No. 7 *Disasters: Image and Context*, ed. Peter Hinton, 1992.

No. 8 *Social Visions*, by Michael Wilding, 1993.

No. 9 *Theatre and Cultural Interaction*, by Maria Shevtsova, 1993.

No. 10 *The Epic Circle*, by Zdenko Zlatar, 1993.

No. 11 *The Epic in History*, ed. Lola Sharon Davidson, S. N. Mukherjee, Z. Zlatar, 1995.

No. 12 *Religious Change, Conversion and Culture*, ed. Lynette Olson.

No. 13 *Citizen Historian: Explorations in Historiography*, S. N. Mukherjee, 1996

IF RAIN DOESN'T COME

An Anthropological Study of Drought and Human Ecology in Western Rajasthan

R.J. FISHER

SYDNEY STUDIES

MANOHAR
1997

If Rain Doesn't Come: An Anthropological Study of Drought and Human Ecology in Western Rajasthan

Sydney Studies in Society and Culture 14

Published by
The Sydney Association for Studies in Society and Culture
PO Box 575, Leichhardt
NSW 2040 Australia
and
Monohar Publishers & Distributors
2/6 Ansari Road, Daryaganj
New Delhi 110 002

ISSN 0812-6402
ISBN 81-7304-184-9

Printed in India by
Replika Press Pvt. Ltd.
Plot No. A 229, DSIDC Narela Indl. Park
Delhi 110 040

Agar barish nahin ayegi to main kya karun?

('If rain does not come, then what am I to do?')

PANCHA RAM NAYAK
Hingãniya, September 1985

Contents

LIST OF TABLES

LIST OF FIGURES

Preface

This book is a revised version of my PhD thesis submitted to the Department of Anthropology at the University of Sydney in 1988. It deals with the human ecology of western Rajasthan, emphasising the strategies by which people adapt to the ever-present threat of drought. The focus is on the village of Hinganiya (and, to a lesser extent, on three nearby villages). The strategies adopted in these villages differ somewhat from each other and from the strategies adopted elsewhere in the region. Indeed, it is a major theme of this book that adaptive strategies are individual responses to specific conditions existing at a particular place at a particular point of time. However, the local processes occur in the context of social and economic forces which are, to some extent, common to the wider region, and the insights gained from the case study throw light on the processes occurring more widely in western Rajasthan and even, perhaps, outside the region. I believe that the value of ethnographic research is that it generates insights (rather than laws), which assist in understanding social phenomena.

In recent years, while again living in Australia, I have been struck by some parallels between the effects of drought on Australian farmers and the situation in Rajasthan during my fieldwork. The drought of the first half of the 1990s has had devastating effects in Australia. Unlike drought in Rajasthan, drought in Australia does not directly threaten human life. But there are similarities in other respects. Drought in both regions is both unpredictable and frequent. While it is uncertain when it will occur, it is certain that it will occur. Farmers and pastoralists, whether Rajasthani or Australian, must cope with both the certainty and the uncertainty.

My fieldwork began in 1983, continuing into early 1984. I spent a further six months in the field in 1985 and 1986 and made a brief visit in 1987. The thesis was revised and a manuscript for this book was prepared in 1990 and 1991. Due largely to institutional changes within the University of Sydney, the publication has been delayed since that time. Although I have incorporated relevant literature published since 1987 and added an Afterword which describes the situation during a further brief visit to Rajasthan in 1994, the book deals almost exclusively with data collected during my PhD fieldwork.

Preface

Researching for and writing my thesis (and, more recently, this book) lead to deep obligations to many people who assisted in one way or another.

My first obligation is to the villagers who fed me, entertained me and endured my endless questions. I am especially grateful to Prem Singh Bhati, who was my friend, informant and sometimes research assistant, and to Udai Singh Bhati and his family, who were courteous and generous hosts in Hinganiya. The people from Hinganiya, Kur, Kukunda and Khokhariya, who helped and befriended me are too many to mention, but my gratitude is profound.

Kailash Rakhecha accompanied me on several field trips and responded to many requests for information after I left India. The late Professor S.K. Lal, Head of the Department of Sociology at the University of Jodhpur, welcomed me professionally and was always helpful. I also wish to thank the following for continuing advice and assistance: Anirudh Krishna, Nahar Singh Jasol, Ganpat Singh Rakhecha and Birendra Singh Tanwar. Rajendra Mehta, J.P. Trivedi, Brigadier and Mrs N.S. Surrey and John and Jan Wilson and their families gave friendship and support to myself and my family in Jodhpur and Delhi. Dr L.P. Bharara of the Central Arid Zone Research Institute in Jodhpur was extremely supportive during my 1994 visit.

Professor Michael Allen, my thesis supervisor, encouraged my work from the beginning and, without his enthusiasm and constructive criticism, it is not likely that the thesis would ever have been completed.

Roger Sandall had the unrewarding job of acting as my supervisor when I was in the field at a time when my project was troubled by problems with research visas and permits. Chris Gregory (Department of Anthropology and Prehistory, Australian National University) visited me in the field and I learned a great deal from him. He provided timely and useful comments on a draft of the thesis and recommended changes as I revised it for this book.

For useful comments and discussion at various stages in the processes of researching and thesis writing I wish to thank Doug Miles, Paul Alexander, Philip Carl Salzman, Max Harcourt, N.S. Jodha, Neil Maclean, Dundi Mitchell, Ana Marko, Kim Paul, Gaye Macdonald, Vivienne Kondos and the late Ed Roper.

My colleagues at the Nepal Australia Forestry Project in Kathmandu (where I worked from 1987 to 1989) provided encouragement and assistance as I worked on thesis drafts. I am particularly grateful to Don and Helen Gilmour for encouraging me to get on with it and for giving me a place to work in Kathmandu. Don also made very useful comments. I would also like to thank Archana Thapa, Andrew Ingles, R.B. Maharjan,

Gary King, Yam Malla, Bill Jackson, Sabita Thapalia and Samasti Bhattachan for help in a variety of ways.

Thanks are due to Professor S.N. Mukerjee, who encouraged the transformation of the thesis into a book and Robyn Wood who applied her skills and artistry to prepare the final copy.

I am grateful to the Carlyle Greenwell Bequest (Department of Anthropology, University of Sydney) for grants to support my fieldwork and to the Commonwealth Department of Education for a Commonwealth Postgraduate Award. The School of Agriculture and Rural Development at the University of Western Sydney, Hawkesbury granted study leave and provided funds which enabled me to visit Rajasthan in 1994.

Finally, but not least, I would like to thank my sons, Luke and Michael, for their sense of adventure and my wife Wil, for the open and generous spirit with which she approached our time in India and for her encouragement, support and patience during all the writing.

Note on Transcription of Non-English Words

In this book all words from Indian languages are italicised except names of people, places and castes or words commonly used as English loan words. All Indian words used are either from the Marwari dialect of Rajasthani or words from other Indian languages used in Rajasthani. For this reason I have not separately indicated origin.

The external boundaries of India depicted in this map are neither correct nor authentic.

Map 1

India, indicating location of Rajasthan

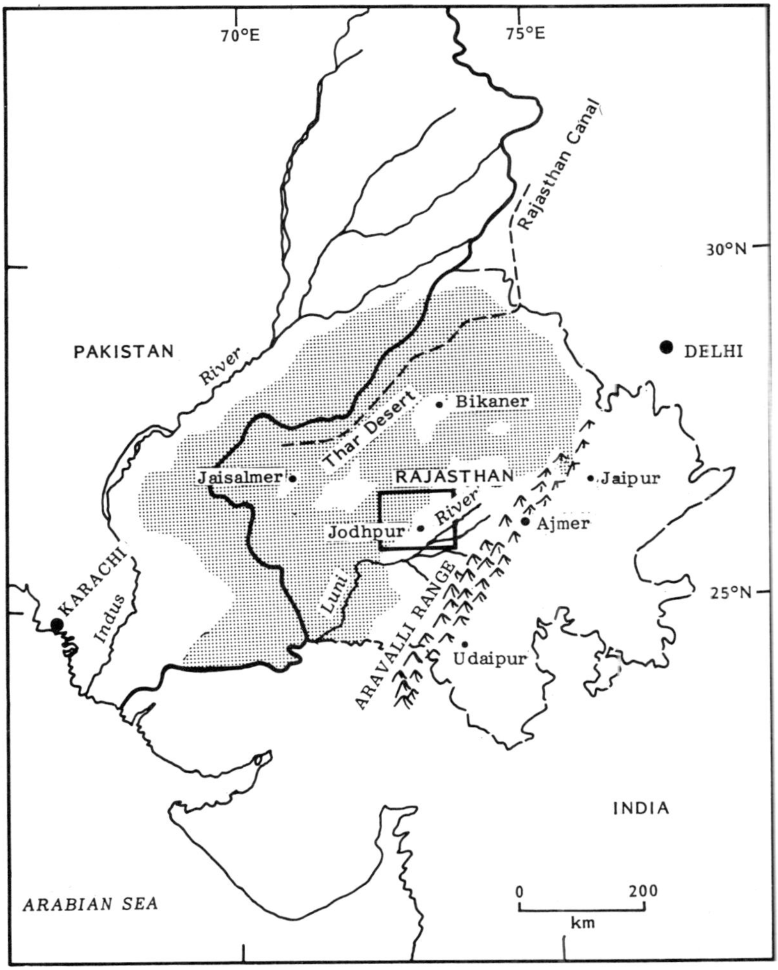

The external boundaries of India depicted in this map are neither correct nor authentic.

Map 2

Rajasthan and adjacent regions, indicating main geographical features. Insert (see Map 3) shows location of Jodhpur District.

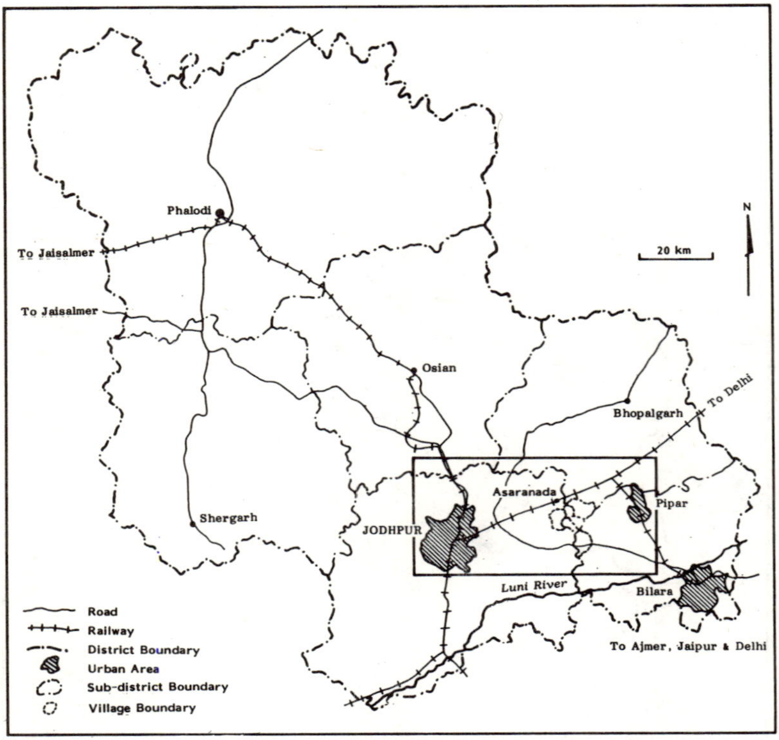

The external boundaries of India depicted in this map are neither correct nor authentic.

Map 3

Jodhpur District, with insert showing location of field site (see Map 4). Based on district map in Census of India 1981a.

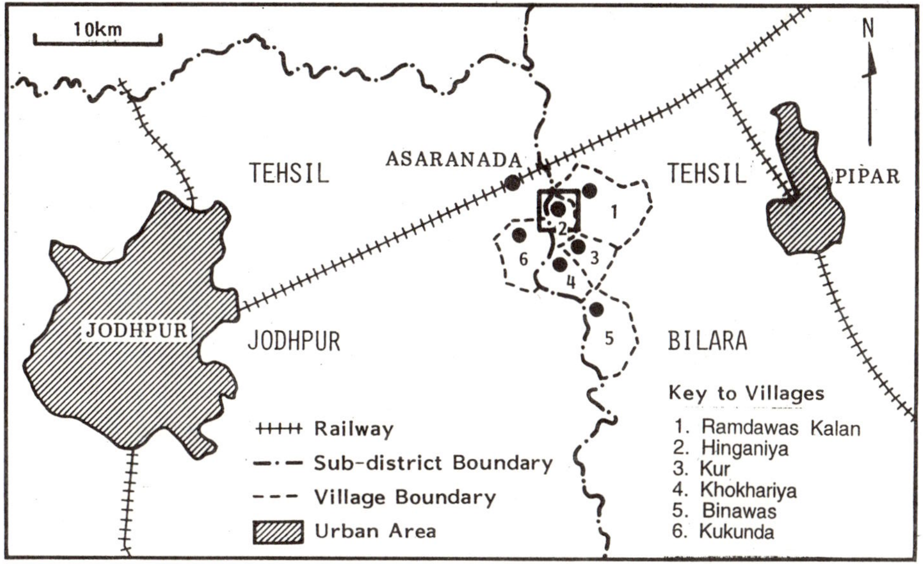

The external boundaries of India depicted in this map are neither correct nor authentic.

Map 4

Locations of villages studied in relation to Jodhpur and adjoining villages.

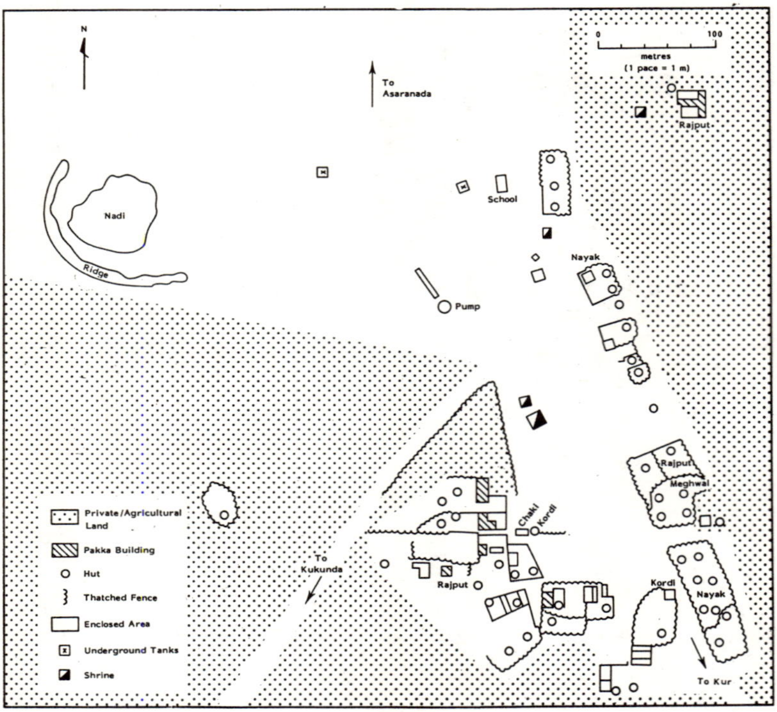

The external boundaries of India depicted in this map are neither correct nor authentic.

Map 5

Sketch map of village core area *(abadi)* of Hinganiya

Chapter 1
Introduction

The environment of western Rajasthan is shaped by predominant aridity, which is broken by moderate and irregular monsoonal rainfall. One assessment of the occurrence and perception of drought by farmers is that in every decade there are '. . . from six to nine severe drought years, from one to three good years, and hardly one average or "normal" year' (Bharara 1982:352). The problem is that no one knows in advance which will be a good year or which will be a bad year.

This study looks at some of the ways in which people survive and organise their economic activities and social lives in circumstances of great uncertainty about subsistence. The examination focuses on a particular agrarian system (or, more accurately, an agro-pastoral system) in a cluster of villages in western Rajasthan.

The focus represents a shift away from my original plan. The reasons for the shift are instructive. In January 1983 I went to Rajasthan to study migratory herdsmen, and, in particular, to look at the relationships between desertification, pastoral land use, market factors and economic strategies. A number of factors led me to change my focus The primary problem was that I was unable to obtain permission from the Government of India to carry out my intended study. There were, apparently, a number of reasons for this, but the main one was that most 'nomads' are found, most of the time, in the politically and administratively sensitive Pakistan Border area. It is a fact, usually denied by officials, that some unauthorised border crossing by herdsmen occurs. Research in such a sensitive area, and by a foreigner at that, was apparently out of the question. In addition 'nomads' are always a sensitive administrative issue, in India and elsewhere.

Even if permission had been granted to carry out the study originally planned, there were practical and logistical problems. Before the good monsoon rains of 1983 western Rajasthan had been subject to a drought for several years. As a result of this most of the livestock, and many of the people dependent on livestock, had migrated. There did not appear to be a clear focus of study. By the time the drought had ended and the migrant herds and herdsmen had returned I had already decided on a new direction. This involved a shift away from livestock herding nomads to an essentially sedentary agro-pastoral village.

Although there are nomads in western Rajasthan, and although livestock are of great importance to the economy, agriculture is also important. For the most part, the economy can be described as agro-pastoral. In an area where environmental conditions are harsh and rainfall is uncertain, a study of the ramifications of such an economy seemed immensely challenging.

I stayed in Rajasthan through the period following the drought-breaking 1983 monsoon into January 1984. When I returned in August 1985 the monsoon had failed. I was impressed by the dramatic contrast between the buoyant mood of the 1983 post-monsoon period and the sense of resignation evident in the 1985 post-monsoon period.

Thus, the focus of this study evolved out of a combination of bureaucratic and climatic circumstances. It was also influenced by essentially fortuitous factors. In particular, I had already established good contacts in Hinganiya, a village near Jodhpur, during an earlier survey visit. I had found Hinganiya congenial, and, when I visited it in March 1983 (during the drought) it seemed essentially pastoral - a factor which remained important, even after nomadism was abandoned as a topic. The importance of agriculture in Hinganiya impressed itself on me only after I commenced my fieldwork during the successful agricultural season which followed the 1983 monsoon.

While a number of unanticipated factors influenced village selection and, ultimately, the focus of study, there is a sense in which a focus on drought, its consequences and its social context, was inevitable. My theoretical interests have always been primarily centred around ecological anthropology. Given this interest and the timing of my stay in Rajasthan to coincide with a drought and subsequently with a drought-breaking post -monsoon agricultural season, I could hardly have failed to focus on drought and famine.

I will now turn to a discussion of previous research and to a more specific discussion of the theoretical issues which this study addresses.

Perspectives on Drought and Famine

Major themes of this study are the extent to which drought leads to starvation and famine, the reasons why it may do so in some cases, but not in others, and the ways in which people deal with the risk or actual occurrence of famine. Rajasthan, as recently as the end of the nineteenth and beginning of the twentieth centuries, has experienced catastrophic famines. Yet, while drought continues to be a frequent occurrence, famine no longer causes massive loss of life. Chronic malnutrition, however, continues to be the lot of much of the population, much of the time.

In this century a great deal has been written about the causes of famine. Roughly, two broad and opposing views have emerged. In one school of thought, famine is seen as the outcome of the failure of crops due to natural disasters (usually drought, but sometimes flood or crop disease) or sometimes due to *abnormal* socio-political events (such as war). Famine is seen simply as the result of a shortage of available food against demand. An implied corollary of this view is that the balance between food production and population is precarious. For proponents of the opposing view, famine is the outcome of unequal distribution within the *normal* socio-political structure. From this perspective, famine may occur when natural fluctuations in climate occur, but when things get tough the poor are the first to suffer. It is also possible for famine to occur in the absence of food shortage (Amartya Sen 1982).

With reference to India there has been a long and often acrimonious debate[1] between adherents to each of these schools of thought. The historian Dutt, writing in the first years of the century (1902-1904), claimed that increases in land taxes, the replacement of subsistence crops with cash crops and the demands of British imperialism generally led to the increasing susceptibility of the Indian population to famine. Thus, even minor droughts led to huge death tolls. McAlpin (1983) disputes this account with special reference to the Bombay Presidency. She argues that famine had been known for centuries, long before the British came, and that, as the economy developed under the British, a reduced susceptibility to drought evolved. At first the British were as ineffective as the earlier rulers (the Marathas) in coping with the unreliable nature of the environment.

Later, according to McAlpin, the development of the economy under the British led to a reduction in the degree to which farmers were susceptible to drought. Among the changes identified were the development of markets and railways. The development of railways led to greater ease and efficiency in the distribution of emergency grain. The development of markets, along with improved distribution, led to greater stability of the prices for purchased grains. This freed farmers 'from the

1 For a review of this debate see Appadurai (1984).

need to store grain as insurance against famines' (p. 154), enabling them to grow non-grain (cash) crops. As far as the agricultural sector of Bombay Presidency was concerned the period 1860-1920 was characterised by a generally improving economic situation, despite some bad monsoons and bad harvests. Transport costs fell (with the development of railways), crops achieved better prices, higher value crops were grown and there was less need for the use of crops as insurance. The increase in the demand for labour (both agricultural labour and non-agricultrual labour) in the newly industrialised Bombay Presidency and the increasing 'absorption of risk by the government' (p. 190) all worked to reduce the connection between drought and famine.

Dutt (1902-1904) argued that the very serious famines of the late ninteenth century demonstrated just how destructive British imperialism had been. McAlpin, on the other hand, argued that these were the consequences of very serious dry spells. The beginning of the twentieth century was something of a turning point after which economic development led to a situation in which serious loss of life due to drought became unlikely. McAlpin suggested that Dutt's time of writing (just after the turn of the century) prevents him from seeing these droughts in perspective. After the end of the first decade of the twentieth century famines ceased to be nightmares:

> Since that period there has been only one famine with major loss of life - the Bengal famine of 1943-1944 - and that one was due in large measure to the destruction of the very systems - transport, economic opportunities, and government relief - that had helped to mitigate earlier crises.(McAlpin 1983:218)

The extent to which McAlpin's conclusions about British Imperialism are valid is beyond the scope of this study,[2] although I must say that I believe her analysis demolishes any *simplistic* account of British imperialism as the main villain. My main concern is that she fails to deal with the distribution of the effects of famine. Some reviewers (Copland 1983; Appadurai 1984) have criticised her, in my view quite correctly, for ignoring internal differentiation within the agricultural sector. McAlpin wrote:

> Given a relatively equal distribution of land in most parts of the Presidency and relatively little tenancy in the period 1876-1889. . . these gains in prosperity were probably widely distributed through the agricultural community. Increasing cultivation of labour-

2 As Copland (1983) says in a review, McAlpin's thesis remains immensely controversial.

> intensive crops, among other factors, probably increased the demand for agricultural labourers, insuring that they also shared in the gains of the sector. (1983:158)

McAlpin's conclusion that land was relatively equally distributed is hardly supported. In any case her figures ignore the landless, so at best her conclusion only applies to distribution of land among the landed. Furthermore, the word 'probably' appears often in the argument that agricultural labourers shared in the gains of the agricultural sector. A major problem is that McAlpin uses figures which exclude agricultural labourers and which do not show much at all about landholdings at the local level. Large scale economic data are of little relevance in showing what happened in villages.

It is odd that McAlpin so easily dismisses the equity question, because she is certainly well aware of the possibilities of unequal distribution of the risks of drought. She discusses (and endorses) material on the Tuareg of the Sahara which sees the hierachical structure of Tuareg society as explicity concerned with ensuring unequal access to resources in drought/famine conditions.

Tuareg society is highly stratified. The most powerful class is the 'noble' class, primarily concerned with camel herding (Keenan 1977). At the bottom of the hierarchy is a slave class. In the middle are goat herding nomads and tenant farmers. Baier and Lovejoy (1977), in a paper cited by McAlpin, argue that the stratification of Tuareg society was related to hierarchically based claims to resources. In good times additional people from the sub-Saharan areas were recruited into the lower Tuareg classes, becoming slaves or tenant farmers for noble Tuareg landlords. In bad times these people again crossed ecological and ethnic barriers. (At the lower levels of Tuareg society the distinctions between Tuareg and neighbouring Hausa were blurred.)

Baier and Lovejoy specifically interpret the Tuareg class system

> . .as a flexible strategy that assured the continued domination by a small class of aristocratic Tuareg of sectors of a highly competitive regional economy. (1977:408)

McAlpin brings in the Tuareg material as part of a discussion of a variety of possible strategies which have been used in drought-prone environments. Yet she fails to explore the implications, raising the question of unequal distribution (both of risks and benefits) but never satisfactorily handling it. I suggest that the primary reason for this failure is that analysis of economic data collected on a large scale tends to disguise internal differentiation. Working as an economic historian McAlpin cannot be blamed for the absence of more detailed data, but she can be criticised for failing to recognise the implications of the absence of such data. Further, McAlpin acknowledges that the available data are not entirely reliable. Nevertheless, she appears to assume that the irregularities all average out and do not amount to systematic errors. As Polly Hill (1984, 1986) has shown in general discussions of economic statistics, this is very doubtful.

Appadurai (1984) emphasises the importance of examining famine and control of resources in terms of moral economy.[3] The emphasis is on the ability 'of an individual or group to obtain legitimately the means of subsistence' (Appadurai 1984:481). A major advocate of this view is the economist Amartya Sen, who developed what he called the entitlement approach.

> The entitlement approach to starvation and famines concentrates on the ability of people to command food through the legal means available in the society, including the use of production possibilities, trade opportunities, entitlements *vis-a-vis* the state and other methods of acquiring food. (Sen 1982:45; emphasis in original)

According to Sen the failure of specific groups to obtain food by legitimate means (as defined by the particular society) is the crucial issue in famine. In other words, starvation is a consequence of distribution, not of availability. This notion is too simple, however. As Sen puts it:

> To say that starvation depends 'not merely' on food supply but also on its 'distribution' would be correct enough, though not remarkably helpful. The important question then would be: what determines distribution of food between different sections of the community? The entitlement approach directs one to questions dealing with ownership patterns. ... .(1982:7)

In arguing that entitlements enable people to 'command' food, Sen stresses that the recognition of the legitimacy of entitlement is specific to a given society. What is a legitimate entitlement in a socialist system may not be so in a capitalist one.

My purpose in undertaking the above discussion is to emphasise the importance of considering the factors which affect the distribution of resources. While overall food availability may be one aspect of famines

---

3 Moral economy can be defined as the set of mutual expectations affecting use of and access to resources.

in some cases, there is no doubt that inequalities of access to resources are crucial. My analysis in this study is heavily concerned with inequality and hierarchy as intrinsic parts of the village agrarian system.

I have been discussing the phenomenon of famine. I will now take a step back from this. In the sense that famine implies catastrophe, then the situation in western Rajasthan in recent years is not famine, although the word 'famine' is used administratively (see Chapter 2). I will be applying the ideas of McAlpin and Sen (among others) to a situation of frequent but irregular scarcity rather than to catastrophic famine. In this context unequal access to (or, in Sen's terms 'command of') subsistence still applies. In fact, an important question is why, despite high and increasing population and great inequality, the catastrophic famines of the past are not being repeated.

Much of the discussion in the literature works at a macro-level, as I have previously pointed out with regard to McAlpin. It is essential to examine the processes of reaction to drought (including distribution and risk management) as they occur in a village setting. That is the justification for this study. The examination of famine or famine avoidance in a village setting is an emerging theme in anthropology. Maclachlan (1983) and Richards (1986) both deal with adaptive responses to drought. Richards examines the way a particular African rice farming system copes with scarcity conditions. Maclachlan deals with agricultural intensification as a way to cope with drought, in the context of high population growth in a south Indian village. I will be referring to his work in greater detail later (particularly in Chapter 8). My approach aims to examine adaptation to drought in the context of inequality. Nevertheless, the emphasis is, as with Richards and Maclachlan, on the micro-level.

In addition to the inequality and hierarchy aspect, there is a second theme related to famine and risk reduction. All people in drought prone areas, whether poor or less so, have strategies for reducing the risk of a bad year (or a series of bad years) turning into food shortages. These strategies will be discussed at various points throughout this book.

An Ecological Perspective

This is a study in ecological anthropology. I use the term to refer to a broad subject area (the interrelationships between human social behaviour and environment), not to define a particular theoretical approach. The most crucial characteristic of the environment in question is the unpredictable rainfall. Not only is rainfall unpredictable, but the human population is rapidly increasing and wider economic and political contexts are changing. For these reasons it is difficult to apply theoretical approaches that have evolved out of simpler contexts. For example, the neo-functionalist approach of Rappaport (1968), depending on more or less repeated cycles with feedback mechanisms, is not appropriate when some variables (population) are changing unidirectionally.

Further, as Orlove (1980) points out, the neo-functionalist approach has generally been applied to small-scale societies rather than 'complex state societies'. The villages of western Rajasthan are certainly part of complex state societies and have been for centuries.

Orlove argues that ecological anthropology has gone through three stages. The first derived from cultural evolutionism and the second included neo-functionalist and neo-evolutionist ecology, epitomised by the work of Rappaport (1968) and Harris (1979) respectively. Orlove calls the third stage processual ecology. In this school the concern is with 'the importance of diachronic studies in ecological anthropology and. . . the need to examine mechanisms of change' (p. 245).

Processual ecology really is very broad in approach and methodology. In fact it is very much what Dwyer (1985) refers to as 'methodological individualism'. As Orlove's review shows, contemporary ecological anthropology consists of a large number of differing approaches, rather than an overriding theory. I believe that this is a healthy situation and reject the view that anthropologists must go to the field to test a particular theoretical perspective. My view of the discipline is that it is problem-oriented or question-oriented. This does not lead to theoretical and methodological anarchy, but rather to an eclectic approach which treats method and theory as tools, not goals.[4]

The essence of the ecological approach which is used in this study is an emphasis on holism. Social behaviour and the environment are not seen as separate interacting systems, but rather as a single system.

Gregory (pers.comm.) points out that interpretive approaches which focus on the interaction between 'nature and culture' suffer from the same limitations as approaches which emphasise the primacy either of culture (idealism) or nature (materialism). Both single-sided and two-sided approaches assume the dichotomy between nature and culture to be 'unproblematic'. Gregory stresses the value of a 'many-sided' approach.

---

4 Eclectic approaches to ecological anthropology cover a whole range of methodologies and issues. See, for example, Kennedy and Edgerton (1982).

The holistic ('many-sided') approach has a long history in anthropology. Mauss's study of Eskimo 'social morphology' (1979) was described by Fox, in the Foreword to his English translation, as '. . . the first ethnographic attempt to adopt a holistic, ecological approach to the analysis of a society' (p. 6). Evans-Pritchards' work on the Nuer (1940) is similarly eclectic and holistic, and Fox's own study of ecological change in Indonesia (1977) follows the same tradition.

A holistic approach takes into account the physical environment, resources, resource use, social organisation, politics and anything else which is relevant. It does not assume causal primacy of one factor over others.

In the largest sense, social behaviour and environment are parts of a single system. Nevertheless, analysis must have a starting point. I have taken Beteille's concept of an agrarian system (Beteille 1972) as the basis of my approach, because it seems most readily to identify most of the elements involved in an analysis of drought in an agrarian society. Beteille identifies technology, the work cycle, the organisation of production and the agrarian hierarchy, as topics of particular relevance. He mentions ecology and systems of land tenure as additional factors. I would add the wider (state and national) political and economic context. Beteille states:

> These major topics are mutually related and each one of them is related to others not listed here.... I have been able to give only a broad indication of these relationships. I doubt that it will be very helpful to go much beyond this because the task of anthropological investigation as I conceive it is to establish the precise nature of such relationships *after* and not *before* field investigation. (1972:171; emphasis in original)

In addition to these focuses of attention there are two further elements in my approach. These relate to two conclusions which arose out of my feel for the field situation.

Firstly, because the physical environment, demography and socio-economic behaviour are all changing, the perspective must, to the extent that the data permit, include an element of historical analysis. The ethnographic analysis must be, to a large extent, historically specific, because the processes under examination are historically specific.

Secondly, the perspective must take account of the fact that the uncertainties of the environment are almost the only thing that the farmer can be certain about. Farming in the semi-arid part of western Rajasthan involves very uncertain subsistence. Thus, we are talking about the ecology of doubt. The anthropological study of such an ecology must be concerned with the strategies used to cope with this uncertainty and with the way people react to specific events.[5]

Anthropological Research and the Study of Agrarian Systems in Rajasthan

In the last thirty years there have been a large number of sociological studies of various aspects of rural life and economy in western Rajasthan. Significant work includes research carried out by scholars associated with the Central Arid Zone Research Institute (CAZRI) at Jodhpur. (See, for example, Bharara 1980, 1982, 1993; Bose *et al.* 1963; Bose and Saxena 1965, 1966; Malhotra and Trivedi 1981; etc.) Some studies have also been done by scholars at the Department of Sociology, University of Jodhpur, although that Department has generally concentrated on urban sociology

These studies deal with a variety of sociological and socio-economic issues, including household composition, status of and attitudes to the child population and the factors involved in the dispersal of dwellings. Important work has also been done on the relationships between social factors and the environment, including the consequences of drought (Bharara 1980, 1993; Malhotra 1977). Some research on the relationships between ecology and social factors has also been done by foreign scholars (Rosin 1968, 1978, 1993).

While much of this work has been useful and important, there are some significant gaps in the research done to date. The crucial point is that most of it has been of a survey nature. The studies have provided a great deal of statistical data, but what is missing is the complementary perspective which requires intensive village-level research - in other words the perspective obtained by anthropologists using the method of 'participant observation' and spending lengthy periods observing day-to-day events and interactions.

In addition to the assistance the field perspective gives to the understanding of the dynamics behind statistical averages, a crucial role of fieldwork is in the way it forces the accuracy of statistical data to be

5 This concern with individual action is important. Haaland (1991:14), in a discussion of the work of Fredrik Barth, points out that: 'To understand these patterns it is necessary to develop a perspective which allows [Barth] to connect the analysis of macro-level ecosystem dynamics with the micro-level analysis of the intentions and perceptions of individual actors.'

called into question. Polly Hill (1984, 1986) has pointed out that economists (she was referring particularly to developmental economists) rarely question the data on which they base their macro-theories and she argues that such macro-theories fail to take account of systematic statistical errors and local variations. My own experience in gathering statistical data in the field led me to an extreme awareness of the arbitrariness of many of the assumptions used in gathering and analysing statistical data. Where I use statistical data in this study I do so because I believe my detailed knowledge of a small area enables me to be fairly confident about their validity.

The relatively small amount of detailed fieldwork carried out in Rajasthan is similar to the pattern for India as a whole. Srinivas (1975) argues that the social sciences in India have generally ignored the importance of field research and that the poor understanding of rural life has had significant effects on policy and administration.

Beteille (1972) has pointed out that Anthropology has an important role. He regrets the fact that some advantages in the anthropological approach have not been fully exploited in India:

> . .anthropologists in this country seem to be ready to abandon their own discipline in order to try their hand at political sociology, the history of civilizations, or something else. This is in many ways unfortunate because the anthropological approach has its own contribution to make to the understanding of the world in which we live. What I consider to be distinctive in this approach is the monographic study of the material culture and social organization of particular communities based on intensive fieldwork. I believe that studies of this kind can tell us much that is of value about human societies and cultures and that no other discipline can take the place of anthropology in making them. (Beteille 1972:151)

In asserting the usefulness of anthropology as a means of gathering valuable information, Beteille argues that anthropology in India can usefully turn to the study of culture, technology and organisation of production in the context of the ecological setting. He calls this the study of agrarian systems.

Very little work has been done at this level in western Rajasthan. One exception is the work of Rosin (1968, 1978, 1981), whose unpublished PhD thesis (1968) is the only substantial anthropological study of anything resembling an agrarian system in arid or semi-arid western Rajasthan. Looking at Rajasthan as a whole, I am aware of no published monographs dealing with an anthropological study of agrarian systems. In addition to a few tribal studies, the major anthropological studies on

Rajasthan are those by Carstairs (1957, 1983), Gupta (1974), Aggarwal (1971), Chakravarti (1975), Chauhan (1967), Erdman (1985) and Gold (1988), none of whom deal specifically with either the arid zone or with agrarian systems. Paul (1992) has written on the ethnography of the Charans who live in the arid zone, but her study does not deal with agriculture or agrarian systems.

There are also some Village Survey Monographs published in connection with the 1961 Census of India. A few of these deal with the arid zone. They are useful descriptive works, sometimes containing detailed data on various socio-economic matters in relation to particular villages. However they do not result from extended research, but from brief survey visits (of several weeks duration). Furthermore they present data and describe physical surroundings, but do not describe or analyse anything in the nature of 'agrarian systems'.

Rosin's PhD thesis (1968) focuses on changing land tenure and village polity. It falls within the tradition of holistic ecological studies and much of what Rosin has to say would apply, to some extent, to my field area. Examples of this are observations about the role of outside employment and about the difficulties involved in determining land ownership. Most importantly, Rosin argues that various castes have different forms of social organisation and that these have differing applications as the basis of strategies for obtaining economic advantage. This argument is similar to one pursued in this study, particularly in Chapters 4 and 9.[6]

It is against the general background of very sketchy anthropological literature and, in particular, an absence of studies of agrarian systems, that this study was conceived. The underlying objective is to describe and analyse the nature of an agrarian system in a rural community in arid western Rajasthan.

6 My argument about various castes having different forms of social organisation which provide opportunities for differing economic strategies, was developed before I saw Rosin's thesis. In fact, when I first saw it and read the abstract, I decided to defer further reading until my own argument was fully developed. I did not read it until after I completed the second draft of my own thesis. Rosin's argument partly confirmed some of my own observations, particularly the general observation about the importance of differences in the structures of various castes. However, there are differences in interpretation which will be discussed in Chapter 4.

Methodology and Fieldwork

(a) Geographic Focus

This study has a number of shifting geographical foci. On the widest level it is concerned with that part of Rajasthan to the west of the Aravalli Mountains. The next level is Jodhpur District and the former Rajput state of Marwar which included all of the modern district and parts of adjacent districts.[7] At a narrower level, the focus is on a cluster of four villages in Jodhpur District. These four adjoining villages are all in a similar ecological setting and, in each case, the economy is a mixture of pastoralism and monsoonal agriculture. Furthermore, three of the villages are linked administratively, being part of the same *gram* (village) panchayat. Within this cluster I have focused very closely on a single village, Hinganiya, the smallest of the four villages. Discussion shifts backwards and forwards between the various levels throughout the study. However, unless otherwise indicated all statistical data refer to Hinganiya.

The purpose of shifting between levels is to develop an understanding of the region as a whole while maintaining a clear perspective on a specific case study. A more detailed introduction to my fieldsite is presented in Chapter 3, following a discussion of environmental conditions in western Rajasthan as a whole (in Chapter 2).

(b) Methodology

The underlying methodology was participant observation. Most interviews, both with villagers and with officals, were unstructured. Apart from a small number of taped interviews I usually relied on notes, taken during a meeting or event, or as soon as possible afterwards. I also collected quantitative data, using semi-structured interviews, about household size, labour migration, livestock ownership and landholdings. Separate surveys were carried out in late 1983/early 1984 and in 1985/86.

Data on landholdings were obtained from official land records held by the Patwari (the official responsible for land records). Two sets of data were obtained, one relating to the position at the time of land settlement in 1947 and the other relating to landholdings in late 1985/early 1986.

I also examined library and archival material in Delhi, Agra, Bikaner and Jodhpur.

---

7 The word *marwar* means 'the region of death'. It refers specifically to the former Rajput state, but is also used more broadly to refer to the arid areas of Rajasthan.

(c) Fieldwork

My fieldwork can be broken up into several stages.

(1) Late December 1982 - early May 1983. My activities in this period included visits to Delhi attempting to arrange approval for my research permit, and also a visit to Bombay to meet my wife and son who were arriving from Australia. Basing myself in Jodhpur I made survey trips to various parts of western Rajasthan (including several days in Hinganiya).

(2) May-early August 1983. This period was spent in Nepal as I pursued my Indian research permit and the alternative possibility of working in Nepal.

(3) August 1983 - January 1984. In this period I carried out fieldwork in Rajasthan. I spent much of my time in Hinganiya but also visited other parts of Rajasthan and spent time in Jodhpur developing an urban and regional perspective. My wife and son remained in Nepal during most of this time and visited the village briefly towards the end of the year.

(4) August 1985 early February 1986. I returned from Australia to carry out follow-up work again concentrating on Hinganiya. I also did library work in Bikaner, Jaipur and Delhi and spent a few days in Manali. My family remained in Australia during this entire period of fieldwork.

(5) I returned to Rajasthan for a few days in August 1987, spending two days in Hinganiya. This brief visit gave me an impression of the effect of the most serious drought in decades.

The fact that I was able to work in, or at least visit, my field area during three separate monsoon seasons (one good, one poor and the third disastrous) has been an important factor in recognising the extent to which conditions vary. Table 1.1 indicates the pattern of monsoons and famines since 1977, and shows the conditions at the time of various stages of fieldwork.

In its combination of a wider study of western Rajasthan and a very localised village study, my fieldwork reflected the balance of the study. On the one hand I concentrated on Hinganiya, and, to a lesser extent, the other three villages in the cluster. On the other hand I developed a fairly broad knowledge of other parts of western Rajasthan. Each level illuminates the other.

Throughout my time in Hinganiya I lived with a Rajput household. The fact that I lived with Rajputs meant that I gained a more detailed knowledge of Rajputs than of the other castes. It also meant that I was associated with Rajputs in terms of commensality. This presented some restrictions on my relationships with members of other castes (particularly with the untouchable castes - the Meghwals and Nayaks), but, in my view, did not lead to any major distortions of my understanding of these castes. I do not think that data on economic matters (such as land ownership) are less reliable for other castes than for Rajputs. In fact some Rajputs seemed less forthcoming in these matters than Meghwals or Nayaks.

Table 1.1

Conditions in Jodhpur District 1977-1987, indicating periods of fieldwork

Year	Monsoon conditions/ famine declarations	Fieldwork
1977	Good monsoon	
1978	Failed/famine declared	
1979	Failed/famine declared	
1980	Failed/famine declared	
1981	Failed/famine declared	
1982	Failed/famine declared	
1983	Good monsoon	In Rajasthan during pre-monsoon (January-April). Returned late monsoon remaining until January 1984
1984	Generally satisfactory - famine declared in some villages	Left field late January (pre-monsoon)
1985	Failed/famine declared	Arrived August
1986	Failed/famine declared	Left January
1987	Failed/famine declared	Brief visit in August

Note: The monsoon period is roughly mid-July to early-September

In personal terms, however, I found the strictures of caste rather unpleasant and inconvenient, and there was an element of subversion and some tension surrounding my relationships with Nayaks and Meghwals. To some extent my frequent visits to the other castes caused concern to my Rajput hosts. While fear that I might breach the rules of commensality were a part of this, there was clearly a concern that I would upset the power relationships between castes. Concern (and jealousy) about my giving gifts and loans was also an element.

The working and living conditions in Hinganiya were very difficult. I lived in a single-room building which doubled as a storeroom, meeting room and sleeping room for myself and a variable number of male members of the household and visitors. Written work was almost impossible at night as electricity was generally unavailable, although there were some spasmodic efforts to make temporary connections to the village power supply later in my second stay.

In both 1983 and 1985 I spent much of the period August to late October in Hinganiya. The heat during these months was deplorable. Fortunately I did not spend the period May to July in Rajasthan at any stage of my fieldwork. Even in August and September the temperature in the shade during the day frequently reached 100°F. Outside it was much worse. I frequently found my notebooks damaged by my sweat as I wrote. Water was often in short supply and very poor.

Fortunately, even in the hot months the nights were relatively pleasant. A great deal of informal 'interviewing' took place during pre-dinner talks with visitors, often over a glass of rum or *desi daru* (local liquor).

In addition to problems with heat and the absence of light, working conditions were affected by the lack of privacy. On one hand this meant that every moment of the day involved participant observation (whether desired or not). On the other hand, while I was able to write field notes (and did so continuously, much to general amusement), I was rarely able to analyse information or to write it up in report form. That sort of task had to be done during my trips to Jodhpur.Visits to the neighbouring village of Kur and Kukunda were fairly frequent, although they were day trips with the exception of a few night stops in Kur. I visited Khokhariya only a few times and also managed to visit several other nearby villages at various times.

Structure of the Book

In Chapter 2, I will describe the environment of western Rajasthan. Then, in Chapter 3, I will give a brief description of my field area. At this point the most natural thing to expect would be a chapter on agriculture and pastoralism. However, an understanding of the way in which productive activities are organised is impossible without a knowledge of hierarchical systems based on caste (Chapter 4) and landholding (Chapter 5). Consequently the description and analysis of agro-pastoral production is deferred until Chapter 6. Chapter 7 deals with demographic issues and includes a discussion of the relationships between economic conditions and population growth. In Chapter 8 labour demands and their relationship to household structure are examined. Chapter 9 examines links between the village and the wider world. Both migration and the developmental role of the state (particularly in famine relief) are discussed. Finally the concluding chapter summarises the argument.

Chapter 2

Ecological Context: The Environment of Western Rajasthan

Introduction

The purpose of this chapter is to outline the main features of the environment of western Rajasthan. The emphasis will be on the macro-environment, setting the broad context, although, where appropriate, I will point out the specific features of my field area. I will also provide a brief account of human occupation and land use.

The Thar Desert

Rajasthan is situated in north-west India [Map 1] and has borders with the Punjab in the north, with Haryana, Uttar Pradesh and Madhya Pradesh in the east, with Gujarat in the south and with the Pakistani Province of Sind in the west.

During the British period the area was known as Rajputana (the land of the Rajputs) and consisted of twenty-two states ruled by Rajas and Maharajahs. Apart from Ajmer-Merwara, which they ruled directly, the British employed a system of indirect rule, controlling external affairs, but allowing (for the most part) the Rajput rulers to control the internal affairs of the states. The various Rajput kingdoms were formally abolished and joined together into the United State of Greater Rajasthan in 1949, two years after Indian Independence.

Rajasthan can be roughly divided into two more or less distinct geographical parts [Map 2]. The Aravalli Mountains (running roughly from the north-east to the south-west) are the important dividing line between the Thar Desert on the west and the more fertile east.

Much of the literature talks about the Indian Desert, or the Rajasthan Desert. Very few writers explicitly acknowledge the fact that eastern Pakistan is part of the same desert. Generally the terms Indian Desert, Thar Desert or Rajasthan Desert are used quite inconsistently in the literature. McGinnies (1979) gives an account which transcends the political boundaries. He describes the Thar Desert (meaning the contiguous Indo-Pakistan desert) as part of the afro-asiatic desert belt which stretches from the Sahara to the Thar.

I use the names Thar Desert and Indian Desert to refer to the contiguous Indo-Pakistan desert and the term Rajasthan Desert to refer to the part within Rajasthan. This study concentrates on the part of the desert on the Indian side of the border.

The Aravalli Mountains, for most purposes, can be described as the eastern boundary of the Indian Desert, although the exact boundaries are disputed depending on how deserts and arid zones are defined. In the west the desert reaches almost to the Indus river in Pakistan.

Between the eastern and western extremes, the main geographical feature is the basin of the Luni River (literally, the salt river). The Luni rises in the Aravalli hills and runs south-west into the Greater Rann of Kutch. To say it runs is merely conventional, as there are no permanent rivers in western Rajasthan. Usually there is little water in the Luni, and even when there is it quickly dissipates in the sands of the desert. The area of the Luni Basin is 57,000 square kilometres and the total length of the river is 805 kilometres (Kaul and Thalen 1979).

The Rajasthan Canal is one very major artificial geographical feature with significant implications to the ecology of western Rajasthan. The construction of the canal commenced in 1958. The major construction work has now been completed. The canal was planned to service the north-western parts of Rajasthan near the Pakistan border. Sen, writing in 1982, stated that the canal would have substantial benefits, apart from the obvious benefits to agriculture, in that a strip 300m wide along the canal would be 'planted over with grasses and trees for the binding of sand and to provide food for livestock and trees for fuel and shade' (D.N. Sen 1982:43).

At the time I completed my fieldwork in 1987 the project, which includes many kilometres of feeder canals, was incomplete. However, the impact in terms of increased irrigation and improved grazing had been felt for some time in some areas. One drought relief project in 1985 involved cutting grass near the canal and shipping it for sale in Bikaner District.

The area to the west of the canal (towards Pakistan) was expected to benefit most, because of natural slope. Some lifts were included in a revised form of the project to provide water to some areas to the east (Khanna 1983). However, as these are relatively small scale most districts on the eastern side were expected to receive no direct impact. (This includes Jodhpur District.) There has been some political debate about the emphasis on agriculture, which favours the western side of the canal. In 1983, state opposition politicians were arguing that greater emphasis should be placed on improving grazing facilities. This was linked to the discussion of lifts and maximising benefits to the east of the canal (Khanna 1983).

While agriculture in my field area has remained monsoon-based and has not been affected by the canal, there seemed possibilities for a spin-off for pastoralism. In 1987 it seemed that the development of good grazing lands to the west could provide an alternative goal for herd migration and could significantly reduce the impacts of drought on livestock. However, long term effects on the impacts of the canal remain to be seen and detailed study of impacts remains necessary. (I have made some tentative observations on the impact of the canal up to 1994 in the Afterword.)

Geomorphologically, the Indian Desert consists mostly of plains, with some areas of sand dunes and low hills (McGinnies 1979). Singh and Ghose (1980) identify two major zones of sand dunes in western Rajasthan, covering 58 per cent of the area. Generally the soil is sandy, of low fertility (high mineral and low organic content) and improves towards the east and north-east (Kaul and Thalen 1979).

At first sight much of the Indian Desert does not look like the popular conception of a desert at all. Even in Jaisalmer District, where the average population is very low (according to Sharma, 1972, it was four people per square kilometre in 1961) it is difficult to go very far without seeing people or villages. The common perception, within India, of Jaisalmer District as having a low population seems odd to those who think of low population density in terms of the Sahara or Central Australian Deserts. In Jodhpur District the population density is much higher being 73 persons per square kilometre for the entire district and 48 per square kilometre for rural areas in 1981 (Census of India 1981a). There were 705 inhabited villages. As the total area of the District was 22,850 square kilometres this gives each village an average area of 32.4 square kilometres.

A second feature which makes the word desert seem odd is that much of the land is cultivated (at least during the monsoon) and fields often less than a hectare in area are usually clearly marked by thatched fences or raised ridges of soil. Sometimes these ridges are deliberately constructed. The unintended effects of the role of man in this desert are highlighted by the way in which sand dunes sometimes follow the boundaries of fields. Sand is blown against thatched fences or raised ridges and gradually (presumably over centuries) the level rises. New thatched fences are placed on top of the new ridge of sand and the process continues.

The popular notion of a desert as an arid, poorly populated waste land needs to be reconsidered in the context of the Indian Desert. Aridity is the only element of this sort of definition which is evident. From a geographer's point of view aridity and other climatic factors are of central concern in defining a desert.

Climate

(a) Rainfall and Moisture

Apart from the physical features of the land itself, the most important characteristic of the Indian Desert is its climate, which is itself characterised by very low rainfall. Whether it should be defined as arid or semi-arid depends on the criteria used.

Degrees of aridity can be defined in a number of different ways. The most simple approach is to take mean annual rainfall as the criterion. Le Houerou (1970) argues (in reference to North Africa) for this approach. He regards areas with less than 100 mm of rain per year as desert; areas with between 100 and 400 mm per year are classified as arid; areas with more than 400 mm per year are semi-arid, semi-humid or humid.

All attempts at definition revolve around mean annual rainfall. Many authorities, however, regard this as an inadequate indicator in itself. Thornwaite (1948) developed an aridity index which measured the amount of water effectively available for plant growth. The index was calculated on the basis of the relationship between mean annual precipitation and the potential for evaporation and transpiration due to temperature, soil type, wind and other factors.

Meigs (1953) followed Thornwaite's approach in producing a series of climatic maps for UNESCO. He admits that the problems of climatic classification are considerable. In a footnote he points out that some writers have called for the abandonment of complex formulae for defining arid areas, and for a return to simple criteria. Meigs replies that the world itself is complex.

Meigs divides dry climates into arid and semi-arid (which, he says, coincide with the common usage of desert and steppe). Arid lands are unsuitable for agriculture, whereas some agriculture is possible on semi-arid lands. Within the arid category it is possible to distinguish extreme aridity. His criteria for defining aridity and semi-aridity are based on the moisture index developed by Thornwaite.

Debates about definition are often not very helpful. For my purposes it is not necessary to take sides. The types of criteria used in defining the boundaries of arid and semi-arid areas can obscure the fact that there are environmental differences within the categories arid or semi-arid. Broad systems of classification are useful in constructing global models, but at the micro-level it is more useful to describe environments than to categorise them within broad types.

For convenience (and following common usage) I will continue to treat the Aravalli Mountains as the eastern boundary of the Thar Desert. Generally speaking, between the Aravalli Mountains and the Pakistan Border rainfall is very low in the west, around the Pakistan border and increases towards the east. Most of the rain which falls is monsoonal and 90% of all rain falls between June and mid-September (Pisharoty 1980).

McGinnies describes the Thar Desert as

> . . .a transition zone between major wind belts. . . . The monsoon movement of moist air terminates in Western India, resulting in a small and irregular rainfall in the Thar. (1979:11)

Pisharoty (1980) describes the dry, stable mass of air over the area which limits the action of convective currents. This type of phenomena is one of the general causes of aridity described by McGinnies.

The general trend of an increase in average rainfall from west to east means that the status of Jodhpur and Jodhpur District is described as arid on the Thornwaite/Meigs criteria or as semi-arid on the criteria used by Bharucha (1955). The mean annual precipitation at Jodhpur is 362 mm (Kaul and Thalen 1979). Within Jodhpur District a shift in mean annual precipitation is evident, following the wider trend of increase from west to east. Useful figures are not consistently available for smaller towns and are not available at all for villages. Nevertheless examination of a map in Sen (1972) indicates that the villages in my field area fall at the upper end of the range between the 300 and 400mm isohyets.

Low average annual rainfall is an important characteristic affecting human ecology and adaptive strategies. However it is the combination of low average with irregularity which is most critically important. This point is fundamental to the argument in this book. Pisharoty has surveyed the literature and concludes:

> There have been several studies looking for a systematic change in the rainfall over these parts during the last hundred years, for which some rainfall records, although not strictly homogeneous, are available. The general conclusion is that there are no systematic trends, and that the rainfall variations have been practically stochastic. Power spectrum analysis have [sic] shown several peaks with several periodicities; but they have been found to be of no forecasting value. Decade rainfall means have not remained the same; they have shown fluctuations; but none that could be anticipated. (1980:42)

Krishnan, Ram Krishna and Rao (1980) examined rainfall data for a number of different stations in western Rajasthan for the period 1901 to 1970. They found that there were two periods when large deficit rainfall was particularly common. These periods were 1901-1920 and, at the other end of the sample period 1961-1970. There was a trend of decreasing rainfall in areas with less than 300mm averages from 1962-1971. However the overall fluctuations were seen as being a result of the randomness and unpredictability of rainfall.

The occurrence of drought in Jodhpur Tehsil (sub-district) between 1901 and 1908 has been analysed in a paper provided to me by the Collector's office in Jodhpur (Collector's Office, Jodhpur n.d.[1]). The paper classifies drought years in terms of the aridity index calculated for each year. A negative aridity index represents a statistically average or better than average year and is defined as a year of no drought. Years with a positive index of aridity (that is, greater than statistically normal aridity) are classified, in increasing order of severity, as years of moderate, large, severe or disastrous drought. The analysis shows that there was drought of one kind or another in 44 years while 36 years were drought free. In other words there was drought in 55% of the 80 years in the sample. (See Table 2.1 for a summary of this information.)

Table 2.1

Occurrence of drought by severity in Jodhpur Tehsil 1901-1980

Classification	*No. of Years*	*% age*
No drought	36	45
Moderate	18	22.5
Large	13	16.25
Severe	13	16.25
Disastrous	0	0
	Total 80	

Two further points about the pattern of monsoon rainfall are important. Firstly there are large variations within comparatively small areas, even within districts. For example, in 1943, the then Famine Minister of the erstwhile Marwar state (roughly equivalent to modern Jodhpur District) gave the annual rainfall averages for various centres within the District (Table 2.2).

1 This paper was an extract from a roneoed report entitled *Identification of the Drought Prone Areas in the District Jodhpur*. No publication or authorship details were provided.

Table 2.2

Rainfall averages for various cities in Marwar

(From Singh 1943:3-4)

Bali (South)	19.65 inches
Phalodi (North West)	9.93 inches
Bilara (East)	19.49 inches
Jodhpur	13.92 inches

The second feature is that the actual annual rainfall in each location varies widely and unpredictably. Furthermore there is a great variation in the pattern of rainfall within a given year - it is not always spread conveniently over the normal monsoon months.

Singh sums it up neatly. Regarding the *kharif* (monsoon) crop he says:

> . .four showers of about 2 1/2 inches each at proper intervals is quite enough. But this is too much to expect of nature. (1943:4)

An indication of the great extremes is that occasionally there are floods in western Rajasthan, centred on the Luni Basin. Although floods are rare, there were serious floods in July 1979 (Kolarkar, Choudhari and Dhir 1981). The floods resulted from 4-5 days of very heavy rain in the Upper Luni catchment. In some places between 600 and 920 mm of rain fell in the period. The result was unprecedented flooding which rendered 160,000 ha of land infertile.

In other words, rainfall is highly variable and unpredictable. A consequence of this irregularity is that famine is common and, like the rain, unpredictable. This is a basic fact that farmers and pastoralists have to come to grips with.

(b) Other Climatic Features

In addition to low and unpredictable rainfall the climate of western Rajasthan has the following characteristics:

(1) Extremes of temperature. The temperature during the summer is very high. In winter months temperature falls considerably and night time temperatures are particularly low. The change in temperature is rapid due to 'the dryness of the atmosphere and lack of vegetation' (D.N. Sen 1982:33). The annual cycle of seasons is quite marked. The cold season lasts from December to February. In March the warm weather starts, cooling somewhat when the monsoon starts (hopefully) in July. The monsoon may last from July to early September. Then, following a few more hot weeks,

the weather starts to cool again. Sen (1982:36) gives mean and maximum temperatures, on a monthly basis, for a number of stations in Rajasthan. Table 2.3 summarises some of this information for Jodhpur, Bikaner and Jaisalmer. In each case the hottest month is May and the coldest month is January.

(2) Humidity. Throughout western Rajasthan the humidity is highest during the monsoon months and lowest during the hot period March to May (D.N. Sen 1982).

(3) Wind. During the period March to May there are frequent dust storms. Wind is environmentally significant for two reasons. Firstly, it is an agent of erosion. Secondly, it encourages evaporation of surface moisture and is thus important as an aspect of the aridity index.

Table 2.3

Mean maximum and mean minimum temperatures at Jodhpur, Bikaner, Jaisalmer in degrees centigrade

	Jodhpur	*Bikaner*	*Jaisalmer*
Full year-			
mean max	33.2	33.3	33.6
mean min	19.2	20.2	18.7
Hottest month *(May)* -		*(June)**	
mean max	40.8	41.7	42.8
mean min	26.3	29.4	26.8
Coldest month *(Jan)* -			
mean max	24.6	22.1	23.8
mean min	9.2	8.3	8.9

* In Bikaner the mean maximum temperature in June equals the mean maximum temperature for May. However the mean minimum (29.4°C) is higher in June than in May (27.7°C)

Source: Abstracted from D.N. Sen (1982:36)

Fauna

In this section I intend to give only a very brief summary of the natural fauna of the Indian Desert. Domesticated livestock and crops will be dealt with later. Natural flora will be dealt with in the chapter on agro-pastoralism, mainly in terms of use as fodder. A detailed study of the flora of the Indian Desert has been published by D.N. Sen (1982). Despite the heavy human population there is considerable variety of fauna. The following account is based both on my own observation and on a monograph by Prakash (1977).

There are numerous varieties of insects, including scorpions. There are many varieties of reptiles, including both lizards and snakes. The most common venemous snakes are the cobra, the krait and the *phoorsa*, or saw-scaled viper. There are also several non-venemous species. The entire desert is rich in bird life, the peacock (Rajasthan's state symbol), the partridge and the vulture being particularly common.

There are also large numbers of mammal species. In a survey carried out between 1953 and 1956, Prakash (1964) collected 38 species and sub-species. Up until twenty or thirty years ago some larger carnivores such as the leopard were found, according to accounts by my informants. Hyenas, wolves and foxes and some smaller species of feline, including the caracal and desert cat, are still found.

The numbers of deer and antelopes have been greatly reduced due to the activities of hunters and poachers. Nevertheless it is possible to find nilgai, blackbuck and chinkara in many areas, particularly where there are members of the Bishnoi caste in the area. Protection of all life is a tenet of the Bishnoi sect and the theme of many encounters between the Rajputs (who tend to see hunting as part of the Kshatriya role) and the Bishnois. I will return to this point later.

Human Occupation of the Thar Desert

Human occupation has been a factor in the environmental history of western Rajasthan since palaeolithic times. The evidence about palaeolithic and mesolithic man in the Indian Desert is covered by Allchin *et al.* (1978) and, briefly, by Dhir (1982). It is sufficient to say that evidence has been found of cultures dating at least to the middle palaeolithic. Allchin *et al.* argued that mesolithic cultural remains found in western Rajasthan are probably the products of pastoral nomads who penetrated the desert. For much of its human history western Rajasthan's population probably consisted of pastoral nomads.

The Indus valley (Harappan) Civilization flourished in what is now Pakistan and north-western India from about 2500 BC until it was destroyed by the Aryan invaders in about 1500 BC (Wheeler 1950). The Pre-Harappan and (later) Harappan cultures extended into Rajasthan along the rivers of the north-western parts of the modern state, especially on the banks of the no longer existing Ghaggar river (Dhir 1982). However, there is no evidence of the Harappan culture spreading to the south away from the rivers and apparently the more arid areas to the south remained accessible only to pastoral nomads and hunter-gatherers (Dhir 1982).

The first major wave of immigrants moved south of the main rivers in the fourth century BC (Dhir 1982). The influx was largely of people from the Indo-Gangetic plains fleeing from waves of invaders, including the Greeks under Alexander (Dhir 1982) and, later, the Huns (Dhir 1982; Sharma 1972).

Despite the predominance of pastoral nomadism as the main economic adaptation, small scale agriculture began relatively early. Dhir (1982:325) suggests that agriculture was probably practiced continuously in Rajasthan following the movement of settlement away from the rivers (about 400 BC). Dhir examined a Gazetteer of Marwar compiled by Muhnot Nainsi between 1658 and 1662 (Nainsi 1968-1974).[2] On this evidence Dhir showed that selected villages in the Phalodi area (in the north west of Jodhpur District) had cultivated land averaging 1.5 ha per household in the period covered by Nainsi's data. Dhir points out that the holding size is very small and that agriculture must have been carried out in combination with pastoralism. Elsewhere, in Merta, agriculture seems to have been much more substantially established at the same time. According to Nainsi there were 6500 wells in use in Merta at the time.

Environmental History

McGinnies, in reference to the claims of some authors that the Indian Desert ranges from the Aravalli to the Sind in Pakistan, expresses some doubt

> . . .as to how much of this area is naturally arid and how much of this arid appearance has resulted from the activities of man.(1979:11)

The question as to whether the desert is natural or man-made is of obvious relevance to this study. There are two sub-issues: (1) is there evidence of recent origin for the Thar? (2) is there evidence of recent desertification (the transformation of arable land into desert)?

---

2 Nainsi was the Diwan (Finance Minister) of Maharajah Jaswant Singh of Jodhpur from 1658 to 1666. For a discussion of Nainsi's work see Bhati (1979).

A number of authors claim that aridity in western Rajasthan is of comparatively recent origin in terms of geological time. Wadia (1960) suggests that aridity was a post-glacial phenomenon. Wheeler (1950) states that the present desert was wooded, marshy and even inhabited by elephants and rhinocerous about 4000 to 5000 BC. He argues that drier conditions gradually developed until desert conditions were established by 1,000 AD and that human behaviour and land use were partly responsible for this change. Bharucha (1955) also claims that the desert is mainly man-made. A recent date for aridity caused by over exploitation of vegetation is supported by Bryson and Baerreis (1967).

There is no doubt that there have been some very significant environmental/geographical changes in comparatively recent times. Allchin, Goudie and Hegde (1978) point out that there were three main river systems in northern India during the late Pleistocene and Early Holocene geological eras. These were the Indus, the Saraswati and the Ganga. At that time the Jamuna flowed into the Saraswati, not the Ganga. By about 1000 BC the Jamuna had changed path and flowed into the Ganga, and by 1300-1500 AD there was no Saraswati at all. These changes were caused, according to Allchin *et al.* by geological changes, not by increasing aridity. This is not to deny that aridity has also increased.[3]

In their comprehensive survey, covering geological evidence and archaeological evidence, Allchin *et al.* (1978) conclude that the Thar is an ancient phenomenon, not a post glacial one. From the analysis of data collected from desert areas in both India and Pakistan, they put forward a picture of a series of alternating wet and dry phases. The oldest identified phase was a major dry phase just before the middle paleolithic period. This was followed by a major wet phase (characterised by humid climate, dune stability, grasslands and through-flowing rivers) beginning possibly less than 40,000 years ago. Sometime before 10,000 years ago there was a further dry phase. Another relatively moist phase, beginning about 10000-9500 years ago, followed this. The current dry phase is, if all this is correct, part of a cycle.

All of this supports the view that the Indian Desert was humid at about the time of the Harappan civilisation (2500-1500 BC), but it differs from accounts which see the desert as a late development in that the basic desert geomorphology is dated much earlier. While some human impact

---

3 Whether the decline of the Saraswati can be attributed to changes to the geological structure of the region, or to increased aridity (due to lower rainfall) there is no doubt that the decline of the Harappan city of Kalibangan in northern Rajasthan is directly associated with changes to the river system. Kalibangan was built on the edge of the river Saraswati (now known as the Ghaggar) and was apparently abandoned when it dried up.

on the ecology of the modern desert is not ruled out, the analysis by Allchin *et al.* suggests that the Thar is essentially a 'natural' desert.

In a review of the literature on this issue Dhir (1982) concludes that

> . . .after traversing the length and breadth of the western arid zone of Rajasthan I have not come across any soil formation characteristic of a humid environment, even on landscapes that have remained stable during late Pleistocene climatic fluctuations... It appears, therefore, that the humidity of the late Pleistocene and Holocene could not have been as high as had been made out. (1982:315)

This supports the view that the desert is not a new phenomenon, but does not support the view that there have been major and cyclical climatic variations. Dhir acknowledges that there may have been more moisture at some stages in the past but believes this has been exaggerated. In other words the area has remained more or less arid.

A related question is whether or not there have been major environmental changes in the present century. Mann, Malhotra and Kalla (1974) examined the common view that the Rajasthan Desert is expanding in terms of parameters such as land use capabilities, crop yield and water availability. They concluded that there is no conclusive evidence of an advancing desert, but warned of future risks. Sen and Mann (1977) state that the question is open, although some features suggest that the desert is not expanding. But, importantly, they point out that conditions within the desert itself are deteriorating. This picture of a desert which is getting worse, but not bigger, is further supported by an interpretation of geomorphological evidence by Ghose, Singh and Kar (1977).

Jodha (1980) regards the 'march of the Rajasthan desert' as an unsettled question, but supports the consensus view that desert conditions themselves are getting worse. He lists a number of factors as demonstrating declining conditions. Factors identified include:

- growth of waste lands due to the covering of soil by sand dunes or the loss of topsoils;
- drying up of wells;
- increasing salinity of water;
- reduced crop productivity.

Jodha sees the changes as being the result of changing land use patterns, particularly associated with the implementation of land reforms (1980, 1985, 1987). I will return to this point in Chapter 5.

In summing up this section, there are some broad conclusions:

- The evidence that the origin of the Thar Desert is a product of human activity is highly doubtful. Some researchers in palaeogeography (e.g. Dhir) suggest that the region has been essentially arid for a very long time. Other research (Allchin *et al.*) suggests that the aridity is natural, environment having gone through major fluctuations not attributable to human activity.
- While the size of the desert may not have increased in the present century, there is considerable evidence that environmental conditions have been getting worse and that the major reason for the decline is associated with human factors - especially increasing land use.

Famines

The result of the extreme unpredictability and unreliability of rainfall in western Rajasthan is that subsistence is risky. At worst it may lead to famine. It is important, however, to remember that drought is not necessarily famine. Drought is a failure of rainfall; famine is a failure of subsistence. Drought is determined by climatic conditions; famine does not necessarily follow from conditions of drought. Food shortage may be ameliorated by transfer of food from other areas, or famine may occur in a situation of overall food surplus.

As this study is centrally concerned with responses to famine and strategies intended to avoid the worst consequences of famine, it is important to put the incidence of famine in historical perspective.

At least from Mughal times some of the Rajput states have had a degree of centralised administration which collected data on income from the various fiefs and which kept records on land grants, taxes and major events, including famine. By the later part of the nineteenth century administration was on a fairly firm footing, with annual reports being prepared by the governments of the various states. Many of the older records are still extant, although the task of cataloguing has not yet proceeded very far. Nevertheless there are a number of reports written in the twentieth century by officials or Ministers of the Government of Jodhpur state which summarise the incidence of famines in Rajasthan from the beginning of the nineteenth century or earlier. There is scattered evidence of famines in Rajasthan at least as far back as what Sharma (1972) calls the Proto-Rajput Period (400-1200 AD). A study of the history of famines in Rajasthan by Kachhawaha (1985) contains a discussion of famines in this period.

Rajasthanis classify famines into four types: *trinkal*, a famine involving fodder shortage; *annakal*, a famine involving grain shortage;

jalakal, a famine involving water shortage and *trikal*, a treble famine, involving shortage of grain, fodder and water (Kachhawaha 1985).

In a report on the Jodhpur Government's Famine Relief Programme, Kothawalla (1939) lists twenty-one famines which occured from 1804 to the time of his writing. There are some inconsistencies between his account and that of Madho Singh, the Famine Minister in his report on the 1939-40 famine (Singh 1943). For the fifty year period preceeding the 1939-40 famine Singh lists eleven trikal (treble famines) affecting Jodhpur State. Several of the famines Singh describes as trikal are given less serious classifications by Kothawalla. Table 2.4 is a composite table listing all of the famines from 1804 to 1938-39 indicating the classifications given by each author.

The word 'famine' usually refers to an extreme food shortage causing hunger and suffering to a population or part of a population. The usual connotation is that a famine is a crisis. As it is presently used in India, 'famine' has an administrative definition which does not necessarily indicate crisis, high mortality or great suffering. Famine is declared on the basis of an assessment that a particular village has a net food deficit, that is, more food is needed for the population than is available from agriculture in a given period. Indian government statistics rely on this definition.

Table 2.5 identifies declared famine areas (by village numbers per sub-district) for Jodhpur district from 1963-64 to 1985-86. The drought that followed failure of subsequent monsoons in 1986, 1987 and 1988 is commonly regarded as one of the worst to strike India this century.

Historically, the most typical response to drought and famine was to migrate. In the famine of 1868-69 there was massive movement from some of the western states, including the migration of one and a half million people from Marwar (Kachhawaha 1980). In the 1891-92 famine 199,600 people (8% of the population of Marwar) left with 661,906 head of livestock (Resident, Western Rajputana States 1893).

Migration remains a common response, but the mass migrations of the past have been largely replaced by rural-urban migration of people seeking employment and by limited migration by specialist herders only.

A major factor in management of famine, at least since the beginning of the Mughal period, has been the response of the state to famine. The practices of the modern Indian and Rajasthan governments centre around grain subsidies and famine relief employment projects, which provide relief labour on projects such as water storage construction. (These responses, and their effectiveness, will be discussed in Chapter 9.) The Rajput states also made attempts to deal with famine.

Table 2.4

Famines affecting Marwar State from 1804 to 1939-40

	Type according to	
Year	Kothawalla (1939)	Singh (1943)*
1804	Annakal	
1812-13	Trikal	
1833-34	Trikal	
1838-39	Annakal	
1848-49	Trikal	
1850-51	Annakal	
1853-54	Annakal	
1868	Trikal	
1869	Annakal	
1877	Trikal	
1891-92	Trikal	Trikal (First year in sample period)
1895-96	Annakal	Trikal
1898-99	Annakal & Trinkal	Trikal
1899-1900	Trikal	Trikal
1905-06	Trinkal	Trikal
1915-16	Trinkal	Trikal
1918-19	Cheap grain shops opened due to high price of grain #	Trikal
1921-22	As above	Trikal
1925-26	Trinkal	Trikal
1928-29	Cheap grain shops opened due to high price of grain	Trikal
1936-37	Various parts of state affected differently	Not Mentioned (Not Trikal)
1938-39	Not included in sample period	Trikal

* Occurences of Trikal Famines only recorded.

From this point Kothawalla tends to switch from use of threefold classification to short descripion of conditions.

Key:

Trinkal	*Annakal*	*Trikal*
fodder shortage	water shortage	grain, fodder and water shortage (triple famine)

Bhati (Introduction to Nainsi 1968-1974), discussing Marwar during the period when it was a Mughal tributary state, points out that land rent was reduced to a nominal level during famine and drought conditions. In the late nineteenth and early twentieth centuries the Rajput states rsponded to famine by the same strategy of reducing taxes. They also provided relief funds which were supplemented by voluntary contributions (often large ones) from merchants. These practices are described by Kachhawaha (1985) in a general study of the history of famine in Rajasthan.

In 1935 famine was declared in a number of parts of Marwar. In an annual administrative report the relief measures taken were described:

> With a view to afford relief to the agriculturalists in the affected parganas the following relief measures were ordered to be adopted:-
> (1) Opening of grass and fodder depots in the affected parganas and selling of grass at the rate of -/8/- a maund and wheat straw at the rate of -/4/- a maund...
> (2) Throwing open of all reserved forest areas for free grazing and making arrangements at a cost of Rs. 3,000 for improvement of water supply for the animals grazing in these areas.
> (3) Remission of fees charged by the Forest Department for grazing cattle in the affected areas...
> (4) Opening of poor houses and grain shops, where required.
> (5) Distribution of... loans to agriculturalists.
> (6) Suspension of all revenue realisations in the affected parganas.
> (7) Starting of Relief works by the P.W.D. where required.
> (8) Stopping the execution of decrees against agriculturalists in the affected areas, and the suspension of all proceedings against them under the Marwar Public Demands Recovery Ordinance for one year.
>
> Three famine Depots of grass were opened in September 1936, and other relief measures were adopted later on whenever they were essential. (Government of Jodhpur 1938:21)

Table 2.5 - Famine-affected villages in Jodhpur District 1963-86

Samvat year affected	Roman year	No. of affected villages by Tehsil						Total No. of villages (725)
		Jodhpur (209)	Bilara (161)	Osian (135)	Phalodi (128)	Shergarh (92)	Bhopalgarh (115)	
2020	1963-64	55	104	99	128	71	-	457
2021	1964-65	nil	nil	6	4	39	-	49
2022	1965-66	4	nil	17	104	12	-	137
2023	1966-67	nil	73	38	43	9	-	163
2024	1967-68	nil	nil	19	43	23	-	85
2025	1968-69	209	161	135	128	92	-	725
2026	1969-70	209	161	132	127	92	-	721
2027	1970-71	nil	nil	nil	38	11	-	49
2028	1971-72	126	79	56	105	51	-	417
2029	1972-73	193	149	130	128	92	-	692
2030	1973-74	nil	nil	nil	nil	nil	-	nil
2031	1974-75	209	161	135	128	92	-	725
2032	1975-76	nil	nil	nil	nil	nil	-	nil
2033	1976-77	nil	nil	nil	nil	nil	-	nil
2034	1977-78	nil	nil	nil	nil	nil	-	nil
2035	1978-7.	114	10	79	125	92	-	420
2036	1979-80	161	161	135	128	92	-	677
2037	1980-81	209	161	130	128	92	-	720
2038	1981-82	209	161	135	128	92	-	725
		(209)	**(78)**	**(103)**	**(128)**	**(92)**	**(115)**	
2039	1982-83	209	78	103	128	92	115	725
2040	1983-84	nil	nil	nil	nil	21	nil	nil
2041	1984-85	101	7	74	110	80	54	426
2042	1985-86	209	77	103	128	92	115	724

Notes:

1. Bhopalgarh Tehsil formed in 2039 from villages taken from Osian and Bilara Tehsils. Numbers of villages by Tehsil at head of columns refer to total pre-2039. Revised numbers in **bold** after 2038.
2. There were some typographical errors on the paper from which this data was abstracted. In each case the totals have been corrected for consistency with Tehsil figures. Any errors are minor.

Source: Collector's Office, Jodhpur

Human Population

I have already pointed out the importance of the human presence in the Indian Desert. The population of western Rajasthan is rapidly increasing. Malhotra and Saha (1985) point out that the population of the Rajasthan Desert increased more than threefold in the period 1901-1981. Consistent with this figure, the population of Jodhpur District increased by a fraction under 293% from 1901 to 1981 (calculated from the Census of India 1981a). Mehta (1984:44) points out that the semi-arid and arid districts more than doubled their population in the period 1901-1961. Five districts in Rajasthan, including three in the arid region (Jodhpur, Bikaner and Ganganagar) have exceeded the state decadal growth rate in each of the last three decades while Jodhpur and Ganganagar have exceeded it 'in every decade in the century' (Mehta 1984:45).

In a study of fertility patterns in selected villages in western Rajasthan, Tewari (1980) found that fertility was lowest in arid and highest in sub-humid villages. However the survival rate is slightly higher in the arid areas. Mehta, without citing figures notes that the survival rate is highest in the arid parts of Rajasthan (1984).

One of the characteristics of population growth in the twentieth century is the change in the balance between rural and urban dwellers. For all of Rajasthan, the percentage of urban population to the entire population has increased. In 1911 it was 13% and it was 17.6% in 1971 (Mehta 1984). Mehta suggests that the earlier increases were due to the inclusion of new towns in the census (partly, I assume, due to the reclassification of larger villages as towns as they reached the critical population level which defines towns for census purposes). However later increases to the growth of the proportion of urban dwellers to the whole population were due to the growth of the existing urban centres. As an indication of the rate of increase in urban populations, Jodhpur city has increased from 79,109 in 1901 (Census of Marwar 1931b) to 506,345 in 1981 (Census of India 1981a), an overall increase of 540%. This is higher than the threefold general increase for western Rajasthan.

Despite the general growth in the population of Rajasthan since 1901 there have been fluctuations. These are usually attributable to migration and mortality associated with drought/famine.

Table 2.6 gives the population of Rajasthan at decennial censuses from 1891 to 1981. Over the sixty year period the overall increase was 23.5%, but there were severe fluctuations. Firstly, in 1901 (following the great famine of 1898-1900) there was a drop of 20.3% compared to 1891. Again, following an increase from 1901 to 1911, there was a drop from 1911 to 1921. In fact, it was not until between 1931 and 1941 that the 1891 population was again reached.

After 1951 there was a sudden take-off, with the 1981 population reaching 34,261,862 (Census of India 1981c). Some possible reasons for this sudden change, after a slow start, will be discussed in Chapter 7.

In addition to general trends of increase or decrease there are fluctuations at the local level. Even in adjacent villages it is quite common for fluctuations to go against the general trends. An examination of population figures for the villages in my field study (Table 7.1) emphasises this point.

Table 2.6

Population of Rajasthan from 1891 to 1981

1891	12,943,836
1901	10,318,677
1911	11,031,827
1921	10,339,655
1931	11,786,004
1941	14,253,901
1951	15,984,169
1961	20,155,602
1971	25,765,806
1981	34,261,862

Note: Populations 1891 to 1951 are taken from Census of India 1951 and figures for 1961 to 1981 are taken from Census of India 1981a. The figures for 1891 to 1951 were calculated by adding figures for Rajputana and Ajmer. There is a discrepancy of just over 15,000 (underennumeration) between 1951 figures calculated in this way and the 1951 figure cited in Table 26, Census of India 1981a. The source of the error is not clear but probably relates to an adjustment of boundaries.

Land Use and Economic Activity

(a) Rural

The main forms of rural economic activity in western Rajasthan are agriculture and pastoralism. Just as the relative rainfall increases from west to east, so does the relative importance of agriculture. Predominantly, agriculture is monsoonal. Irrigation is rare. Nevertheless, apart from the extreme west where semi-nomadic and nomadic pastoralism are predominant, agriculture and pastoralism co-exist in some mix or other throughout the entire region.

It is important to stress this point because the Census of India tends to distort this picture. Sometimes the inconsistencies involved are quite blatant. In 1983 I visited several villages in Jaisalmer District. Agriculture was obviously not a more significant occupation than pastoralism in these villages or, for that matter in the district as a whole. The 1961 Census of India explicitly states that 'animal husbandry is the main occupation of the people living in the district' (Census of India 1961a: Introduction, para. 18).

The same Census handbook says that the net sown area of Jaisalmer was 3.7% of the total area in the district. Yet according to the census tables there were 34,744 cultivators, 350 agricultural labourers and only 8461 workers in Category 3, which includes pastoralists. I would suggest that the large proportion of cultivators to pastoralists is quite inconsistent with the small proportion of agricultural land. This is particularly important given that the agricultural land is only useful in monsoon periods anyhow, and given that the monsoon in Jaisalmer is particularly unreliable.

Regarding my field area, the Census of India (1971 and 1981a) gives the main occupations of all four villages as cultivation and agricultural labour. This is quite inconsistent with observable facts and reflects a systematic bias towards the overemphasis of cultivation and agricultural labour in the reporting of the Census of India. Table 2.7 abstracts the main occupations for each of the four villages in 1981.

The failure of census respondents to describe either their primary or secondary occupations (in terms of time spent) as livestock husbandry, is odd. Agriculture, in Hinganiya particularly, is never more than a seasonal activity, while pastoralism is a significant aspect of economic activity and is the only one of year round importance.

A partial explanation for the undervaluing of pastoralism may be in terms of a tendency to confuse cash income and days worked as criteria for determining primary occupation. For most (not all) of the household heads in Hinganiya, agriculture, or wage labour may be the main sources of cash income, but not necessarily the main type of activity in terms of total days worked. Pastoralism requires a steady input of labour, but does not earn as much. Yet, according to the census criteria (Census of India 1981b) categorisation should be on the basis of days worked, not on the basis of income.

There is a further explanation for the undervaluing of pastoralism. A significant amount of the work involved in pastoralism is done by children, particularly by young unmarried girls. Although all people who do some form of work apart from domestic work should be accounted for in the census, in practice the work of women or children is largely ignored or undervalued. In Table 2.7 the numbers of 'non-workers' of

Table 2.7

Hinganiya, Kur, Khokhariya and Kukunda - types of workers in 1981

Village	Cultivators		Agricultural Labourers		Household Industry Manufacturing Processing services and repairs		Other Workers		**Total** Main Workers		**Total** Marginal Workers		**Total** Non-Workers	
	M	F	M	F	M	F	M	F	M	F	M	F	M	F
Hinganiya	91	77	-	-	-	1	2	-	93	77	-	6	116	117
Kur	293	31	7	3	12	1	41	6	353	41	-	116	344	358
Khokhariya	155	3	-	-	2	-	27	-	184	3	-	164	151	151
Kukunda	228	-	4	-	1	-	52	-	285	-	8	286	244	261

Note: Workers in pastoralism are recorded under 'Other Workers'

Source: Census of India, 1981a

each sex are approximately equal in each of the four villages and it seems reasonable to assume that the figures largely represent children. As they are not counted as workers, pastoralism is undervalued. As a general point it is also worth noting here that female labour is also systematically undervalued as women are largely categorised as marginal workers. This does not accord with reality.

The variables, nomad, pastoralist and agriculturalist can be combined in a number of ways to describe types of land use or economic activity.

(1) Nomadic Pastoralism

This is now a rather rare adaptation, except in areas such as the highly arid parts of Jaisalmer, Barmer and Bikaner districts. Even in these areas, because of the low population densities, the absolute numbers of nomadic pastoralists are small.

(2) Semi-nomadic pastoralism

Throughout western Rajasthan there are pastoralists who live in permanent villages, but who migrate with their herds on a seasonal basis. In many districts there are specialist pastoralist castes. The Raikas (also known as Rebaris) are the best known Rajathani pastoralists and who have been the subject of recent research by anthropologists (Srivastava 1991, Köhler-Rollefson 1992, Agrawal 1993, 1994). Sometimes members of castes not traditionally pastoralists will individually become specialists. This is comparatively common among the Bishnois, although their traditional caste occupation is agriculture. In the far west members of all castes tend to be pastoralists and an analysis of census figures carried out by Sopher (1975) suggests that specialist pastoralist castes are not found in the region.

The extent and frequency of migrations by semi-nomadic (or migratory) pastoralists is highly flexible. It depends very much on annual conditions. For example, in times of water or fodder shortage large numbers of livestock are taken on migrations, within, through and out of Jodhpur District. There is no fixed annual pattern: in very bad years the migrating herdsman may stay away throughout the whole year; in some years they may take their herds only short distances and/or for short periods; in other years they may move to other states; in particularly good years they may not go anywhere at all. The range of migrations may be immense, with journeys into Gujarat or Madhya Pradesh being common. Although the Pakistan border is a legal barrier to herd migration, in fact some illegal migration does occur.

Among semi-nomadic pastoralists it is common for for the herds to be accompanied only by men. Women and children tend to remain in the village to which they will return after the migration. In fact some men also remain in the village, either because they are old, unwell or because they have other occupations.

(3) Non-pastoralist nomads

There are a number of castes in western Rajasthan which are fully or substantially nomadic and which travel around performing a number of different (and often peripheral) economic roles. These include the Banjaras (who trade in salt and bullocks/donkeys), the Gawariyas (merchants dealing in trinkets including bangles and cheap toys), Gaduliar Lohars (nomadic blacksmiths) and Joghis (snake charmers and musicians). There have been several papers on non-pastoralist nomads in India (Misra 1969; Hayden 1979; Fisher 1981) and there are monographs by Misra (1977) and Ruhela (1968) on the Gadulia Lohars (a caste of nomadic blacksmiths). Apart from Misra's and Ruhela's work the literature specifically on Rajasthani non-pastoralist nomads is sparse.

(4) Agro-pastoralism

Where people are agriculturalists they generally also participate to some extent in pastoralism. The mix ranges from people who are primarily farmers, but keep a few goats or cows for milk, to those who concentrate on livestock but also own small amounts of land. Unless an agro-pastoralist depends significantly on livestock, he is unlikely to migrate with his herds. If migration is necessary due to drought conditions, it is likely that the animals will be placed in the hands of a paid shepherd (usually a Raika) who takes the animals with him, leaving the owner to sow his crops if (and when) the monsoon next comes. Alternatively, several households may combine herds under the control of one or more men who migrate with them.

(5) Pure agriculture

Pure agriculture is a possibility, but very few rural people actually own farming land without keeping at least a few animals for milk. The largest proportion of agriculture, whether pure or mixed with pastoralism, is monsoon dependent. It is for this reason that pure agriculture is rarely viable. Dependence on agriculture is most viable when land is irrigated. In 1971-72, only just over 2% of the cultivated area of Jodhpur District was irrigated (Agarwal 1979).

I am not suggesting here that agriculture is not important. Rather, I am stressing that the agro-pastoral mix is a characteristic and essential aspect of the economy. In fact, there is a great deal of agriculture in the arid zone, and this is something of a paradox. Jodhpur, for example, is within the arid zone according to Meigs' criteria (1953), and Meigs says that one of the defining characteristics of arid areas is that they are unsuitable for agriculture. Yet, in 1972-73, 49.12% of land in Jodhpur District was cropped (Agarwal 1979).

There is considerable evidence that the extent of agriculture is increasing, and that this is leading to an environmental crisis. Jodha (1980) emphasises the recent trend of increase in area under crops. He cites a 49.5% increase (for the arid region of western Rajasthan) from 1951 to 1961, with a further increase of 13% by 1971. Land which was earlier classified as 'cultivable wastes and barren lands' is now used for agriculture.

It is tempting to argue that the increase in agriculture represents a movement towards the sedentarisation of pastoral nomads. To a certain extent this is correct, as there is considerable evidence for a process of sedentarisation and sedentarisation is an underlying theme of government policy. It appears that pastoral nomads occupied parts of eastern Rajasthan, or at least the eastern fringes of the desert, into the early years of this century. Most of these have now settled. Inder Dan Detha, a farmer with a very informed interest in anthropology, told me that his grandfather was a pastoral nomad (a Charan) who settled in Borunda in eastern Jodhpur District about sixty years ago and became a farmer, despite conflict with the landlords.

While agriculture has been a factor for some time in western Rajasthan, it has increased immensely in recent years. But, to what extent has this been at the expense of pastoralism? Both agriculture and pastoralism have, in fact, increased in intensity. Marginal lands have been taken over for agricultural purposes, but, at the same time there has been a massive increase in livestock numbers. Jodha (1980), while describing the expansion of agriculture, also points out that livestock numbers increased by 45% from 1951 to 1961 and by another 5% by 1965. The result is not just a crisis in agriculture, but, as Salzman points out, there is a crisis in pastoralism as well. The crisis involves

> . . .increasing costs per livestock unit and concomitant reduction in return, social conflict resulting from competition over scarce resources, and environmental degradation as the limited resources available are over-exploited. (1986:49)

(b) Urban

Much of the population of western Rajasthan is rural and thus primarily concerned with agriculture or pastoralism. Nevertheless, a significant and growing number of people live in cities or large towns. Jodhpur and Bikaner are the largest, but there are also a significant number of middle size towns distributed throughout the region. The raison d'etre of most towns is as market and service centres. In many cases the prominence of towns as trading centres has great antiquity and is related to positions on caravan routes. The prominence of Jodhpur and Bikaner was associated with their status as capitals of major states, but they are also significant as market centres and Jodhpur, in particular, is becoming something of an industrial centre.

In this century western Rajasthan has been the source of much of the merchant wealth in India. Throughout India many of the largest merchants are called Marwaris, highlighting their links with Marwar (see Timberg 1978). Many of these Marwaris maintain ties with their home towns and villages. In Jodhpur today there is a powerful merchant class made up of various castes of Jain merchants, as well as some Hindu castes (including the Sonis, or goldsmiths).

One of the features of the cities of western Rajasthan (again, I am referring particularly to Jodhpur) is their rapid growth. The huge growth of the population of Jodhpur has been associated with increased industrialisation. The thriving building industry in Jodhpur has meant that work requiring unskilled wage labour is available and this has been a powerful force attracting the rural poor to the city, either temporarily or permanently.

Another major factor in the growth of urban centres is the heavy military presence associated with proximity to Pakistan. Both Bikaner and Jodhpur have large military establishments. The Indian Western Air Force is commanded from Jodhpur and there is a large permanent army presence. This factor has affected the economy of the city, in the sense that service industries and businesses have developed accordingly. Military service (in the Army or Border Security Force) is a common career choice for villagers, although the great majority of villagers who join the services are Rajputs. Service in the Police or the Rajasthan Armed Constabulary is also common.

The final factor in urban growth is the increasing tourist industry. In the last few years a popular picture of Jaisalmer as an exotic medieval paradise in the desert has led to a rapid development of tourism. Jodhpur, being on the most convenient route to Jaisalmer, has experienced changes, mostly in terms of new hotels and restaurants. Outside of Jodhpur, Bikaner and Jaisalmer the impact has been small, apart from those villages which are on the routes for tours and camel safaris. Nevertheless jobs in hotels, tourist bungalows and tour agencies are increasingly attractive to those villagers who have been to school (usually from the higher castes) and they present yet another aspect of the interrelationship between the cities and the rural hinterland.

Conclusion

In this chapter, I have discussed the major features of the environment of western Rajasthan. In summary, the climate is characterised by low annual rainfall which is both variable and unpredictable. There is some evidence that the environment has become arid in the last two or three thousand years and there is considerable evidence that the desert conditions have deteriorated within the present century. The human history of the region paradoxically shows a shift from a sparse population of pastoral nomads during the humid period about 4000 years ago (the Harappan civilisation did not penetrate the desert itself) towards a large and essentially sedentary agricultural population in all except the most arid areas in the last few centuries, at a time when the environment has been arid. In the current century population increase has been very rapid and there has been an increasing urban population and a growth of industry.

The critical problem faced by the rural population is how to cope with the inevitability and unpredictability of drought conditions, and the famine which is related to drought. I have described the opportunities for wage labour opened up by increasing urbanisation; I have described the role of migration; I have also described the broad parameters of the mixture between agriculture and pastoralism which are the main components of rural economy. The focus for the rest of this study will be to show how the changing socio-economic conditions are related to environmental parameters and particularly to the uncertainty of the environment. The interaction between these factors can best be seen at the village level. In the next chapter I will introduce a particular village setting in which these interactions occur.

Chapter 3

Fieldsite: Hinganiya and the Surrounding Villages

Introduction

This chapter is intended to provide a brief introduction to the villages in which I carried out fieldwork. Map 4 shows the locations of the four villages and important adjacent villages. The description in this chapter describes the situation up to the time of my field visit in 1987. Subsequent developments are not discussed.

Prior to administrative changes in 1982 Hinganiya village was in Bilara Tehsil of Jodhpur District. In the changes of administrative areas it was included in the newly created Bhopalgarh Tehsil. The village is located about 40 kilometres to the east of Jodhpur. Asaranada railway station, on the main line linking Jodhpur with Delhi (and, by branch line, with Jaipur), is 4-5 kilometres to the north. A network of cart tracks links Hinganiya with Asaranada and with nearby villages. A few kilometres to the south is the main highway from Jodhpur to Ajmer, Jaipur and Delhi.

Hinganiya is the smallest of the three administratively defined villages[1] in the Gram Panchayat of Kur. The other two villages are Kur itself, about 4 kilometres to the south-east, and Khokhariya, about 4 kilometres to the south. The nearest village is Kukunda, about 2 kilometres to the south-west of Hinganiya. Kukunda is, administratively, in a separate panchayat. There is quite a lot of visiting between villages and one or two-day trips to Pipar City or Jodhpur are quite common. On such trips villagers do banking, marketing or other tasks. Both Pipar City and Jodhpur are accessible by train from Asaranada, and Jodhpur is accesible by truck from Kukunda.

The economy of the four villages in the study area is based on mixed farming and herding. Pastoralism is a year-round activity, but, apart from a few irrigated hectares in Kur, agriculture is entirely monsoonal. Some irrigation, using underground water, occurs in other nearby villages.

---

1 A Gram Panchayat is a village or multi-village level political division with an elected Panchayat (or council). The Panchayat is headed by an elected Sarpanch and Up-Sarpanch (deputy Sarpanch). A village, administratively defined, is the smallest area for which separate land records are kept.

Within six or seven kilometres to the east (at Ram Ravas) and to the south (at Binawas), irrigation is reasonably common.

It is important to stress that much of the description of agro-pastoral activity which follows later in this study refers to the combination of rainfed agriculture and pastoralism which occurs in Hinganiya. The situation is different elsewhere, even in patches quite close to Hinganiya. This is not to suggest that Hinganiya is, in this way, unusual. Many villages with similar lack of irrigation exist throughout western Rajasthan. An important result of the dependence on rainfed agriculture is that farmers in rainfed areas tend to be poorer, on average, than farmers in irrigated areas.

Hinganiya

There are members of five castes resident in Hinganiya. Of the so-called 'clean' castes there are Rajputs, Jats and Bishnois. The other two castes, Meghwals and Nayaks (often called Bhils), are scheduled castes. At Table 3.1 is a list of all castes present in the village. The population, in 1981 was 409 (Census of India, 1981a). In 1985/86 when I carried out a village census there were 433 residents including 29 'part-time residents'. (I will explain this term fully in Chapter 9. In essence it refers to people who move between the village and a residence at the place where they work.)

A pond which collects run-off rainwater, two underground tanks, a water reservoir and a two-room school are all situated on panchayat (common) land to the north of the village. The residential core (the *abadi*) has as its centre an open area roughly triangular in shape (see Map 5). Two sides (the western and southern) are fringed with the houses of the Rajputs. The Nayak and Meghwal huts are situated on the third side. The separation of castes into distinct areas is not completely rigid. There is one Rajput household in the middle of this area (it was established in late 1983) and the Meghwal cluster adjoins this single Rajput household. The Nayak houses extend more or less in a line on either side of this enclave.

All Bishnois living within the borders of the area administratively defined as Hinganiya, live in *dhanis*, which are hamlets dispersed throughout the agricultural fields away from the *abadi*. The single household of Jats and some households from each of the other castes also live in *dhanis*. The four households of Rajputs from the Soda clan (all other Rajputs resident in Hinganiya are Bhati Rajputs) live in a single *dhani* known as Soda-ki-dhani. Other *dhanis*, whether inhabited by a single household, or several related households, are known by the name of the household or lineage head.

Table 3.1

Castes present in Hinganiya, Kur, Khokhariya and Kukunda

Hinganiya	*Kur*	*Khokhariya*	*Kukunda*
Rajput	Rajput	Rajput	Rajput
Jat	Brahman	Jat	Jat
Bishnoi	Jat	Bishnoi	Bishnoi
Meghwal	Bishnoi	Goswami	Goswami
Nayak/Bhil	Goswami	Daroga	Suthar
	Daroga	Raika	Nai
	Raika	Meghwal	Meghwal
	Nai	Nayak/Bhil	Nayak/Bhil
	Suthar		Mirasia
	Bania		
	Sadh		
	Darzi		
	Dholi		
	Meghwal		
	Nayak/Bhil		
	Harijan		

Note: Castes are listed in approximate descending order of caste ranking. Brahmans, locally, are commonly ranked below Rajputs

Generally speaking the houses of the Meghwals and Nayaks are simple huts. They are round, made of mud-brick and have thatched roofs. There are, however, a few structures made of stone and one or two comparatively substantial, albeit single-roomed, rectangular houses have been constructed. The houses of the Rajput section are quite different, and generally far more substantial. There are far more *pakka* buildings, made of stone blocks and with stone, concrete or corrugated iron roofs, although even these buildings are mostly single-room constructions. Throughout the Rajput section thatched roof huts and rectangular buildings are intermingled. Frequently individual households include separate buildings of both types, used for various purposes at different times of the year. Huts are ideal for cooking and are also preferred for sleeping in warm weather. *Pakka* buildings are ideal for storage and are much warmer in the winter.

Rajput houses tend to have a fortress like appearance, with high walls at the front and often with locked doors barring entrance to the central area of the village. However, this is largely for appearance. There is rarely any wall behind the houses and access from the fields, or from other Rajput houses, is relatively simple. The symbolic aspect of this false-fronted fortress-like style of architecture is, I suggest, related to the self-image of Rajputs as Kshatriyas (warriors).

Within the triangular village centre is a thatched roof hut known as the *kordi*. This functions as a guest hut and as a meeting place. Two other buildings are known as *kordi*, a term which can be glossed as 'meeting place'. A second, more substantial meeting place is located on the perimeter of the central area in a plot adjoining the house of the ex-Thakur (ex-landlord) of the village. This open-fronted building and a separate hut nearby are considered to be the property of the Thakur and, in the period before the incorporation of the state of Jodhpur into independent India, was apparently the location of official activity. A third building at a *dhani* owned by the current Up-Sarpanch (deputy mayor) of the Village Panchayat, and located only a few hundred metres from the residential village, is also known as a *kordi*.

A small temple (dedicated to the folk-deity, Ram Devji) is situated within the village centre. Other temples and shrines are scattered throughout the village and surrounding fields.

Also in the village centre is a *chaki* (an electric powered mill) owned by one of the Rajputs. It is the only building in the village which is used for commercial purposes. There are no shops at all, although one of the Meghwals keeps supplies of bidis (cheap cigarettes made from rolled tobacco leaves) and matches which he resells. At the time of my departure in January 1986 one of the Rajputs (the son of the owner of the mill) was preparing to purchase some goods to set up a small shop.

To the north of the village, near the two underground tanks, is a two-room school building. This building was constructed during my stay in 1983, but there was difficulty in finding a teacher willing to stay and, until January 1986, the school was only very occasionally in operation. In January 1986 a new teacher took up his appointment and he was still there in August 1987. The Hinganiya school caters only for junior primary classes. Older children attend school in Kukunda (up to class eight) and those few who pursue further education travel to Jodhpur.

Electricity has only recently become available. Supply lines had already reached the edge of the village at the time of my first visit in March 1983, but no connections had been made prior to the end of my first period of fieldwork in January 1984. By August 1985 a connection had been provided to the mill, but no other connections had been approved. Several households had made 'informal' connections for household lighting. The situation was essentially unchanged at the time of my brief visit in August 1987.

There is no system of sanitation. However, as the village is small, visits to the fields are not too inconvenient and Hinganiya, unlike larger villages, is fairly clean.

Drinking water is piped to the village. Water is stored in two large underground tanks. (The second was built in early 1983, as a famine relief project.) There is also an above ground reservoir connected to the pipe. The supply of piped water is inconsistent due partly to dependence on a very unreliable electricity supply for the pump located some kilometres away. During the extremely hot weather following the failed monsoon of 1985, the high level of demand for water for domestic purposes and livestock led to a severe, if temporary, shortage. The pumping stations were simply unable to cope with the greatly increased demand in the district. Water was brought several kilometres from excavated dams or small natural wet-season lakes (both called *nadis*) containing permanent or semi-permanent water. This water was carried in tanks hauled by camel or tractor. At this time the limited water in the underground tanks was very brackish and dirty. In 1987 the situation was much worse. The Sarpanch was, at his own expense, providing daily tank-loads of water to Hinganiya even in August.

Even after the good monsoon rains of 1983, there was a mild shortage of water during the period of hot weather which followed the monsoon. However the problem was not anywhere near as serious as that of 1985 or 1987, due largely to the the persistence, for several months after the end of the monsoon, of surface water as an alternative source of drinking water for livestock.

In the drought-stricken pre-monsoon period of early 1983, a *nadi* (a pond for the collection of rainwater) was dug as a government funded famine relief project. This, filled with run-off water during the subsequent monsoon, served as a supplementary source of water (mainly for livestock), and lasted from the end of the monsoon (in early September) until early November. In 1985 it was virtually dry when I arrived in August and it was completely dry in August 1987.

Some *dhanis* are located on the pipeline and have direct access to water without the need to carry from the village by hand (or rather, by head) in pots or in water-bags carried on the backs of camels.

Prior to the building of the pipeline most water was carried from the well in Kukunda by one of these methods. Water is still sometimes obtained from the Kukunda well in exchange for an annual levy which is used to pay the well contractor. The levy is based on a fixed price per household and supplementary charges per head of livestock of various types. The levy is charged only if water is taken in a given year, but informants claimed that use on a single occasion led to the full annual charge.

There are in fact two wells in Hinganiya. One has been there for hundreds of years,[2] but yields water which is completely undrinkable and which is also useless for irrigation due to salinity. This well is a substantial stonework construction. The other well is of fairly recent construction and is situated near a Bishnoi *dhani* some distance from the village. Again due to salinity the water is unusable except for making mud bricks.

There is very little information on the history or origins of the village. It certainly existed in 1662, the last year of the survey by Muhnot Nainsi (Nainsi 1968-1974). According to Nainsi it was a Bishnoi village at that time. Oral accounts of villagers claim that the original Bishnoi inhabitants abandoned it prior to it being destroyed by the Mughals.[3]

Kur

Kur and Khokhariya are the other two villages within the Kur Panchayat. Kur is a comparatively large village with a population of 1312 in 1981. It has several small shops, a mill, several wells, a school, a post office and even a newly constructed hospital - unstaffed at the time I left the field. It is a multi caste village.

The immediate appearance of the village suggests far greater wealth than Hinganiya. There are several quite substantial multi-roomed *pakka* houses, including the family home of the current Sarpanch (a merchant who has a business in Jodhpur where he spends much of his time) and the home of the descendant of the Thakur (landlord). Around the village are a few vegetable gardens made possible by well irrigation. The amount of irrigated land is, however, quite small. In 1981 only fourteen out of Kur's total area of 1707 hectares were irrigated (Census of India, 1981a). A few more hectares (probably less than ten) were apparently opened for irrigation between the census and 1985. These few hectares are the only irrigated land within the panchayat.

Hinganiya residents frequently visit Kur in order to obtain supplies, including rationed goods (sugar and, following declaration of famine, wheat). The Brahman who serves the Hinganiya Rajputs as a priest lives

2 Oral history asserts the considerable age of the well. A reference in Nainsi's Gazetteer indicates that it was there as far back as 1662 (Nainsi 1968-1974).

3 No date was given for the sack, nor was it linked by my informants with any specific Mughal incursion. In fact The Mughals invaded Jodhpur on three occasions (in 1544, 1563 and 1679).

in Kur and also serves Khokhariya and Kur. Some other ritual specialists, including Dholis (drummers), serve Hinganiya from their homes in Kur. (A detailed discussion of caste interaction appears in Chapter 4.) The Patwari (land officer) for the Kur circle, which includes Hinganiya, has his office in Kur.

An all-weather road connects Kur with Binawas and with the paved road from Jodhpur to Pipar City.

Khokhariya

Khokhariya is between Hinganiya and Kukunda in size (population 653 in 1981). Like Hinganiya it has relatively few facilities and most goods and services are obtained from Kur. There is a junior primary school at Khokhariya. The older children travel to Kur.

The landscape around Khokhariya is, like Hinganiya sandy and barren. However there are far more trees in the area. There is a well, but no irrigation. Among the castes present are Raikas, a caste of specialist herdsmen, and the village is far more oriented towards pastoralism than any of the other three villages.

Kukunda

Kukunda (population 1084 in 1981) is the nearest village to Hinganiya. Although it is in a separate Panchayat, it is frequently visited by people from Hinganiya. It has a Government Upper Primary School (Classes 1 to 8) and older children from Hinganiya study in this school. Kukunda has two shops, although much less is available here than in Kur. There is also a daily milk-truck from Kukunda to Jodhpur. As this truck carries passengers it provides an alternative to the train from Asaranada as a means for Hinganiya residents to go to Jodhpur. In late January 1986 a bus service from Kukunda to Jodhpur commenced operations.

Special Characteristics of Hinganiya

It would be wrong to over-intellectualise the reasons for choosing Hinganiya as a field site. As I have pointed out in Chapter 1, the village was chosen for a number of very practical reasons. In retrospect, however, the choice of a small village threw up a number of interesting questions. Most village studies in India have concentrated on larger villages. Typically a population of about 1000 and about twenty different castes are given as explicit criteria for the selection of a village for study. Hinganiya is much smaller and has members of only five castes actually resident. An advantage of this small size and relative caste homogeneity was that it was possible to spend a considerable amount of time concentrating on the ethnography of each separate caste (as well, of course, as examining the relationships between the castes). What emerged was a picture of 'communities', which, to a considerable extent, had different values and practices. While the village itself could meaningfully be described as a community of people with common interests, whose social life was substantially focused within the village boundaries, it is also important to recognise that much of the social life of members of particular castes was focused on interaction with members of their caste in other villages.

I believe that the importance of separation of, and differences between, castes has been obscured by the emphasis on studying larger villages with greater numbers of castes. In these cases, it is the interactions between members of different castes, and the resulting hierarchical arrangement of castes, which have been emphasised. I do not wish to dispute the importance of hierarchy, but I wish to correct what I see as an overemphasis on interactions between castes at the expense of the internal social organisation and functioning of particular castes. Both aspects are an essential part of analysis. Apart from the ethnographic significance of the differences between castes, there are some practical implications of the distinctive social organisation of various castes which are relevant to their economic strategies, including the way that they respond to drought. The question of differing forms of social structure in various castes will be discussed in the next chapter.

Chapter 4
Castes and Caste Relationships

Introduction

In order to understand the agrarian system in any Indian local community it is necessary to understand the workings of the caste system, since caste patterns much social and economic behaviour.

The major responses to the uncertain environment of western Rajasthan involve utilising a wide variety of resources, either by spreading risks within the agro-pastoral economy, by moving into other physical regions (through nomadism) or by tapping in to the national economy, through civil service, military service or other employment.

In this chapter I aim to show how tapping in to diverse resource levels can be facilitated by some aspects of caste organisation. To a certain extent members of different castes have different strategies consonant with their economic status and with organisational features of their caste. One aspect of this is that the higher castes, which constitute an upper class at the village level, are able to utilise alternative resources more easily than the lower castes, because the options are more restricted for those castes which own little land. This aspect will be raised in this chapter and developed later.

I wish to emphasise that the use of the term 'class' in this context refers to a local level class structure defined in terms of economic criteria (essentially land ownership). All of the people in Hinganiya, and most of the people throughout the village cluster, would rank very low in a class system defined nationally or even on a district basis. While the differences loom large on a local level, they are relatively minor in the wider context.

In the pages that follow I will first describe some of the features of each of the five castes present in Hinganiya; secondly I will describe the main forms of caste interaction.

Rajputs

(a) Background

There are two distinct groups of Rajputs present in Hinganiya. The main Rajput population consists of members of the Bhati clan. The others are of the Soda clan. The Bhati Rajputs are descendants of one of the two original Thakurs (landlords) of the village. The four households of Soda Rajputs are descendants of one of two brothers (the other died childless) who moved to Hinganiya from Pali District about sixty years ago. In a census which I carried out in 1985-86, the four households of Soda Rajputs accounted for twenty-eight individuals; there were nineteen households of Bhatis (127 individuals).

In Rajasthan, Rajputs (literally *raja putra*, son of a king) are the principal representatives of the Kshatriya varna in the Hindu varna system, although some non-Rajput informants claim that some non-Rajput castes also have Kshatriya status. Most Rajputs would hotly dispute any such claims. For practical purposes, the words Rajput and Kshatriya are seen as equivalent by most Rajasthanis.

During the period when Rajasthan consisted of a number of princely states, all except two of these states were ruled by Rajputs. The Rajas were supported by other members of the warrior Rajput caste.

Tod, the British Political Agent to Western Rajputana early in the nineteenth century, wrote an account (1894, first published in 1829-32) of the history of the major Rajput kingdoms. He argued that the socio-political system of Rajasthan, even up to his own time, was similar to European feudalism. Without going into a debate about the utility of the concept of feudalism for comparative analysis, it is true to say that there were considerable similarities. Maharajahs were linked with local Rajput landlords, sometimes through various vassal intermediaries

In exchange for an annual rent and taxes and the provision of troops, the Rajas made grants of land to prominent Rajput lords. There were a number of distict types of grants, all involving different obligations and rights in the relationship between landlord and Raja. A system called *Jagir* was particularly common. (I shall be dealing with the landholding system in greater detail later.) Such a grant (usually hereditary) carried the title Thakur (or *Jagirdar*) and almost complete power over the residents of villages on the land. The Thakurs sub-let portions of land to various tenants in exchange for a share of production. From the other Rajputs resident in his domain (often, but not necessarily, from his own clan, sub-clan or lineage), the Thakur maintained a fighting force for the use of the Raja on call (and often for his own use).

Just as in feudal Europe, the ties were the subject of frequent rebellions and shifting alliances. The origin of ties between farmers and local chiefs seems to have involved something of a 'protection racket'. The development of large scale territorial units linking local chiefdoms under feudal lords was no doubt part of the same process. This is not to deny that the relationships between Maharajahs and vassals were highly ritualised and idealised.

The village Rajputs were themselves often tenants of the Thakur, and further sub-let land superfluous to their own needs. The extent to which Rajputs actually worked land held for self-cultivation themselves, or had it worked on their behalf by landless labourers, varied depending on the wealth of the individual Rajput. The *Jagir* land was something of a feudal estate, with a ruling Rajput caste headed by a Thakur, tenant farmers, artisans and landless labourers. An additional category of land (*khalsa*) was land directly controlled by the ruler. It tended to be at the centre of the kingdom.

The Rajputs, as Kshatriyas, included Rajas, courtiers and officials, Thakurs and the warrior cultivators in the villages. Increasingly the last group became cultivators, but a strong consciousness of warrior identity persists.[1]

Related to the socio-political structure described briefly above, was a set of values emphasising valour, honour, fame. The Rajput military tradition still exists at the village level. In Hinganiya, in 1985/86, six men were in the armed forces, and there were six retired servicemen. All of these (except one Bishnoi ex-serviceman) were Rajputs.

Rajputs have an elaborate egalitarianism in terms of food sharing. This can be seen as a form of camaraderie. Rajput men, irrespective of individual rank or prestige, eat from a common plate. When important guests are dining with their hosts both sides may force food into the mouths of the other, then proceed to eat, by hand, out of the common plate.[2] Rajputs are also characterised (and think of themselves as) meat-eaters and drinkers of wine, and often as womanisers.

Despite their self-image as womanisers, the Rajput attitude to the purity of their women seems similar to the chivalric code associated with feudal Europe. One Rajput told me of a Hindi saying which he translated as follows:

---

1 The Rajput's self-image as a warrior has been discussed by Hitchcock (1959).

2 The general meaning of this as a sort of aggressive display of egalitarianism was always obvious to me. However, since working in Nepal where ritual purity is much more seriously preserved than it is in Rajasthan, I have realised how radically this sort of behaviour departs from the Hindu concern with pollution. I am not sure whether the behaviour indicates a lack of concern with pollution or whether it is a symbolic statement about Rajput solidarity which *depends* on a breach of normal purity based behaviour.

When someone is spoiling your religion,
when someone is taking your property by force;
or when someone is insulting your ladies,
that is the day to fight.

All of these things are symbols of dignity and honour for a Rajput. Having and defending property and defending 'ladies' and religion are the basis of Rajput perceptions of status and self-image.

The concern with the virtue of Rajput women is evident in the legend of the famous fort at Chittorgarh. On three occasions the fort was under siege. The Rajput men rode out to certain death, while the women committed ritual suicide (*jauhar*), throwing themselves on a huge funeral pyre. Rajput legends often refer to bloody events like this, all demonstrating the ideal of Rajput behaviour and often emphasising glorious defeats rather than glorious victories.

Part of the underlying theme in this legend is virtue, but also evident is a distaste for subservience. Carstairs quotes from an interview with a very senior Rajput (the former holder of what Carstairs compares to a 'dukedom'):

> We had great times when he [the speaker's father] had his birthday. There would be a feast with wine and dancing girls. Yes, from 5 to 6 years old. I remember that. They were so well-dressed. We admire beauty but we do not touch it. They came from a servant caste or Beragi Saddhu caste, or Mahammedans. If a woman of high caste chose to do this work she would soon be killed. We think it is the lowest work, to be a puppet in another's hands. (Carstairs 1957:183)

Carstairs, who describes the distinct values of Rajputs, and their drinking, meat-eating and use of prostitutes, suggests that 'there is a conflict between a Rajput's caste and his religious values' (1957:124). While there is a recognition of conflict with Hindu values, this is rarely seen as important. At the same time, some Rajputs avoid meat and alcohol for religious reasons. Carstairs pressed the informant quoted above about the inconsistency of drinking and so on with 'spiritual rise' The informant argued that

> . . .so long as your spiritual rise is the most important thing for you, you can engage in everyday affairs... without being deflected from the most important purpose. (Carstairs 1957:194. The direct quote is from Carstairs, not his informant.)

This is, of course, the doctrinal Hindu position for Kshatriyas.

The existence of a characteristic set of Rajput values is an important determinant of Rajput behaviour. The most significant element economically is the impetus this gives to Rajputs towards taking up military service. The conception of Rajputs as being naturally good fighters enhances the chances of recruitment.

(b) Organisation of the Rajput Caste

The Rajput caste is sub-divided into three *vamsh* (lines). These are the the Suriyavamsh (sun-line, claiming descent from Rama), the Chandravamsh (moon-line, claiming descent from Krishna) and the Agnivamsh (the fire-line, claiming descent from Agni). Each *vamsh* consists of a number of sub-divisions. There are ten sub-divisions in the Suriyavamsh, four in the Chandravamsh and four in the Agnivamsh. In English translation these sub-divisions are usually called clans. In local usage the word *jati* (caste) is often used, although *jati* also refers to the category/group 'all Rajputs'. At first I believed that the most suitable term for these sub-divisions was sub-caste, but these groups are exogamous, which means that they do not meet an essential factor in the definition of sub-castes. A further feature of these sub-divisions is that the members claim descent from a common ancestor. For this reason, and because it is a commonly used translation, I use the term clan.

Clans are further sub-divided. The lower level of sub-division is, according to some informants, called a *khamp*. Other informants use *khamp* (usually less confidently) to refer to the clan. This confusion even exists among the more scholarly Rajputs. At the village level people very rarely use the term at all and few recognise it. As this level of sub-division usually consists of people claiming descent from a common ancestor (ocasionally the group is named after a place of origin), the term sub-clan is the most useful for analytical purposes.

Sub-clans are further sub-divided into lineages of various sizes. The word *awlad* (lineage) is used when individuals are referring to the descendants of a particular ancestor. The term does not refer to a lineage of any particular depth. It simply refers to all the patrilineal descendants of X For example, all Bhati Rajputs in Hinganiya are descendants of Sundar Dassji (the founding Bhati Thakur) and are thus part of *Sundar Dassji ka Awlad* (Sundar Dassji's lineage). At another level it is possible to talk about all of the descendants of Moti Singh (the third last Thakur) as *Moti Singh ka Awlad*. An *awlad* is not usually a permanent named group, but a descriptive device used in specific contexts. In some cases, however, maximal lineages are permanent named groups.

There are two other structural terms that must be briefly mentioned: *gotra* and *nukh*. The *gotra* is an exogamous category theoretically quite distinct from the clan and lineage system. A *gotra* was described to me as a group descended from ancient gurus (*Rishis*) and this is close to the original (and formal) meaning in Hinduism. It, said one informant, was originally a matter for Brahmans and Kshatriyas, but other castes now have *gotras*. In fact, outside Brahman castes *gotras* are not well known. Many village Rajputs seem not to be clear about what the word *gotra* refers to and my own observations support Blunt's statement that 'Rajput clans... possess *gotras* but ignore them for marriage purposes' (1931:45). Similarly my observations are consistent with his view that the term *gotra* (or *got*) has lost its original meaning in many (non-Brahman, non-Kshatriya) castes and is used as the term for the exogamous sub-divisions of a caste (Blunt 1931:44). In fact, it refers to exogamous clans in most castes and is used more or less interchangeably with *jati*. It is quite clear that the term *gotra* no longer has a single shared meaning, precisely because it is no longer structurally important within most castes.

Some Rajput informants told me that *nukh* is a sub-division of *gotra*, but others used it to describe the level of sub-division below sub-clan (that is, a maximal lineage). No informant was, however, ever confident about what a *nukh* is. It is also quite obvious that many Rajputs do not know their *nukh* - at least by that name.

The essential point about all of these various levels of division is that there are either no indigenous general terms for a level of division, or the term is rarely used and often not known even by people who regard themselves (and are regarded by others) as experts on Rajput history and culture. While there are no widely used generic terms, the levels of division are socially recognised.

As Blunt points out (1931:10), the lack of consistently used indigenous terms for caste sub-divisions is true of castes generally in northern India. Different terms have different meanings to different people within a caste and are used differently between castes. A consequence is that the technical terms used by anthropologists and other scholars are also inconsistent.

In the absence of any consistently defined terms for the structural sub-divisions of castes, it is important to specify my own 'technical' definitions. The terms are used consistently in this study, but sub-divisions coinciding with each term do not exist for every caste.[3]

---

3 My usage is another attempt to get over a problem that has plagued scholars for some time:

'The terminology of subdivisions of the caste is extremely vague. In 1885 Sir Denzil Ibbetson, Sir Herbert Risley and Mr Nesfield laid down certain English terms for use in ethnographic enquiries called "subcaste" and "subtribe" respectively; the largest exogamous groups were designated "section" and "sept". The attempt failed largely because there were no general vernacular terms to correspond.' (Blunt 1931:10)

I use the term caste to refer to an endogamous unit and, where they exist, I use sub-caste to refer to the smallest endogamous sub-divisions of that unit. Branch refers to major sub-divisions within the major unit (caste). Clan refers to a named exogamous unit which asserts descent from a common ancestor. Sub-clan refers to a named exogamous division asserting descent from a lower level common ancestor. Lineage refers to lower level descent groups, which might or might not be named, according to context.

Table 4.1 summarises Rajput caste structure on the basis of my terminology and indigenous terminology. I must stress that Rajputs often don't know the indigenous terms for structural divisions, (as opposed to the names of specific groups) and rarely use them anyhow. Rajputs (and members of other castes for that matter) use a sort of segmentary logic when talking about castes and lineages.

Rajputs do not ask 'What is your *khamp*?' They ask 'What is your *jati*?'[4] Sometimes the answer will be 'Rajput'; at other times it will be a clan name; sometimes it will be a sub-clan name. It may be a sub-clan name on the assumption that the questioner will know to which clan a given sub-clan belongs. For example, in Jodhpur District a large proportion of Rajputs are from one of two clans, Rathor and (to a lesser extent) Bhati. Within the region, resident Bhati or Rathor Rajputs will usually identify themselves by their sub-clan (for example, Jodha, a Rathor sub-clan or Jaisaha, a Bhati sub-clan). Any other Rajput living within the region will be familiar with the sub-clans of Rathors and Bhatis. Members of other clans (for example, Inder or Parihar) would usually identify themselves by the name of their clan, since questioners might not be familiar with the sub-divisions. Whatever the response, if the questioner wants further detail he will simply ask 'Which Inder?' or 'Which Parihar?'

This can all be rather subtle. The Bhati Rajputs in Hinganiya are of Bhati clan, Jaisaha sub-clan, Bera Dasot maximal lineage. If a stranger was attempting to place one of them socially the conversation might go like this:

---

4 In my view *jati* has often been mistranslated. It usually is taken to mean an endogamous unit and is glossed as 'caste'. In practice it means something like 'group', and has shifting references according to context. It often actually refers to exogamous groups. Rajasthanis also use it to refer to religious affiliation, as in the following series of questions put to me.

Q. What is your jati?
A. No jati.
Q Muslim?
A No.
Q Christian?

Table 4.1

Rajput caste structure

English Term	*Indigenous Term*	*Example*	*Structural Importance*
line/division	vamsh	Chandravamsh	No structural importance apparent
clan	jati (also used for all Rajputs)	Bhati	Exogamous
sub-clan	khamp	Jaisaha	Exogamous
maximal lineage	awlad?	Bera Dasot	Exogamous
lineage	awlad	Sunder Dassji-ki-awlad	Not corporate group, nor permanently named group

Q. What is your jati?
A. Rajput.
Q. Which Rajput?
A. Bhati.
Q. Which Bhati?
A. Jaisaha.
Q. Which Jaisaha?
A. Bera Dasot.

Occasionally major steps are left out. On one occasion one of the Hinganiya Rajputs met a group of Rajputs migrating with herds from Jaisalmer. Neither side knew the other side's affiliations. The questions went like this:

Q. Where do you come from?
A. Jaisalmer.
Q. What is you jati?
A. Rajput.
Q. Which Rajput?
A. Bhati.
Q. Which Bhati?
A. Bera Dasot.

In other words the respondent omitted the sub-clan level. Presumably it was understood that the questioner would know that Bera Dasot was a sub-division of Jaisaha. Perhaps it was also assumed that any Bhati from Jaisalmer would necessarily be a Jaisaha.

This exercise, and the description of Rajput caste structure which preceeds it, demonstrates the operation of the lineage principle within the Rajput caste. Rajputs are not divided into endogamous sub-castes, but into exogamous clans, sub-clans and lower level lineages. Particularly below the level of sub-clan what we find seems something like a segmentary lineage system, at least in the sense that lineages have shifting boundaries. The boundaries depend on whichever level of ancestor is thought to be significant for whatever reason. Internal Rajput caste structure is based on a segmentary, fissioning principle, not a principle of endogamy.[5]

(c) Marriage Exchange

- The main functions of clans and sub-clans is to regulate marriage exchange. Rajput marriage rules are as follows:
- The Rajput caste as a whole is endogamous.
- Clans are exogamous.
- Sub-clans are, as sub-divisions of exogamous clans, also exogamous by definition.
- There are also rules prohibiting a man from marrying into his mother's sub-clan or his father's mother's sub-clan. (These are

---

5 While compiling genealogical data for the Jaisaha Rajputs in Hinganiya I was able to produce six separate charts linking members of various households into minimal lineages of varying depths. Despite the claim of common descent from Sunder Dassji (as members of his lineage) and common sub-clan membership, I was unable to obtain even a tentative guess from any informant as to how these descent groups might be linked. No informant had any claim of genealogical knowledge beyond three ascending generations. Most have even less knowledge. One Rajput informant explained that detailed knowledge of such matters is unnecessary, because each clan has a genealogist who knows the details and keeps written records. Genealogists visit all members of the clan for which they are responsible every three years to keep their records up to date. The genealogists for Bhati Jaisaha are from the Rau caste and live in Udaipur District.

The shallow genealogical knowledge and apparently low level of concern for genealogical knowledge is emphatically different from the situation regarding the other castes in Hinganiya. In the cases of the Nayaks and Meghwals genealogies covering all members of each caste in the village were relatively easy to compile. In the case of the Meghwals, with a total population of under thirty, this is not, perhaps, surprising. But in the case of the Nayaks, with a population only slightly less than that of the Bhati Rajputs, the difference in knowledge is striking. Oddly, the linking Nayak genealogy was provided by a Nayak informant in the presence of Rajputs who seemed substantially aware of the genealogical details of the Nayaks, to a much greater depth than the genealogical knowledge they held of their own caste.

fairly standard Hindu rules. but they are usually applied to a clan not a sub-clan.)

The various lower level lineages (i.e. below sub-clan) are, by definition, also exogamous (as sub-divisions of exogamous groups). They have no significance for marriage, except that marriage into a particularly prestigious lineage (for example the lineage of a Maharaja or Thakur) might be sought after. The *vamsh* have no structural significance in marriage, as they are neither endogamous or exogamous.[6]

The most apparent feature of these Rajput marriage rules is the emphasis on exogamy below the level of the entire Rajput caste (effectively the entire Kshatriya varna). What is striking is the size of the category of potential marriage partners. It is not a case of having only a few tens of thousands of potential marriage partners within a sub-caste, but a case of having perhaps hundreds of thousands of potential marriage partners, with a few tens of thousands restricted because they are too closely related.

Despite the implications of these formal rules, there are two ways in which it could be argued that there is endogamy operating at a lower level than the category of 'all Rajputs' in some sort of *de facto* sense.

Firstly it could be argued that marriages occur within a locality and that this creates *de facto* local sub-castes. It is easy to reject this argument. It is true that people in villages tend, for practical reasons, to marry people who live reasonably close. However, while I do not have detailed data on all Rajput marriages (marriages-in and marriages-out) involving Hinganiya, I know of only two cases of a marriage involving a partner from an adjacent village. I am aware of no other marriage involving a partner from a village less than ten kilometres away. On the other hand I know of several marriages involving partners from greater distances. The tendency is to marry outside of a core circle of nearby villages and within a larger circle loosely defined by practical factors such as cost. Because the same approach applies in other villages, this does not create a local endogamous unit since the boundaries (loosely defined anyhow) vary for each village and thus overlap. Hinganiya Rajputs may be able to marry into village A sixty kilometres to the south-west, but not into village B one hundred and twenty kilometres in the same direction. Rajputs in villages A and B might, however, find it practical to marry each other.

---

6 Whatever its original significance, the *vamsh* now seems to be significant only in terms of religious affiliations. The clan gods are determined by the *vamsh* affiliation of the clan. Bhatis, as Chandravamsh, are officially followers of Krishna. In fact the greeting used by Bhati Rajputs is 'Jai-sri' or 'Jai-sri-Kishan' (victory to Lord Krishna) as opposed to the general Rajput greeting 'Jai-mata-jiri' (victory of the Mother Goddess).

The second possible argument for *de facto* endogamous sub-groups is that clans tend to restrict marriages to a limited number of other clans. Rathors and Bhatis will marry, but marriage between either and an Inder Rajput would be unlikely because the Inder clan is not at all prestigious. The prestige of various Rajput clans varies immensely. Clans which have royal lineages (such as the Rathors, who ruled both Jodhpur and Bikaner, and the Bhatis, who ruled Jaisalmer) are usually given high prestige. Even a poor Bhati Jaisaha Rajput in Hinganiya shares some of the prestige associated with having a royal lineage within his sub-clan. The question arises: to what extent could clusters of clans with similar prestige become effectively endogamous?

At first sight endogamous clusters of clans with similar prestige seen very plausible. In fact, of twenty-five Bhati marriages in Hinganiya for which I have data, all involved marriages with men or women from various sub-clans of the Rathor clan. Nevertheless, I would argue that this does not set up endogamous sub-castes because Rajput marriages are non-localised and the boundaries are not fixed. The high incidence of marriages between Bhatis from Hinganiya and Rathors from other villages is probably related to the very high proportion of Rathor Rajputs in the area, as well as to their high prestige.

As wife-taking is more prestigious than wife-giving there is a tendency towards hypergamy. Bahadur (1978) sets out in great detail the clans from which each Rajput clan will take wives and the clans to which it will give wives. Blunt (1931) sums up the situation, and the crucial limiting factor:

> Amongst Rajputs, the relative rank of the various clans is carefully determined; every Rajput knows into what clans he may marry a son or daughter. If the practice were uniform everywhere, it would be possible to lay down an exact warrant of marriage precedence: but a clan ranked high in one district is often ranked low in another, and in the second gives brides to clans from which in the first it accepts them.(Blunt 1931:47)

As endogamy associated with a tendency towards hypergamy (high status groups taking women in marriage from lower status groups) is commonly associated with caste (Dumont 1970), some hypergamy could also be accommodated within a model of ranked clusters of clans approximating sub-castes. However, the variability of ranking between regions, combined with inter district marriages, means that clan clusters based on similar prestige levels could never effectively become endogamous groups, or even endogamous groups with a tendency towards hypergamy.

The reasons for selecting a certain marriage partner are connected with obtaining prestige and creating alliances. Village Rajputs with relatively high prestige will seek marriage alliances with people with similar (or higher) prestige, and this often means having to go fairly far afield. The question of creating alliances is important in terms of establishing a network of people who can provide accommodation and hospitality (inter-village visiting being a favourite Rajput occupation). Affines may even mind livestock in conditions of local shortage of fodder, water or labour. Affines may also assist in obtaining positions in government or private service. For this reason a marriage with connections in Jodhpur is particularly advantageous. The general adaptive advantages of such networks are obvious.

The objectives of making prestigious marriages and creating alliances are particularly evident among the wealthy, educated Rajputs in the cities. Rajputs from the ruling lineage in Jodhpur (a branch of the Rathor Jodha sub-clan) have made marriages with Rajputs as far away as Nepal and Gujarat. In Chapter 9, I will be examining one household cluster of Hinganiya Rajputs which has placed great importance on marriage alliances as a strategy for developing economically useful urban connections.

The importance of alliances is reflected in the exchanges of gifts and money associated with marriage and in the cost of ceremonies. Exchange at marriage consist of a variety of gifts. The *dayza* consists of gifts from a father to his daughter. These are in the form of useful items (beds etc) and jewellery. The *dayza* also includes gifts to the bride from the husband (perhaps in the form of jewellery or watches). *Tika* is money from the bride's father to the bridegroom. It is usually given at the time of engagement and acts as a guarantee that arrangements cannot be broken. Various other exchanges of gifts occur. For example, the bridegroom's side gives clothes (or money for clothes) to the bride. Jewellery can be given, but clothing is essential. The bridegroom's father gives no gifts to anyone. The bridegroom gives money to the bride before the marriage is consummated.

Costs of the marriage are shared by the two sides. The costs of the wedding (payment for Brahman etc.) are paid by the bride's father, whereas the costs of the *barat* (the journey by the bridegroom's party to the girl's village) are paid by the groom's father. The share of the costs to be paid by each side are decided at the *sagai* (engagement). The breakdown and total to be spent depend on the details of this agreement and the availability of money. Among Rajputs, the larger share usually (but not invariably) falls on the bride's side. One of the Hinganiya Rajputs, married in 1984, claimed that his father-in-law paid about Rs 50,000 (including about Rs 20,000 in jewellery) whereas the groom's side spent only about Rs 8000. Generally the greater share comes from the girl's side, although this is apparently not always the case. The absolute cost and the costs to each side naturally depend on the relative wealth of the two parties and the relative desirability of the two partners, especially in terms of the potential long-term benefits to be gained through affinal ties.

In this section I have briefly mentioned the existence of characteristic Rajput values. I have also argued that the structure of the caste consists of segmented lineages (with named groups at the upper levels). Within the context of the wider endogamous caste the structure emphasises lineage exogamy rather than sub-caste endogamy. This structure facilitates quite widespread networks of marital alliances which would have been useful in the days when Rajputs were mostly concerned with fighting wars, enforcing the wills of the rulers and with feuding. The same networks now provide contacts which can be utilised in seeking employment and in opening economic options in other ways. All of this happens at the cost of substantial ceremonial expense as well as the costs of dowry and travel.

Bishnois

In the Rajput period the Bishnois were tenant farmers. Now they are a politically influential and fairly prosperous caste, still primarily involved in agriculture. In the following pages I will pay some attention to Bishnoi history (and mythology) because much of the current status of Bishnois can only be understood in terms of their history, their distinctive religious beliefs, and their use of religious beliefs as political symbols. A discussion of their caste structure will follow.

(a) Ecological Saints or Kingmakers?

The Bishnoi caste was originally a Hindu sect which took members from all castes, although Jats (the main caste of tenant farmers) were predominant. While it remains a sect concerned with the worship of Vishnu, it has become endogamous and is now regarded as a caste. Blunt (1931) refers to the Bishnois as a sectarian caste and I will adhere to this usage.

The sect originated near Nagaur, between Jodhpur and Bikaner, and the Bishnoi population is now mostly concentrated in the arid parts of Rajasthan. Erskine wrote in 1909 that Bishnois in Rajputana were concentrated in only four states: Jodhpur, Bikaner, Jaisalmer and Udaipur. Bishnois are also found outside Rajasthan, particularly at Hissar (in Haryana, originally the Punjab). Bania Bishnois (that is of merchant caste origin) are reported at Muradabad (the former North Western Provinces) (Maclagan, 1892) and as far away as Bijnaur (near Meerut in Uttar Pradesh) (Sherring 1974).

The Bishnois are well known in Rajasthan, and are an important caste politically. However, while there are many references to them in various gazetteers and glossaries of tribes and castes and in the popular press, relatively little of substance has been published, at least in english. A Village Survey Monograph in the 1961 Census of India series (Gupta 1965) deals with the village of Mukam, a major Bishnoi centre, and provides the only monographic publication I have seen on the sect. In Hindi there are several biographies of Jambhaji, the founder of the sect, by his followers, plus a collection of his sayings called the 'Jambh Sagar'

According to Rose (1911) the name Bishnoi comes from the connection with Vishnu worship. Rose adds, however, that the Bishnois themselves '...sometimes... derive it from the twenty-nine (*bis-nau*) articles of faith inculcated by their founder' (Rose 1911, vol II:111). In every interview I have had with Bishnois the name was related to the twenty-nine rules.

The founder of the Bishnois was Jambhaji (or Jambheshwar), who was born at Pipisar (near Nagaur) in 1451 AD (Samvat 1508). His father was a Rajput who was the *Jagirdar* (landlord) of Pipisar. Jambhaji died in 1536 AD and was buried at Mukam, a few kilometres from Pipisar. He is worshipped as an incarnation of Vishnu. These dates are fairly certain, but the rest of the life of Jambhaji is an uncertain mixture of history and myth. The following is an account of the early life of Jambhaji.

> In his childhood Jambheswarji is said to have begun tending his cows which he continued upto the age of twentyseven. After the attainment of this age he is said to have propagated the teachings of his sect. According to another legend Jambheswarji was dumb upto the age of twelve. The parents were greatly worried on account of this disability of their son and they sought the services of a learned person from Nagaur to perform some ceremonies for curing Jambheswarji of this trouble. Some earthen lamps put at the place of worship by the learned man could not be lighted. Jambheswarji is then said to have lowered an unbaked earthen pot in the well with the aid of an untwisted thread and to have drawn out water from it. As soon as the water was sprinkled on the earthen lamps arranged by the learned man they began to burn spontaneously. All those who witnessed this miracle were wonderstruck and from that moment onwards Jambheswarji was taken to be an incarnation of Lord Vishnu.(Gupta 1965: para 26)

I have already mentioned that the defining characteristic of the Bishnois is that they are a sectarian caste devoted to the worship of Vishnu and that Jambhaji is regarded as an incarnation of Vishnu. The code of twenty-nine rules is the cornerstone of the sect's social and religious life. (The rules are provided as an Appendix.)

The rules include references to the purity of women after child-birth and menstruation, the requirement to bathe daily, to be faithful to one woman and so on. A number of rules show a high regard for the protection of life. For example, Bishnois are instructed never to take life, and, as far as possible to stop others from doing so; to never cut a green tree; never to geld a bullock; and to examine wood before burning to remove any insects or living things from it. This emphasis has recently led to a conception in some publications (e.g. Malhotra 1986) of Bishnois as some sort of ecological saints, profoundly concerned with conservation. This view has been picked up by many articles in popular publications (see, for example, Morrison 1985). While this is perhaps romanticised, there is obviously an extreme concern with the sanctity of life within the Bishnoi sect.

The Bishnois are particularly concerned with the preservation of the *khejri* tree and of the blackbuck. Deer are not specifically mentioned in the twenty-nine rules. The protection of the deer seems to fall under the general admonition to never take life, but there is no doubt that deer have a special place in the Bishnoi world view and the relationship with deer is one of the defining characteristics of the Bishnoi in the minds of other castes. While deer are legally protected they are nevertheless commonly hunted by members of other castes. Hunting trips are a popular past-time of Rajputs and Nayaks. For all that, great care is taken to hide hunting trips from Bishnois, or at least to refrain from making them too obvious.

Hunting is usually an activity of the late afternoon and early evening. At this time the concentration of deer around the Bishnoi *dhanis* is overwhelmingly obvious. It is popularly believed that deer know they are safe near *dhanis*. From my own observations I have no doubt whatsoever of this. I know from at least one first hand account of a wounded deer actually going inside a *dhani* to escape a hunting party.

The protection of animal life is the basis of several other customs. While the twenty-nine rules suggest only that sheep and goats should not be sold to a butcher, only one sheep was owned by a Bishnoi in Hinganiya. One informant said it was a rule of the Bishnois to keep no sheep and goats at all. A Bishnoi woman said that any Bishnoi who kept sheep and goats would be fined by the caste. The fine would be in the form of grain left out for birds.

Clearly a general rule has developed into something much more specific. On the other hand the rule that Bishnois should not eat opium is openly ignored, even flouted. Public gatherings at which opium is taken are among the occasions when Bishnois conspicuously interact with other castes. The opium used in Hinganiya (by all castes) is actually grown by and obtained from Bishnois in Kota District. The fact that the rules which might be described as 'conservationist' are taken very seriously, whereas the rule about not taking opium is not, cannot be dismissed as an accident. Nor is it an accident that the broad respect for life has become focused around a specific concern for the well-being of the deer. There is clear evidence that the ecological consciousness (or conscience) of the Bishnois has been used as a political symbol both recently and in the medieval period. This is not to say, of course, that the consciousness is not genuine.

While some Bishnois seem reasonably tolerant about hunting (it is difficult not to notice the sound of muzzle-loaders being discharged in the fields at dusk), others are disliked because they have reported poachers to the police. In fact one Rajput expressed generally negative views about Bishnois, citing this as a reason. As the matter was pursued it became clear that his general condemnation allowed for exceptions. The grounds for being counted as an exception were related to tolerance of hunting. If one of the political symbols which defines a Bishnoi is the protection of deer, it is equally true that love of hunting is part of the rather macho *Kshatriya* self-image of many Rajputs and that ability as a hunter is seen as something of a defining characteristic of Bhils. One case of conflict emphasises this point.

Several years ago, in Hinganiya, a deer was killed by two Rajputs (one a soldier on leave, another a retired soldier). The Bishnois found out and took the body of the deer and buried it under a pile of stones. Large numbers of Bishnois came from various villages, incensed by the killing. They threatened to call the police, or to beat both the Rajputs if they did not pay a fine of one or two thousand rupees. (My informant was unsure of the amount.) One of the Rajputs simply refused to pay (I do not know about the other). Everything eventually settled down, without the police being called and without the beating being administered. It is difficult to say why the Bishnois backed off. Perhaps the pressures of village solidarity won the day; alternatively a full-scale inter-caste dispute may not have been an attractive proposition. The point is, however, that conflict between the castes was centred around deer-hunting. Protection of the deer was invoked as a political symbol by the Bishnois.

I would argue that the early development of the sect was very much concerned with political symbolism. Before developing this case, it is necessary to establish the historical context in some detail. The fifteenth and early sixteenth centuries in western Rajasthan were characterised by continual feuding between Rajput clans and the consolidation of a number of petty chiefdoms into Rajput states. I am referring particularly to the two major Rathor states of Marwar and Bikaner. In the early fifteenth century, the Rathor leader Rao Chunda captured Marwar. At that time its capital was at Mandor, a few kilometres from Jodhpur. Rao Chunda was murdered in 1423. Years of feuding and wars of succession followed his death. His grandson, Rao Jodha, eventually gained control of

Mandor in 1458 and in 1459 he laid the foundations of Jodhpur Fort and shifted the capital from Mandor to Jodhpur. Rao Jodha's son Bika founded Bikaner state and another son, Rao Duda, annexed Merta.

What we have, then, is a number of cities ruled by Rathors. The surrounding areas were under variable degrees of control. Some were more effectively under control than others and the extent of effective control varied from time to time. The previous political structure seems to have been based essentially on small chiefdoms and to some degree this remained the case. Many of the people in the area between Bikaner and Jodhpur were pastoralists, often nomadic. It is understandable that they would not have been easy to pacify or control.

Max Harcourt (pers. comm.) argues that the development of the Karani Mata cult at Deshnoke, in the desert about thirty kilometres from Bikaner (and on the modern road between Bikaner and Jodhpur), was supported by the Rathors as a way to extend control over the rural population. It is surely no coincidence that the Bishnoi sect developed a few kilometres away in the same period and it is possible to show links between the consolidation of the Rathor states and the growth of the Bishnoi sect.[7] One aspect of this is the apparent attempt in a myth about Jambhaji, to provide a charter for Rao Duda's conquest of Merta.

In 1486 (or, perhaps, 1485)

> . . .Merta was taken from Rao Duda by Mohindra and he was obliged to fly; he happened in his flight to alight at the village Peepasar; and at the time of his arrival the dumb Jamba was watering his flocks and herds at the village well. Duda observed that as he made a sign by lifting up his hand only so many of the cows as there was room for at one time at the well came to drink, as one set finished he again held up his hand when another lot of animals came forward to drink and this went on until all had quenched their thirst. Duda thought this a very wonderful proceeding and concluded that the cowherd must be imbued with supernatural powers; he did not like to speak to him there, but when he drove off the cattle, followed him on horseback. He found that when riding though always keeping in sight he could never overtake him; this again appeared most extraordinary. So dismounting he followed on foot and came up with him. Duda then put his hands together in a position of entreaty and asked his name. The man who had been dumb for thirtyfour years then spoke, said

7 Jambhaji was a contemporary of founders of other major sects: Kabir (1440-1518); Nanak (1469-1538). Michael Allen (pers. comm.) has drawn attention to the significance of this. It is quite possible that the appearance of a number of major sects at the same time is related to the same processes of state building and consolidation that I have described in regard to the Bishnois.

his name was Jamba, and in return asked Duda what he wanted. Duda related all that had occured, How he had lost Merta and asked his advice as to what he should do to recover it. Jamba had a small... [axe] in his hand, and with this he cut a piece of stick from a Kher tree and out of it manufactured a straight sword, this sword he gave to Rao Duda, told him at once to proceed to Merta and retake it, and that so long as the sword remained in his family he would hold Merta.... Duda did as he was told and was successful.

From that time Jamba abandoned his occupation of shepherd.... In the same year... there was a great famine in the land. The Jats of all the countries round about where Jamba was living, began to make preparations to emigrate to more favourable lands. Jamba, however, told them that if they would become his followers he would feed them and that there was no necessity for leaving their country. They obeyed his instructions and became his disciples. . . . (Walter, n.d., quoted in Gupta 1965.)

The implications of this legend as a myth of charter (for Rao Duda) are obvious. The first words spoken by Jambhaji in his lifetime are a promise to a dispossessed ruler who goes off to regain his kingdom. The gift from the prophet is a cutting from a *khejri* tree and prohibition of the cutting of live trees (particularly the *khejri*) later becomes one of the twenty-nine tenets of the sect. Further, the connection beween Duda and the prophet is dated to the same year as the foundation of the sect.

A further story (this one with a definite historical basis) shows the political aspect of Bishnoi sectarian practices. In 1631, during the reign of Maharajah Abhay Singh, troops were sent to the Bishnoi village of Khejarli about 20 km south of Jodhpur to cut timber for renovations to the palace. According to the story 363 Bishnois, mostly women, put their arms around the trees in order to protect them. At the orders of the Maharajah's official they were slaughtered. The Maharajah was so touched that he vowed that the beliefs of the Bishnois would thereafter always be respected. At the present day village, the massacre is commemorated with a monument, a temple and a nursery where *khejri* seedlings are grown. A fair held there in 1985 was attended by large numbers including a Bishnoi who was a government minister.

The Bishnoi rules are used in two ways in this story. Firstly, for the Bishnois themselves the *khejri* tree is a symbol of political resistance to the Rajputs. Secondly the story suggests that the Maharajah apparently decided that honouring the beliefs of the sect would be a better way of establishing control than by attempting to over-ride them. Again the story presents a charter for a special relationship between the state (this time Marwar) and the Bishnois.

There appear to be two related processes at work in the period. Firstly, the ruling Rajput clans attempted to neutralise the potential for revolt by using the sect (and other sects such as the Karani Mata sect) as a means of validating power, perhaps by enhancing their own credibilty with the population at the expense of the credibility of rival Rajputs. Secondly, the Bishnois used the tenets of their sect as a symbolic focus for resistance, or self-assertion. This process, I have suggested, continues today.

If, as I have argued, the Rajput clans used the sect to validate their power, it is possible that the Mughals may have done the same thing, perhaps after Jambhaji`s death.

According to Walter (n.d., quoted in Gupta 1965), the Muslims, who ruled over Nagaur in Jambhaji's time, forced Jambhaji to include some Muslim tenets in the sects rules. Among the practices cited was the practice of burial of the dead rather than burning. This suggestion is given some support by the fact that burial is normal Bishnoi practice even though it is not prescribed in any of the twenty-nine rules. Another was the use of readings from the Qu'ran at weddings. Blunt (1931) also refers to Muslim influence.

I have seen no evidence whatsoever of Qu'ran readings or Muslim greetings. It is quite possible that such practices have occured in the past. It is also likely that any Muslim influences would have declined since partition. Gupta says that Bishnois at Mukam deny any memory of Qu'ranic recitations at the time of marriages. He suggests that the absence of any reference to Muslim practices in the twenty-nine principles or 120 *sabdas* (sayings) attributed to Jambhaji combined with evidence that he was a bitter critic of Muslim practices makes it appear certain

> . . .that the introduction of the Muslim rites in the ceremonies of the Bishnois. . . which are conspicuous by their absence now-a-days, relates to a period after the death of Jambhaji. . . . (Gupta 1965:9)

(b) Caste Organisation

The caste structure of the Bishnois is much simpler than that of the Rajputs. Essentially the whole caste is divided into exogamous clans (called *gotra*, *got* or, occasionally, *jati*). Some of the *gotras* are divided into two sub-divisions called *nukhs*. According to some informants, these *nukhs* developed simply because the particular *gotras* got too big and were split.

There is also a category of Bishnoi priests, since the Bishnoi do not regard themselves as inferior to Brahmans. These are the *gaenas*.[8] The

8 A second category of holy men, called *sadhs* is often referred to in the literature. See for example Blunt 1931:108). As far as I was able to ascertain the term merely refers to any sadhu who also happens to be a Bishnoi.

gaenas have separate exogamous clans (eleven according to one *gaena* informant). While the *gaena* clans are exogamous, the *gaenas* as a whole are an endogamous sub-section. A *gaena* must marry outside his or her clan but into another *gaena* clan.

Besides this endogamous priestly sub-section, Bishnois assert that all Bishnois can marry into any clan besides their own. This contradicts some of the early accounts of Bishnois. According to Fagan (1893) the Bishnois maintain the caste of their ancestors before conversion to the sect. Thus we have Jat Bishnois, Rajput Bishnois, Bania Bishnois. Blunt says there are 'eight endogamous sections', corresponding to original caste (1931:134).

There is an ambivalence about the way Bishnois handle this contradiction. A Bishnoi will assert that the Bishnoi sect is a religion (*dharam*), not a caste (*jati*), thus paying lip-service to the anti-casteism of Jambhaji. Yet the same person will slip into using the term *jati* in reference to the Bishnois. Similarly one individual boldly asserted that there were no Rajput Bishnois or Chaudhary Bishnois; later in the same interview he described himself as a Chaudhary Bishnoi. When this inconsistency was drawn to his attention he said he was a Bhadu Bishnoi. Many Bishnoi clans have the same names as Jat (or Chaudhary) clans, and Bhadu is listed by Gupta (1965) as one of these. Awareness of Chaudhary origins of his clan would not automatically mean that my informant regarded Chaudhary Bishnoi as an important social category, but the fact that he initially identified himself as a Chaudhary does. Other Bishnois consistently deny any implications of endogamy within caste of origin.

The fact that some Bishnois obviously recognise caste of origin while there is a general assertion that this does not form a meaningful social category is an obvious inconsistency. How can it be resolved? My view is that the caste of ancestry is sometimes (perhaps often, but this is not certain) remembered and less often used as a basis for *preferential* endogamy. It clearly does not represent a basis for sub-dividing all Bishnois (or even most) into endogamous sub-sections. Chaudhary Bishnoi is, then, a category, not a bounded group. In some contexts preferential endogamy may lead to something approximating a bounded group, but this is rare and of fairly local significance. In other areas and contexts, endogamy by caste of origin is simply not structurally important.

Beyond the essential clan exogamy, modified by the existence of a sub-division of *gaenas* and the possible occurence of occasional preferential endogamy in terms of caste of origin, the marriage rules are those of Hindu law/convention, prohibiting marriage within the *got* of mother, mother's mother and father's mother.

The tendency of these rules is broadly similar to those applying to Rajputs: potential partners are available from a large proportion of caste members. But the size of the group prohibited by rules of exogamy is much smaller than that of Rajputs because there are a very large number of Bishnoi clans and they are smaller than those of the Rajputs. The effect is that, while the Rajputs are *forced* into wider ranging marriage alliances, the Bishnois are *able* to make marriages much less wide-ranging. Consistent with the structural possibilities, marriage practices and preferences reflect quite different strategies from those of Rajputs.

Wide-ranging marriages are not often sought after by Bishnois, as marriages tend to be made with Bishnois from relatively nearby villages. A direct exchange of sisters for brothers is a quite common, even a preferred arrangement. In this arrangement X marries Y's sister and Y marries X's sister. This sort of marriage is sibling-set marriage, described by Kolenda (1978).

In stark contrast a direct exchange of sisters is unthinkable for Rajputs. A direct exchange of cousins is 'legal', but highly disapproved of.

According to Blunt (1931) the levirate occurs among the Bishnois. In fact, he says that sometimes widows marry an elder brother, as well as the more common form of the levirate, that is marriage to a younger brother of a deceased husband. Again, any question of widow remarriage is unthinkable to Rajputs.

Bishnois are popularly thought to be very promiscuous. The continued practice of polygyny, although illegal and probably not common, seems to contribute to this image. (On the part of Rajputs there is some inconsistency here, as polygyny was quite common among Rajputs in the recent past.) There was one Bishnoi man in Hinganiya who admitted to having two wives. One wife normally lives in her own village. The two wives apparently do not get on together - the older wife certainly does not like the idea. When she mentioned the second wife in discussion there was an atmosphere of embarassed amusement in the conversation between her and my Rajput companion which suggests that the practice is now unusual.

This exchange highlights another Bishnoi characteristic. Bishnoi women have high status within their caste and act relatively independently. They are often quite relaxed in conversation with outsiders, in sharp contrast to Rajput women.

Child marriage is very common among the Bishnois and may well be the norm. However, it tends to be under-reported, because it is illegal.[9]

9 The illegality of both practices (under *The Hindu Marriage Act 1955*) probably explains why the census monograph on Mukam (Gupta 1965) reports high age of marriage and no 'bigamy' (polygyny).

Regarding Bishnoi marriage practices in Mukam, Gupta states that there is no brideprice and that dowry is not stipulated. The bride's father presents whatever he thinks is proper. Caution is needed here. What Gupta describes is the legal situation under the *Hindu Marriage Act 1955*: dowry and brideprice are illegal, but gifts are legal. It is quite possible that the census investigators were simply given a description tailored to the legal requirements, rather than a description of actual practices.

Nevertheless, I think Gupta is correct about the low level of exchange of gifts and dowry associated with Bishnoi marrage, despite the problem of obtaining unambiguous data. It seems to me that the practices of child marriage and sibling-set marriage are generally related to low or nil dowries. Bishnoi child marriages are often organised as mass-marriages at *nyarts* (feasts held about ten days after a death). Keeping the cost down was given as one reason for Nayak mass-child marriages, which I will discuss later. If, as Gupta says, dowries are relatively unimportant, this is consistent with the high incidence of child marriage and preference for sibling-set marriage.

The pattern which ties all these Bishnoi marriage practices together is that they all tend to consolidate inheritance and property and to avoid undue redistribution of property at marriage.

A considerable degree of political unity exists within the caste. This is achieved largely by shared religious identity. Further, unlike the Rajputs, the Bishnois have caste councils. There are caste assemblies (panchayats) which are held at the four important annual Bishnoi festivals - two held each year at Jambha (a village founded by Jambhaji) and two held each year at Mukam. These caste panchayats have judicial functions relating to breaches of the twenty-nine rules. The functioning of caste councils is explicitly focused on religious matters, but the outcome is a relatively homogeneous political interest group.

In my view, religious beliefs and practices provide a symbolic medium for the expression of Bishnoi caste solidarity, which is not at all to say that one causes the other.

The former tenant castes (particularly Jats and Bishnois) have been a very powerful force in post-Independence Rajasthan. The Bishnois have been, given their numbers (perhaps one or two hundred thousand in Rajasthan), disproportionately prominent. Generally the ex-tenant castes have been strong supporters of the Congress Party and Bishnois have held important ministerial posts in both Rajasthan and Haryana. Interestingly Bishnois have held posts which fit the Sect's concerns with trees and animals: Bishnois have been senior Ministers, both in the Haryana and Rajasthan Governments. One has been Minister of State for Animal Husbandry (Ram Singh Bishnoi in Rajasthan), another for forests.

The Rajputs, have (particularly in recent years) generally been supporters of the BJP (Bharatiya Janata Party), largely because the Congress Party has always been seen as an opponent of Rajput class interests, especially in supporting land reform as a major policy. In the Rajasthan State Parliament the Congress Party was in power throughout my period of fieldwork. The BJP was in opposition.

I have argued that Rajput caste structure allows for (and encourages) territorially dispersed marital alliances, which are utilised to widen the range of economic options open to an individual. These are, however, individually-centred networks, and there is little focus for a sense of corporate solidarity among Rajputs as Rajputs. The caste structure and marriage practices are essentially divisive, placing great importance on membership of lineages rather than caste solidarity. Among the Bishnois, on the other hand, wide-ranging alliances are less evident and important. The focus is on marriage practices (some of which Rajputs would regard as incestuous) which emphasise conservation of resources. Through their identity as a religious sect, however, the Bishnois are able to achieve a sense of caste solidarity which the Rajputs lack. Historically, their sectarian beliefs have been used as a political weapon against the Rajputs as well as having worked as a symbolic base for caste solidarity.

Jats

There is only a single household of Jats resident in Hinganiya (a total population of seven). I do not propose to discuss the Jats in detail because I have already mentioned them in the section on Bishnois, because the caste structure is relatively simple and because I am less familiar with Jat social structure than that of the other four castes. In the period of Rajput rule the Jats were tenant farmers. Now they are, like the Bishnois, a comparatively prosperous caste of cultivators, politically aware and influential.

Within the endogamous Jat caste, there are a large number of *gots* (clans). The clans are exogamous. Most of the generalisations made about Bishnoi marriage practices are equally applicable to the Jats: child-marriage is common; sibling-set marriage is also common and was first described for the Jats (Kolenda 1978). Like the Bishnois the Jats are regarded (by Rajputs) as being somewhat incestuous in their marriage practices.

Rosin (1968) argued that the social organisation and marriage practices of the Jats were an important factor in the emergence of the Jats as a major political force in post-Independence Rajasthan. The argument is that the marriage practices led to networks of kin ties which provided the organisational basis for Jat political solidarity.

Given a similarity between the social organisation and marriage practices of Jats and Bishnois, a similar argument could be made for the Bishnois. (Rosin does not mention the Bishnois.) It might, however, be a mistake to take this argument too far. By placing heavy emphasis on the role of Jat marriages in building networks of kinship ties, Rosin rather misses the importance of consolidating property and avoiding redistribution of property at marriage. (Of course, the marriage practices could do both things at once.) In any case, it is difficult to see what sibling-set marriages (common among both Jats and Bishnois) could contribute to building *networks* of kin, since they are direct exchanges between two families.

Meghwal

The Meghwals are also known as Bambhis and are a scheduled caste. In 1985/86 there were five households in Hinganiya, comprising twenty-five individuals. Traditionally Meghwals were leather workers or carpet makers, although, with the exception of one part-time resident who works as a labourer in Jodhpur, all of the Meghwals in Hinganiya are small-scale farmers and agricultural labourers.

There are three branches of Meghwals: the Basira Meghwals claim Rajput ancestry; the Jata Meghwals claim Jat ancestry; the Jatiya Meghwals are descended from Jata Megwals. Traditionally the Basira Meghwals and the Jata Meghwals are blanket makers. The Jatiya Meghwals are shoe makers. Each of the three branches is endogamous and marriage outside a branch allegedly results in excommunication.

Each branch is divided into exogamous clans which are named after an ancestor or the Rajput or Jat clan they claim descent from. The Meghwals in Hinganiya are Basira Meghwals of the Anikpal clan claiming descent from a Rajput called Anik Singh.

There is a local level political structure which is effectively a local sub-caste. For each branch there is a sub-division into local areas (*keraa*, lit. area) consisting of 10-20 villages. Each clan from each village has a 'Pradhan Panch' (headman) and all the 'Pradhan Panches' from the 10-20 villages meet as a caste panchayat. Their role includes matters of caste discipline. The *keraa* can be thought of as a local sub-caste. It is important to note that a local sub-caste is specific to one of the three branches, which maintain their separateness at this level. If all three divisions of Meghwals were present in an area there would be three local sub-castes.

Marriage is usually within the local sub-caste but this is not a rule. Marriage outside the local sub-caste is difficult and expensive, but quite alright for a '*paisewallah*' (rich man) according to one informant.

Marriage with someone from ego's own clan, mother's clan or paternal grandmother's clan is prohibited.

Nayak/Bhil

Nayaks are included on the list of scheduled castes for Rajasthan. On the separate list of scheduled tribes the Bhils are a scheduled tribe. Yet, the Nayaks in Hinganiya use both names. Most higher caste villagers assert that Bhils and Nayaks are the same thing, something which, administratively and legally at least, is impossible. Furthermore, according to the 1971 Census there was no scheduled tribal population in Hinganiya; the 1981 Census recorded a scheduled tribal population of 101 (Census of India 1981a). It appears that the Nayaks had been reclassified or had reclassified themselves.

Much of the confusion exists because the names are used in different ways in different localities. Kothawalla (Census of Marwar 1911) notes that the Bhils of the hill areas of Rajputana are distinct from the Bhils in the north eastern parts of what is now Jodhpur District (Hinganiya is in this area). In north eastern Jodhpur State the Bhils are also known as Nayaks, Thoris and Aheri. This confusion in names is tied up with a debate about whether Nayaks are true Bhils. There are some suggestions that Nayaks are descended from marriages between tribal Bhils and caste Hindus. It is also quite possible that the Nayaks are the descendants of Bhils who came from Mewar as guides for Rao Jodha (B.S. Tanwar, pers. comm.). This is plausible, as the name Nayak literally means watchman or guide.

In Gujarat the 'Naiks' (also called Naikdas or Naikas) are regarded as a separate tribe from the Bhils (Shah 1959). However, Shah refers to linguistic evidence which supports the view that, in Gujarat, 'the two groups are probably only local variations of one tribe' (1959:251). In Rajasthan the term Bhil seems to have a specific reference to the tribal Bhils of southern Rajasthan and also to be a general term for people of tribal descent. I am not sure whether the Nayaks of Hinganiya are genealogically related to the tribal Bhils of southern Rajasthan.

Culturally, there are close similarities. Among the Bhils of southern Rajasthan there is a category of shamans called *bhopa* (Doshi 1971). Among the Nayaks there are two types of people called *bhopa*. The first group can be described fairly simply as shamans. They participate in rituals in which they dance and apparently whip themselves into trances. There second type of Nayak *bhopa* (*bhopi*, fem.) is a performer who sings an epic to Pabuji, a Rajasthani folk hero.[10]

---

[10] Smith (1986) has given a detailed account of these epic performances.

Whether the Nayaks were originally tribal or whether they are just loosely categorised as Bhils is impossible to judge. In any case they are now clearly Hindu; they regard themselves as being part of the caste system and the others in the village (untroubled by theoretical distinctions between caste and tribe) regard them as a caste, nevertheless usually calling them Bhils.

The ambiguity seems to be inherently administrative, not social. Shifts in which category was reported in censuses are evident in the early censuses of Marwar, so the switch in Hinganiya between 1971 and 1981 was not a new phenomenon. I suspect that the reclassification from 1971 to 1981 reflects the assumptions of the census collector at the particular time, rather than any attempt by the Nayaks themselves to profit from a change in status, either in terms of prestige related to caste ranking or in terms of seeking advantages from the scheduled tribe quota. A Nayak informant attributed the classification to the Patwari (land registration officer), who was the 1981 census collector.

I have gone to some length to discuss this issue because I wish to demonstrate that many divisions and sub-divisions, which the various glossaries of tribes and castes and early census reports describe, are attempts to construct a model which includes every group in a bounded universe. In fact, attempts to look at the whole population from the outside and to divide it into coherent groups are misleading. A Nayak in Hinganiya sees himself as one of the larger category of Bhils, but a Bhil from Udaipur might not recognise this claim. Thus, the boundaries of the group shift depending on the point from which it is defined.

The extent to which categories are consistent depends on the extent to which social intercourse and ties extend. In the case of the Meghwals and Nayaks, this goes little beyond the local sub-caste and adjoining sub-castes. Beyond these boundaries the category tends to be 'other Nayaks' or 'other Bhils'. There is no need to classify people with whom you are unlikely to have contact or, especially, who you are not going to marry. In the case of Rajputs, where marriage ties are comparatively extensive, systems of classification are much more consistent. The role of genealogies and the importance of alliances between lineages, clans and states, underly this difference.

Thus, within the north eastern parts of old Jodhpur State the Nayaks are regarded as one of at least two groups who are loosely called Bhils (the Thoris are another). Each of these branches is endogamous. Below this division into endogamous branches are exogamous clans (called *nukh* or *gotra*). The Nayaks are also divided on an area basis. The local division is called a *nyart*, has a panchayat (council) and is headed by a *nyart* Sarpanch. The *nyart* has a diameter of around 20 *koss* (60 km). Most marriages take place within this local sub-caste, but this is not essential and depends on practical considerations. Unlike the case of the Rajputs the tendency to local marriage leads to preferential endogamy because the local area is bounded and has a political identity.

Other marriage restrictions exist. As is common in Hindu society, a man cannot marry into his mother's clan or his father's mother's clan. There is a further Nayak restriction. While a man can marry a woman from his mother's mother's clan, he cannot marry into her village of origin.

Like the Bishnois and the Meghwals, the Nayaks have a political structure which gives a strong element of caste solidarity, but only at the *nyart* level. One of the important functions of the *nyart* is to gather together when a member of the *nyart* dies, for the funeral feast (also called a *nyart*) held up to twelve days after a death, depending on auspicious dates. On these occasions child marriages are sometimes arranged. On two of the occasions during my fieldwork when Nayak men died in Hinganiya, multiple child marriages were arranged and held some weeks later. On the occasion of the first mass marriage I witnessed (December 1983) there were eighteen child brides from Hinganiya married to boys from other villages. On the second occasion (1985) there were two brides from Hinganiya. Following the marriage the bride and groom visit their respective in-laws and get to know each other, but they do not cohabit until a *mukhlawa* is held when they reach puberty.

Mass child-marriages are common practice among the Bhils. Many other castes also have child marriages, usually *en masse*. It is difficult to obtain much firm data on this because child marriage is illegal. (Rajputs do not have this practice in Hinganiya nowadays and assert that it is not a Rajput practice at all.)

I was told that the main reason for mass marriages is that it is cheaper to hold them since all parents share the cost of festivities. Furthermore, no dowry is involved and gifts are divided among the participants. That is to say that gifts to the brides and their families are divided equally and gifts to the husbands and families are divided equally. At the *mukhlawa* stage a dowry is provided by the girl's father to set her up for her future life. There is no indication that this is paid to the husband or his family.

The marriage rules, the caste structure, the practice of child marriage and the tendency towards marriage within the local area, show a concern for marriage as a way of holding limited resources within narrow boundaries. At the same time the major ceremonials and the role of the Nyart both demonstrate and reinforce solidarity at the supra-village level, but not at the level of Nayaks as a whole.

Patterns of Interaction Between Castes at the Local Level

In Chapter 3 (Table 3.1) is a summary of the castes present in each of the four villages in the cluster. To a varying degree all of these castes are involved in the social, economic and ritual lives of the people of Hinganiya. The village is also visited by groups of migrating Raikas and members of other nomadic castes including Banjaras, Gadulia Lohars, Gawariyas and Joghis. All of these have economic roles as petty traders, craftsmen or entertainers.

Caste interactions are shaped by the rules of commensality. As the general nature of such practices is well known, I will not describe them here, although I would argue that one of the functions of the rules is to divide the population into two broad categories (ritually 'clean' and 'unclean') which are closely related to economic and political power.

While there are subtleties involved in commensal interactions between various clean castes at the top of the purity-based structure (Brahmans, Jats, Rajputs, Bishnois), these subtleties involve food, not tea, cigarettes, bidis (local cigarettes), pipes, or opium. All of these things are conspicuously shared at gatherings called *sabha*. Tea is taken from enamel cups, which are washed and passed around freely among the clean castes. Opium is particularly significant. It is taken in liquid form (crushed and mixed with water). All of the clean castes sit around the filtering apparatus which is usually operated by a senior Rajput or an honoured guest. When taking liquid opium, a member of the clean castes always drinks it from the cupped hand of another clean caste participant. The important thing is that there are no caste restrictions about members of one clean caste taking it from members of another. The Bishnois, who are very fussy about following strict rules of commensality as regards food, are fully involved in the opium ceremonies, even though taking opium is specifically against one of their twenty-nine rules.

Members of the unclean castes sit outside the main semi-circle. As the *sabha* usually takes place on a platform, this means that they sit (squat) below the platform. A clean caste person pours the opium from the container into their hands and they drink from their own cupped hands.

The symbolism is strikingly obvious. An in-group (the ritually clean castes) make no distinctions among themselves in sharing the opium and conspicuously demonstrate their broadly equal status in terms of purity by drinking from each other's hands. The out-group (the ritually unclean castes) passively receive the opium in a way that symbolically isolates them from the higher castes, and even from their own caste fellows, since they do not take opium from each other's hands in this context. All of this is an implicit statement to the unclean castes that they are dependent and have an inferior place in the society.

In fact, the dependency carries over to the economic system. The two unclean castes in Hinganiya are the Nayaks and the Meghwals. Their average landholding by household is much less than that of the other castes (see Chapter 5). To a large extent the unclean castes are heavily dependent on wage labour on the land belonging to the clean castes. There is some patronage involved in providing employment. Furthermore, patron-client ties often mean that food (or even cash) will be available in times of emergency. The implicit threat of the withdrawal of patronage encourages conformity. Both Nayaks and Meghwals in Hinganiya treated me as a Rajput, because I was living with Rajputs, but when they realised that rules of commensality were not of concern to me personally, some individuals made it quite clear that their reason for keeping the rules was based on concern with not rocking the boat. On several occasions the rules were broken, but always when Rajputs were not nearby.

The threat of withdrawal of patronage usually remains implicit and latent. Frequently patrons and clients have relationships which are based on mutual respect and friendships across the caste barrier are quite common. Nevertheless, breach of rules of commensality, or taking too many liberties, can lead to problems for lower caste people. As a comparatively prestigious visitor, with huge resources by local standards, I found that I caused some conflict myself. On one occasion a Nayak who was both a close friend and a frequent informant was told not to visit a Rajput house because I was 'giving too much to him'.

The second aspect of caste interaction is the question of caste economic specialisation and the *jajmani* system. The main economic activity of most of those who live permanently in any of the four villages is a combination of agriculture (including, in many cases, paid agricultural labour) and pastoralism. The Raikas in Khokhariya specialise in pastoralism, but have some involvement in agriculture. There are a few full-time merchants in Kur and in both Kur and Kukunda there are some people working in their caste specialties as carpenters (Suthar), tailors (Darzi) and barbers (Nai). In these villages, but not in Hinganiya, a few Meghwals engage in their traditional trades (shoe-making or blanket-making). However, even those who work as specialists are often involved in some agriculture and pastoralism. To a large extent caste specialties are secondary to agro-pastoralism, or at least carried out in some combination with agro-pastoralism.

Ritual roles are carried out by one of the Brahmans in Kur (who covers Khokhariya and Hinganiya as well), by Dholis (drummers) from Kur and by the barber (Nai) from Kukunda. For the Meghwals and the Nayaks ritual specialists come from other villages further afield.

Although there are some remnants of the *jajmani* system, they are now fairly minor. Where payments are made on the basis of the traditional system they tend to involve the ritual specialists performing ritual roles. The barber continues to be paid in grain for routine barbering, at a rate of ten kilograms of grain per adult male per year and five kilograms per child per year. Most other payments are made in cash. Outside of the few cases of *jajmani* payments in kind there is a second category of payments in kind. I am referring to the practice of paying for goods or services, for which cash is normally involved and for which there is a specific cash value, in grain. The value of the grain is the equivalent of the cash price asked for goods or services. For example two rupees worth of vegetables may be sold in exchange for one kilogram of millet, which has a cash value of two rupees. The underlying medium of exchange is cash in these situations. The millet is used because there is a shortage of cash.

Jajmani appears to have been in operation up until the time of Independance. The 1947 Settlement Report for Hinganiya (Chand 1947) contains some snippets of information regarding *jajmani* relationships. According to this account the Bambhis (described as 'village servants') receive ten measures[11] of grain per year as salary from Rajputs. The Thori (Nayak) described as 'chowkidars' (watchmen) received five measures per year from Bishnois and other castes. There are also references to the *jajmani* payments due to Suthars (carpenters), Lohars (blacksmiths) and Nais (barbers). The report seems to suggest that these three castes were resident in Hinganiya, but all my informants insist that they were not resident at all. Presumably, then, the reference is to a *jajmani* system which included other villages and itinerant service castes (such as Lohars).

The decline in the *jajmani* system since independence is hardly surprising given the massive social changes of the last thirty-five years. Land reform, in particular, has changed the entire balance of power in Rajasthan. The transition of tenant farmers to self-cultivators and of lower caste village functionaries and wage labourers to at least partial dependence on self-cultivation made a transition to cash inevitable. Further, the *jajmani* system depended on a social structure revolving around a semi-feudal estate.

Elder, in reference to the link between land ownership and successful attempts to improve caste status in Uttar Pradesh, shows the connection between centralised land control and *jajmani*-type services:

> Why might rural land control be so important in improving one's ritual status? One reason may be that in an agricultural setting, land

[11] The measures were translated as kilograms, which seems very unlikely given the date of the report. However I was not able to obtain a copy of the report and cannot check.

> is the major commodity for establishing relationships of continuing dependency. Thus, the family which controls land controls, in part anyhow, the lives of those who ultimately depend for their survival on that land - agricultural laborers, artisans... and any who trade their service for grain. Furthermore, in an agricultural setting, resident dependents have few alternatives. They either work for the local landlords, or they don't work - at least in that locality. (Elder 1977:205)

Conclusion

In this chapter I have shown some differences between the internal caste structure of the Rajputs and of other castes represented in Hinganiya. The Rajput caste is a large caste divided on a segmentary fissioning principle, into exogamous clans with various lower levels of sub-division. The Rajput marriage rules, combined with the structure of the caste, lead to the opportunity to form wide ranging marriage alliances. On the other hand, they work against Rajput solidarity. Historically, Rajput kingdoms and chiefdoms were built and maintained by clans and lineages, partly on the basis of their ability to muster allies. Marriage alliances were a part of that process. Nevertheless, as units competing for land and power, they never achieved any cohesiveness at the level of the entire caste. This lack of permanent cohesion as a caste continues. The strategy of seeking wide ranging alliances is useful now as a means of opening employment options. The fact that marriages of Bhati Rajputs in Hinganiya tend to be exchanges between Bhatis and Rathors reflects the relative prestige of the two clans, the predominance of the two clans in Jodhpur District and the advantages associated with alliances between clans well placed politically and economically.

On the other hand the Bishnois have a caste cohesion which is largely the result of their religious identity. Through this they have become a significant factor in State and even National politics. Their marriage practices suggest concern with maintaining resources rather than with building alliances.

Both Bishnois and Rajputs are 'clean' castes; both castes consist largely of landed peasant farmers; in Hinganiya, both have similar average land holdings per household (see Chapter 5). However, they approach problems of politics and economics rather differently and these varying approaches are related to caste structure and value differences.

The Nayaks and the Meghwals are 'unclean' castes; they are marginal peasants or near-landless labourers, or something between the two. As castes they are quite cohesive at the local level, but do not have any corporate organisation at the level of the whole caste. Their marriage practices tend to be very much concerned with preserving scarce resources. Marriage ceremonies, among the Nayaks, are occasions for expressing sub-caste solidarity rather than for establishing wider alliances.

I have mentioned briefly the breakdown of the *jajmani* system as the basis of inter-caste economic relationships, while emphasising that a broad line between clean and unclean castes continues to exist. In Chapter 5 I will examine the extent to which the caste system and land ownership are connected.

Photo 1

Photo 2

Photos 1 & 2: A graphic illustration of the effects of variable monsoons. Similar views of Hinganiya taken in late August of two different years, 1983 (Photo 1) and 1987 (Photo 2).

Photo 3: Rear view of Rajput houses taken in September 1983 (post-monsoon).

Photo 4: Area to the rear of Rajput houses, November 1985. Note the very limited natural, vegetation in comparison to Photo 3.

Photo 5: The village centre of Hinganiya.

Photo 6; A cluster of Rajput huts.

Photo 7: Gathering (*sabha*) of Rajputs under verandah at time of a marriage.

Photo 8: The Meghwals and Nayaks remain squatting outside.

Photo 9: An *adola* (1983).

Photo 10: Winnowing *bajra* (1983).

Photo 11: Livestock being watered from underground storage reservoir (*tanka*).

Photo 12: Camel transporting water to Bishnoi *dhani*.

Photo 13: Emergency drinking water delivery during the failed monsoon (1987).

Photo 14: The *nadi* in August 1987. In good seasons it holds rainwater for several months after the monsoon.

Photo 15: A private underground tank, with concave surface for collection of rainwater.

Chapter 5

Land Ownership: Caste and Economic Status

Introduction

In this chapter I will be examining some of the features of the system of land tenure in Rajasthan and analysing the distribution of land ownership in Hinganiya. The underlying aim is to demonstrate the biased distribution of land ownership particularly along caste lines and to examine the extent to which landownership and caste are related. The working hypothesis is that there is a land-wealth nexus. In later chapters I will examine the points at which wealth and landownership diverge.

One of my aims is to show how hierarchical systems based on caste and landownership are related and how they diverge. From the point of view of the study as a whole, I wish to show how the higher positions in these hierarchies provide advantages in situations of recurring drought. This is readily understandable in the case of landownership: it seems reasonable to expect that those with more land are in a better position to cope in bad years. In later chapters I will bring together the other strand of the argument which I have been developing: that membership of particular castes (especially higher ranked castes) may also provide economic opportunities distinct from those associated with landownership. However, it is first necessary to show the relationships between the two hierarchies.

The chapter will begin with a discussion of systems of land tenure and the history of land reform in Rajasthan. A section on the relationship between the household as an institution and land ownership and inheritance will follow. I will then discuss the nature of the land records and some of the problems in interpreting them. Some of the theoretical problems involved in establishing a model of the rural class system in western Rajasthan will also be considered before I turn to a description and analysis of land distribution in Hinganiya itself.

Land Tenure and Land Reform in Rajasthan

(a) The Jagir System

In my discussion of the Rajput Caste (Chapter 4), I briefly described the relationship between the Thakur landlords and the Maharajah under the *Jagir* system. I will now discuss land tenure under the system in greater detail, before looking at land reform legislation in Rajasthan.

Prior to the land reforms of the 1950s, land tenure in western Rajasthan was characterised by a complex variety of grants from rulers to various local landlords, who acted as intermediaries between the rulers and the people who actually farmed the land as tenants. The history of the development of the Rajput states is in large part the history of the development of loose ties between local chieftains and rulers into a fairly rigid hierarchy.

It is possible to simplify this and to look at the process as essentially a two-stage one. Sharma (1977), in a history of the State of Marwar, sees the restructuring of Marwar polity along the lines of the Mughal *jagirdari* system as the crucial turning point in this process. From the beginning of the thirteenth century there were a number of small principalities spread throughout western Rajasthan. The boundaries of these small principalities were ill-defined and often ill-defended. The Maharajahs of Marwar appointed *sardars* (mostly from members of their own clans) to rule over villages. Rao Chunda (c1383-1423 A.D.) created another category of fiefs by recognising existing chiefs as *bhomias* and established marital ties with these *bhomias*. This early system was called *bhai-bant* (literally 'brother-bond') and was the rule, through brotherly ties, by members of the royal clan, or by affines of the ruler.

Under the Mughals the system was replaced by a more rigidly hierarchical one. The previously loose and shifting territorial divisions became clearly defined and named divisions (*parganas*) and sub-divisions (*tappas* or *patti*). The local Rajas became *mensabdars*, with obligations to the Mughal state. The ruler himself became a *jagir* of the Mughals and, in turn, made *jagir* grants to nobles within his territory. Thus the system of *bhai-bant* was replaced by an internal hierarchical system within the Rajput client state which developed to meet the external military and financial obligations (Sharma 1977).

Although the position of the ruler as a *jagir* of the Mughals changed after Mughal times, the main elements of the internal hierarchy survived. Essentially the system persisted until the land reforms of the 1950s. Except where specified, the following account refers to the position just prior to Independence.

There were two broad types of land within the Rajput state: *khalsa* land was held for direct use by the ruler; all other land was given in grants to various types of intermediaries. In fact there were many types of grant with different rights and obligations. One important form, dating back to the recognition of *bhomias* by Rao Chunda, was *Bhomichara* tenure, under which the descendants of Rajputs who 'held the lands prior to the Rathore conquest of Marwar' (Upadhaya 1973:160) held tenure.

Apart from a small fee due to the ruler, *bhomichara* holders had no other obligations (Upadhaya 1973:161).

There were other forms of tenure, based on different rights and obligations. These, however, need not concern us here. I will confine discussion to grants to *jagirdars* (otherwise known as Thakurs), since that was the dominant system in Marwar and was the system applying in Hinganiya.

A *jagirdar* received a grant of a specific territory with an assessed annual income called *rekh*. Upadhaya separates the term *rekh* into three distinct aspects, although most authors use the single word, blurring the three aspects. *Patta rekh* was the assessed annual income specified in the grant deed. Actual income varied from year to year in practice. The *jagirdar* annually paid a tax called *rekh bhartu* which was a fixed proportion of the *Patta rekh.* Rajput *jagirdars* (there were some non-Rajput *Jagirdars*) also had to provide a fixed number of troops in proportion to *jagir* income. This military *rekh* was called *rekh chakri* (Upadhaya 1973). In earlier times the *rekh* was assessed in terms of military obligation (the provision of a fixed number of horsemen or infantry), but later a lump sum was paid to the ruler in lieu of this, or in addition to it (Sharma 1977). There were other types of taxes and obligations which the *jagirdars* had to meet, but these are not important here.

As an intermediary, the *jagirdar* then allocated land to various tenants who paid him rent from which he paid the *rekh* to the Maharajah, supporting himself and his supporters from this income and from the produce of land kept aside for his own private purposes. Land kept for the landowner's private purposes was farmed by hired or bonded labourers, members of the Thakur's own family, or by share farming tenants. It was also possible for the *jagirdar* to make *jagir* grants of land to others, usually close kinsmen and/or retainers. These people could themselves use the land for self-cultivation or rent it to tenants. While the position of *jagirdar* itself was passed on by primogeniture, the younger sons of a *jagirdar* received a small proportion of the *jagir* land for their upkeep (Upadhaya 1973).

According to Upadhaya, *jagir* grants were effectively hereditary, although, when a *jagirdar* died his land technically became *khalsa* (i.e. under the direct control of the ruler) until the heir's claim was recognised. In fact inheritance by a direct lineal heir was refused only in very rare cases.

The obligations placed on tenants were extensive. Besides rent, usually paid as a share in kind, there were a large number of other obligations. In Marwar, between fifty and one hundred and fifty different levies and taxes applied in different parts of the state in 1941 (Jodha

1985). They included grazing fees, levies on livestock and compulsory labour.

It is not easy to describe any particular individual as the landowner, since everyone within the hierarchy held or used land within a complex network of rights and obligations. In one sense it would be appropriate to say that the land was vested in the State, in the person of the ruler. In Upadhaya's view it was actually considered to be vested in the ruling Rathor clan, of which the Maharajah was the first among equals (1973:166). In practice, I suggest, the *jagirdar* can usefully be described as the 'landowner' since his rights were essentially hereditary and alienable at his discretion. Tenants might, in fact, use land passed on from generation to generation, but this was at the discretion of the *jagir* holder.

Clearly, a major function of the *jagir* system was to provide for the needs of the rural nobility at the cost of tenants and labourers. However, it has also been argued that the *jagir* system was an ecologically effective land management system. Jodha, in a series of papers (1980, 1985, 1987), claims that land reforms in the 1950s led to a breakdown of controls on land use. This led to an increase in the cultivation of marginal land and livestock grazing on common land. Degradation of the quality of the land was a result. Jodha argues that, under the *jagir* system, access to grazing land was controlled by the landlord, who charged fees for grazing. Landlords also controlled cultivation, preventing cultivation of marginal land. After land reform these controls were lifted, with the result that marginal land was increasingly cultivated and livestock numbers increased. Jodha stresses that this management system emerged 'as a by-product of [the] . . . exploitative mechanism' (1987:203).

As far as my field area is concerned, there is no evidence in favour of Jodha's thesis regarding increased use of marginal land after land reform. In Hinganiya, as I will show, land classified as cultivable did not increase from 1947 (before land reform) to 1986. However, Jodha's case for an overall increase of cultivated land in western Rajasthan since land reform is convincing and there is no doubt that the proportion of cropland to all land has increased. In my view, however, the efficiency of the *jagir* system as a form of land management should not be overstated. There is an alternative view which blames desertification on the *jagir* system, rather than on its removal. Purohit (1978) argues that the demands of *jagirdars* on tenants led to overexploitation of land resources and that this was a major cause of desertification.

(b) Land Reform

During the 1950s land reform legislation was passed in many states of India. In Rajasthan a series of Acts, beginning with *The Rajasthan Land Reform and Resumption of Jagirs Act 1955*, and including the most important *Rajasthan Tenancy Act 1955*, abolished the position of intermediaries such as *jagirdars* and transferred effective ownership of land to the user. The user was given *khatedhari* rights, under which land could only be taken from the cultivator by the state. Those with *khatedhari* rights no longer had to pay rent to the former landlords. The previous landlords themselves maintained a right to *khudkusht* land (that is, land used for personal cultivation, including land cultivated by hired labourers, but not by tenants). There were, however, limits placed on the amount of *khudkusht* land which could be claimed. A number of other features of the package of land reform legislation were:

- There was an overall land ceiling, to be gazetted for each district or sub-district. The ceiling applied to a household of five members. Larger households were entitled to exceed the limit.
- Land in excess of the land ceiling was to be transferred to poorer farmers. Members of scheduled castes and scheduled tribes were to receive preference.
- Once land was held by a person from a scheduled caste or tribe it could not be sold to anyone not also from a scheduled caste or scheduled tribe (depending on which category the seller himself came from).
- Land could only be leased for a maximum of five years. There were some exceptions here: land owned by minors, students, widows, mentally or physically disabled people, military servicemen and people in a small number of other categories, could be leased for a longer period.
- A land tax was to be paid to the state based on the area of land and its assessed quality. There were provisions for suspension of tax liabilities at times of natural disaster (such as drought). The amount of liability was, and still is, actually quite nominal. For example, in 1986 the tax for the best quality of unirrigated land was Rs 0.47 per bigha (about three rupees per hectare) per year.

The main legal effect of the land reform legislation was to transfer the 'fruits of the land to the cultivator' (as it was put to me by the Sub-Divisional Officer responsible for Hinganiya). Subject to limitations on the amount of land which could be owned and the restriction on selling land outside the categories Scheduled Caste or Scheduled Tribe, the user of land had rights of hereditary ownership and the right to alienate the land. The previous tenant effectively became the owner.

It is significant that rights to land were conceived in terms of enjoying the products of the land. This way of looking at things persists from the period before land reform up to the present. In the 1947 village settlement papers for Hinganiya, the land register refers to the *bhokta* and the *up-bhokta* for each piece of land. The word *bhokta* means literally 'one who enjoys'. The terms thus mean, respectively, the one who enjoys the fruits of the land and the subordinate enjoyer (*up-bhokta* means sub-*bhokta* or vice-*bhokta*). The terms can be glossed as landholder and tenant, respectively, in reference to the period before land reform. After land reform their referents shifted. The *bhokta* is now the state (the *bhokta* column actually being left blank in the register) and the *up-bhokta* is now the landowner.

(c) The Effectiveness of Land Reform

The India-wide movement towards land reform following Independence can be seen as the result of a philosophical commitment by the Congress Party, particularly of Jawarharlal Nehru (Harcourt 1986). It is worth examining briefly the practical effects of land reform legislation.

It is something of a commonplace observation of land reform in India generally that the people who most profited were the previous tenant classes. Large owners lost land, and, more critically, the income from land previously farmed by tenants. The landless remained landless, or gained comparatively little (see, for example, Kamal 1984). In the case of Rajasthan, it is clear that major changes took place, but the extent to which they might be described as revolutionary is questionable.

Sharma (1970), in a comparative study of six villages in eastern Rajasthan, found that there had been no significant change in the class structure, despite the abolition of the *zamindary* (another type of tenure) and *jagir* systems. There had been some new developments. For example, the higher classes mobilised other resources in the post reform period (for example, in money lending), but the basic structure remained essentially unchanged.

Kamal (1984) cites evidence that 2.91% of rural families in Rajasthan remain landless while 9.84% possess as little as one half of an acre of land (0.02 ha). The top 3.33% of families own 24.34% of the total land, with more than 50 acres (20 ha) each family. The bottom 46.83% own five or less acres (2 ha) and less than 9% of the total land. While I am very doubtful about the precision of such figures, based on my own experiences in trying to obtain similar data for a very small area, even the general order of magnitude demonstrates that the distribution of land ownership remains desperately skewed, despite land reform.

Kamal attributes the inadequacies of the reforms to the fact that the Congress Party, once it ceased to be a nationalist movement and became a political party, was forced to include the former feudal elite in its fold. Thus the State Government lacks political will in enforcing land reform. I think that this somewhat distorts the process of land reform. It emphasises the role of those who had most to lose in blocking effective land reform, but ignores the interests of the tenant classes who gained most. Land reform legislation was explicitly concerned with transferring land to the people who were cultivating it, that is, the tenant farmers. Attempts to distribute land to the landless were a somewhat secondary concern. The lack of political will in enforcing land reform is, I suggest, not so much a result of the incorporation of the feudal elite into the Congress Party, but the result of the fact that the leaders of movements towards agrarian reform (the former tenant classes, particularly the Jats) have got what they want.

Rosin reports on an analysis of reform in various parts of Rajasthan. His findings support

> . . .the general success of the initial Rajasthan land-reform program in removing intermediaries and eventually giving title to land to those who cultivate it, whether previous tenants or resident landlords. (1981:76)

Rosin's study suggests 'that absentee landlords were more readily divested of their estates' than resident landlords (p.76).

To me the crucial issue is the notion that the original tenants *largely* gained from land reform (Rosin talks about some ways in which its purposes were side-stepped), but the pre-Reform landless seem to be left out of the equation. I think there is a problem in the way Rosin attempts to measure the success of land reform.

He identifies two indices for measuring its effectiveness. Both indices are conceived of as statistical tools for comparing different regions. One is the 'percentage of cultivators who had not previously been landlords [now] holding proprietory rights' (p.75). The other index is the extent of subleasing. The significance of this second index is rather ambiguous in my view. A high rate of subleasing could be as much an indicator of the failure of land reform as of its success. I therefore intend to leave it out of the discussion.

But what of the other index, Rosin's percentage of cultivators holding proprietorial rights? It is, in practice, rather difficult to express changes in the numbers of people holding proprietorial rights as a percentage. In fact, I am a little uncertain as to what is supposed to be a percentage of what. If we are talking in terms of the percentages of pre-reform households which held proprietorial rights in comparison to the number of post-reform households which hold proprietorial rights, we would need to know the actual number of households at some specific time immediately prior to reform. The records, for Hinganiya at least, do not tell us that. They only say which individuals held property rights and which individuals were tenants. Brothers can own land individually in terms of the register, but whether they are members of a combined household is not shown. The records don't mention landless households and they don't help us to distinguish between individual tenant households and clusters of tenant households.

I prefer to talk about the transfer of proprietorial rights as an indicator rather than as an index and to look at whatever evidence is available to see whether it does suggest a transfer of proprietorial rights. Have the descendants of the old landholding class avoided land ceilings?

There is a more fundamental problem. Emphasis on proprietorial rights obscures the key issue: to what extent have more people gained access to land since land reform?

I suggest that the most useful indicator of the success of land reform is the pattern of land distribution among rural households. Thus, in terms of the transfer of proprietorial rights, land reform has been largely (although to different extents in various parts of Rajasthan) successful. However, in terms of the actual distribution of land amongst households it has not been particularly successful, as Kamal shows.

An increase in the spread of proprietorial rights is not, in itself, a trivial thing. I do not wish to imply that a change in status from a tenant paying substantial rent (perhaps as much as a half share)[1] to that of an owner paying only token land tax to the government is not a major change. However it is the extent of distribution of land accompanying the new status that completes the process of revolution. In discussing the figures for Hinganiya, I will be examining the extent of changes in the social structure since 1947 in terms of both criteria.

The Institution of Household and Inheritance of Land

As a pre-requisite to understanding land ownership an essential starting point is the concept of household. I would like to digress briefly to describe the main attributes of the concept of household and the related concept of household cluster. Both terms are useful glosses for indigenous terms, not mere anthropologist's abstractions.

The term *ghar* (literally 'house') is used to describe the basic domestic and economic unit in western Rajasthan. A household may be a simple nuclear family, a patrilineal extended family (comprising the household head, his wife, married sons and various wives and children) or some other form of composite household (such as a household head, his nuclear family, and an un-married brother or sister).

---

1 Just prior to land reform, tenants of the Kur *Jagirdar* paid one third of all crops to the landlord. He, in turn, paid Rs 150 per year to the Maharajah as tax.

Essentially the household is a domestic unit, although some individuals are effectively part-time members, since they are frequently, even usually, resident elsewhere because of career or employment requirements. The most obvious indicator of household membership is that members share food cooked from a common heath when they are together. The Census of India bases its definition of household on eating together (Census of India 1981b).

The economic focus of the household is primarily obvious in terms of shared consumption. The household boundaries do not necessarily limit cooperation. Even though extended families might be broken up into separate households in a formal sense (with all parties asserting this separateness), a great deal of cooperation (such as sharing herding or farming tasks) occurs between households, particularly those related through a proximate common ancestor, living or dead. A cluster of related households, approximating a minimal lineage, is simply described as *ek parivar,* which can be translated literally as 'one family'. I translate *ghar* as 'household' and use the term 'household cluster' for *ek parivar.*

Theoretically, all income earned by members of a household should be given to the household head to control and distribute. In practice, this does not always occur, particularly when some members of a household are resident elsewhere and have separate expenses and separate income from wages or salary. However, even in these cases, much of the income is used for household purposes.[2]

The pooling of resources is perhaps the most essential characteristic of a household (Neil Maclean, pers. comm.). One way in which members of a household resident elsewhere contribute is by purchasing goods (including foodstuffs) for which they are not reimbursed. When goods are purchased on behalf of others outside the household, even from closely related households, the buyer is usually reimbursed.

The relationship between the household and land holding is crucial, but highly complex. Where the household holds land the household head (usually a male) is responsible for its management. This does not mean that he is the owner of the land, since he may merely hold it in trust for other members of the household. This may occur either because the owner is relatively young or, sometimes because the owner is frequently absent, perhaps on military service. I must stress that in this context I am referring to land ownership in terms of rights recognised by the parties. These rights usually conform to the rights which would apply under the

---

2 As Hill (1984) points out, in reference to the concept of household in many agricultural societies, the degree of economic individualism in a household may be such that the household head can become a very unreliable source of data, simply because there is much about the economic affairs of the household that he doesn't know.

Hindu Succession Act 1956 (at least as far as males are concerned), but do not necessarily do so.

Land is often legally registered in the household head's name, but this is not always the case. Sometimes, particularly in a joint household, land may be registered in the name of another member or more than one other member. While the household remains together, land can be regarded as the property of the household. Nevertheless certain individuals are regarded as having an entitlement to specific shares and land is partitioned on the basis of those shares when new households are formed. The household head effectively holds land, whether legally registered in his name or not, in trust according to legally and/or traditionally defined shares.

Land, is inherited in the male line, being shared equally by sons.[3] (Customarily, a father's house is inherited by his youngest son.) Land is vested in an individual, not in a household. The household, while it is not the landowning unit, is the land-using unit. The production from the lands owned by a member of a particular household is used for the household as a whole as long as that person remains a member of the household.

While the household can be conceived of as a unit which uses land jointly, there are some intermediate forms which confuse the relationship between housholds and land.

One intermediate form occurs in the situation in which land is held by a household head, but some sons (or siblings) own separate livestock and operate as independent households in other respects. This can happen when the head of the non-landholding household is normally absent from the village (on military service or working in Jodhpur) while his wife and children remain in the village and operate as a separate household. Land which will ultimately be partitioned may be held in trust by a resident father or brother. It is also possible for land to be held by a senior, despite the existence of otherwise separate households, in order to prevent or delay the sub-division of land into very small holdings.

The household may be intermediate in a chronological sense as well as a structural one. On one occasion I was interviewing one of two brothers. He said that there were two separate households, yet the other brother held all the land. At that time I was accompanied by an informant who explained that they were 'just going separate'. The brother who had no land had recently retired from the army.

The existence of separate households is normally quite clear-cut, being based on self-identification. However there are some ambiguous cases.

3 Under the *Hindu Succession Act 1956* the property of an intestate household head is divided equally amongst his wife, sons and daughters. The shares of female offspring are generally ignored, in practice, at least as far land is concerned.

People outside a particular household cluster sometimes assert very confidently that a particular group comprises a single household in cases where the parties themselves assert that there are two or more separate households. On one occasion my statement that 'X says that he and Y are heads of separate households and Y says so too', was simply dismissed by a third party who insisted that they belonged to a single household. This is hardly surprising, given that household membership is largely a matter of self-definition. However, there are two cases in which there seems to have been some genuine ambiguity about household membership because people made differing assertions about their relationships to each other.

In one case, involving two Meghwal brothers, the elder brother said there was one household, while the other claimed that they were separate. This occured during my 1983-84 fieldwork. By 1985 the households were unambigously separate. I interpret this as another case of 'just going separate'. Each of the parties had different views about the status of the intermediate form and about the exact point at which separation was complete. One regarded the transfer of land as the conclusive issue, the other did not. It is also possible that there may have been some conflict about the process of separation.

For present purposes, the important point about the household is that one of its main functions is the control of land, although control of land does not define the household. Similarly, the process of household formation is related to the inheritance of land, although the inheritance of land is not a necessary pre-requisite for household formation. Land and property can be divided between sons while a father is still alive (depending on the agreement of the parties concerned) or after his death. Sometimes one brother (often, but not necessarily, the elder) becomes household head and holds land in trust for younger brothers, or for those doing military service. It is quite possible for other brothers to head their own otherwise separate households while land remains in trust. This would normally occur when they are 'part-time residents' (see Chapter 9) or frequent absentees from the village. It is common for the shares of some siblings to be held in trust while the shares of others are distributed (partitioned).

As will become clearer later, reference to holding in trust relates to effective control of a share, not necessarily to legal *registered* ownership.

Under local practice, land originally owned by a father will be divided equally among his sons. Wives can hold land in trust, but in practice widows usually transfer responsibility to the eldest son, or adopt a son if there is no natural son. If sons are very young, temporary absorption of the household into the household of a relative of the deceased father may occur. The three cases in Hinganiya of households headed by women are rare examples.

Two of these simply relate to a situation in which a male household head has died , leaving sons, but the widow has held land in trust rather than choosing to have her household absorbed into another. One case is that of one of the four households of the Soda clan, which is headed by the widow of the previous household head. The household consists of the woman and one young son. Her name appears on the village land register as a landowner. The other case is a Bishnoi woman with four adult sons and a younger daughter.

In these two cases the role of the mother as household head is not necessarily a deviation from the normal practice of dividing land only among male offspring, since the function of the arrangement is to hold the land in trust until the sons come of age.

The other case, an all female Bishnoi household, was derived from unusual circumstances. The woman's husband died in 1983. As their only son had been murdered some time before, no male descendant was available. Normally the household would have become assimilated into the household of a near male relative of the husband, or the wife would have adopted a young male kinsman (usually a son of the deceased man's brother) to inherit both the property and position of the deceased household head. In this case the woman refused to nominate a successor because of the tensions which existed over the death of her son, who had been murdered by a young kinsman of her husband.

In 1983 a Rajput informant told me that he thought the woman would probably sell her land, because she would not choose someone to take over. This informant assumed that she would either have to select someone or sell the land. He apparently did not regard permanent leadership of a household by a woman as conceivable.

In 1985 the household continued to exist as an all female household, consisting of the woman, a married daughter and three young girls (one of the household head's own daughters and two daughters of her married daughter. The married daughter continued to live separately from her husband, who lived in another village.

The appearance of women's names on the 1947 land register for Hinganiya suggests the possibility of women heading households even before the period of modern law, but this is uncertain and, even if it were so, such cases appear to have been just as rare then as they are now. The reasons for women heading households were probably similar to the first two contemporary cases mentioned above.

Despite the local practice of distributing land equally among sons there are several ways in which unequal holdings between male siblings may develop. Firstly, new land acquired during a period of trusteeship is regarded as the property of the household head. It can be retained and divided at his discretion.

Another source of potential discrepancy is the institution of *khola* (adoption). When a household head dies without male offspring the widow may adopt a younger male kinsman (normally a brother's son of the deceased household head) as *khola bacca* (adopted son). Adoption can also be arranged during a landholder's lifetime, if he has no natural heirs. The *khola bacca* inherits land and the position of household head. He is not normally eligible to inherit land from his genitor as well as his adopted father, although there are one or two cases in the land records where this appears to have happened. I am unable to explain these exceptions.

There is one other way in which unequal holdings among male siblings may originate, although this relates solely to the descendants of the *jagirdars*. Under the *jagir* system inheritance of *jagir* land was by primogeniture. As some of the old Thakurs (a more common local term for *jagirdar*) are still alive, unequal land holdings between ex-Thakurs and their siblings are often evident.

Although the *jagir* system has ceased to exist legally, the title Thakur (or Thakur-sahab) is still inherited by the process of primogeniture and those who hold the title still attract considerable prestige.[4] English speaking Thakurs often describe themselves as 'ex-Thakur', just as the Maharajah is described as 'ex-Maharajah'. The 'ex' does not imply that the holder of the title has personally retained it from the pre-reform period. He may have succeeded long after the legal abolition of the position of Thakur (or Maharajah). The 'ex' seems to have become an intrinsic part of the title, as it is used in English. (The English prefix 'ex' is also used in the vernacular.)

The current Thakur of Hinganiya inherited his title only a few years ago. His predescessor was a paternal uncle who died childless and passed on his role and his remaining land (this all happened after land reform) to the current Thakur as *khola bacca*. The previous Thakur's brother (genitor of the present ex-Thakur) is still alive. Due to the fact that the current ex-Thakur is himself very ill and rarely leaves his house, the brother of the former Thakur is himself often called Thakur-Sahab, as if this fills a gap among the roles available in the prestige hierarchy. This case, of what seems to me to be very loose usage, probably would not have been possible if the position had any legal authority.

---

4 The rule of primogeniture was explicitly intended as a means of protecting Thakurs from assassination by siblings. It also minimised partition of land.

Land Ownership Today: Interpreting the Register

The analysis of land ownership in Hinganiya later in this chapter is based on data obtained from the register of landholdings kept by the Patwari (the land registration officer, who is ultimately resposible to the District Collector in Jodhpur). In 1985-86 the Patwari for Hinganiya was stationed in Kur and was responsible for the three villages in the Panchayat. A separate register was maintained for each village. Administratively speaking a village is the smallest area for which separate land records are kept. I was able, with the assistance of the Patwari, to abstract details from the register for Hinganiya. I also examined and copied extracts from the 1947 settlement records kept in Jodhpur.

The basic land register is in the form of a set of columns. The first column is a tax account number, but it acts simply as a serial number. The second column is the *bhokta*. In the 1947 Land Settlement records the *bhokta* was either one or both of the Jagirdars, or a close relative of the Jagirdars. In 1985 it was left blank, the government being regarded as the *bhokta*. The third column identifies the *up-bhokta* (the sub-bhokta). Effectively this refers to the tenant of the Jagirdars in 1947 and to the land holder in 1985.[5] Following this are listed the plot numbers of fields held within the account, the area of each plot and the category and quality of land. The categories of land refer to the assessed quality of land in the case of farming land, or to any other purpose for which it is used: road, wells, cremation ground, *abadi* (village residential area) or *dhani* (dispersed residential hamlets). The classification of land is based on a dichotomy between irrigated and unirrigated land. Within each of these categories there are a number of grades. Land tax varies according to the grade. All agricultural land in Hinganiya is unirrigated (*barani*). The four grades are BA (tax Rs 0.47 per bigha), B1 (Rs 0.32 per bigha), B2 (Rs 0.25 per bigha) and B3 (Rs 0.15 per bigha). While this amount is referred to as a tax, it is entirely nominal and should probably be regarded as a registration fee. Nevertheless, during declared famine it is not collected. In 1985 there were ninety-four account numbers and 355 numbered fields.

While the register is the official record of landholdings there are substantial difficulties in using it to compile breakdowns of individual holdings or holdings by household. I shall discuss these difficulties in some length here because assessing the reliability and usefulness of my data on landholding depends on an understanding of these points.

---

5 While theoretically the state owns all land it is convenient to gloss the term *up-bhokta* as land owner because the *up-bhokta* can alienate the land or pass it on to his descendants.

For each account a number of blocks of land are listed and the individual or individuals who hold this land are identified. An individual may appear in several accounts, since he may have joint shares with different combinations of partners. Often, the land is held by a number of people (sometimes ten or eleven) on a share basis. The problem is that the size of the shares is not always clear. Where several names (usually of brothers) are listed without a share being defined it is possible that the division of shares is not equal, but it is reasonable to assume that it is equal in most cases. In some cases shares are made quite explicit: for example the entry may read 'so-and-so one third share and so-and-so two thirds'. The most complicated cases combine the two types of entry. For example three brothers are identified as holding a one-third share between them, but no details are given as to their individual shares. Another set of four brothers shares the other two-thirds share. Thus, assuming equal sub-sharing between owners of fixed shares, we have a case where three people each own one ninth of the land nominated and four others each own one sixth. The land in question may be in several dispersed blocks of unequal size. It may also be extremely small, as plots are often less than one hectare in area. If one of the nominated share holders is deceased then the sub-division of his one ninth share becomes very complex. In the case of the 1947 Settlement Records the situation is further complicated by the fact that the same sort of sharing of rights to land can relate to both the *bhokta* and the *up-bhokta*. In other words a number of people are joint owners and several other people are, jointly, tenants.

In the case of jointly owned plots of land, the plots are not normally farmed cooperatively, unless shareholders are members of the same household. Rather, some sort of sub-division of plots is made between the people involved. The land register does not operate at this level of detail.

An underlying problem is that the record itself, despite the efforts of the Patwari, is not always completely up-to-date. Sales of land appear to be updated promptly, but changes of land ownership following a death are often not recorded. The register lists several deceased people as landholders or holders of shares in land. Reluctance to get too involved in the paperwork of re-registering land may be a factor in this. When a plot, or several plots, are identified as the property of a single deceased owner, the current situation can be fairly easily calculated on the basis of known modes of inheritance. However, when the deceased person held the land jointly with a number of others (in sometimes unequal and sometimes unspecified shares), it can be exceedingly difficult to calculate the sub-shares of heirs.

There is not always a co-incidence between *de jure* (legally registered) and *de facto* ownership of land.

- Sometimes land is legally transferred by a father to his sons (or to some of them) before his death. This, presumably, is done to avoid complications later. The father may continue *de facto* to manage some of the land himself, while remaining nominally landless.
- It is quite common for people who do not legally own land (i.e. land is not registered in their names) to be landholders in fact. Partition of land between brothers may have taken place, but because a transfer hasn't been recorded one brother appears as the legal owner.
- People who are registered as legal landholders (including small children) may be members of another household (father's, brother's or father's brother's). Land is *de facto* held by the household head in trust.

From the point of view of compiling data on *de facto* landholdings the issue is quite complex. It is necessary to use the land register and then to make certain assumptions about the actual divisions of land owned by individual household heads. The inheritance practices are the basis for making these assumptions and knowledge of genealogical relationships and household status (derived from a full census of the village) are essential.

The principles I have used in analysing the records from Hinganiya are as follows:

- Where the register names an individual as landholder or as holding a defined share, I have simply recorded that share against his or her name, unless
  - he or she is deceased, in which case land is equally apportioned among living male descendants;
  - he or she is not recognised as a household head, in which case the land is recorded against the name of the household head.
- Where the equal share inheritance rule is used, but some heirs are still members of another household, the share is included as part of the ownership of that household. (For example, three brothers may be entitled to equal shares, with the second brother having separated from the eldest brother and the youngest still living with the eldest. In this situation the household of the middle brother is assessed as having one share whereas the eldest brother's household has two.)
- Where two or more names are listed as sharing land, but the details of the shares are not defined, I assume it is an equal share. Similarly where a specified share is further sub-divided among two

or more individuals without details of the sub-share, I assume that the sub-division is equal.

- Where my own local knowledge suggests that these conclusions do not apply, I have made adjustments accordingly.

In summary, the analysis gives priority to recorded *de jure* ownership, modified according to inheritance rules and my own knowledge of *de facto* variations.

An obvious objection to the priority given to legally registered landholdings is that a thorough survey of households for *de facto* holdings would have been more useful. That might be true in theory, but, in fact, such data is very hard to obtain for a number of reasons, not least of which is the fact that many people are reluctant to say how much land they own and may distort figures for one reason or another. Another reason is that concepts of area are very vague. People tend to think of landholdings in terms of location of plots rather than in terms of gross area. The register records land in hectares and bighas, but these terms are not used by many villagers. There is a local measurement (*halki*) which is perhaps better known. Attempts to obtain data on landholdings through a semi-structured survey in 1983 provided me with data which I regard to be completely unreliable. Approaching the question of land ownership through official records seems to be the only viable approach, whatever its limitations.

Despite the use of these principles there are some cases where ambiguities exist and other cases where obvious irregularities occur. However, I maintain that the overall exercise is fairly accurate. Firstly, ownership by caste is completely accurate, as there are no cases where land is shared by members of two or more castes. Secondly, because of the accuracy of caste totals, averages per head of population and averages per household within castes are accurate. Thirdly, the larger landholders tend to own land individually and in easily assessible shares. It is mainly in the case of middle and smaller landholders that complex sharing of holdings exists. The ambiguities thus affect relative ranking of individual households, not gross categorisation as larger, middle size and small landholders. Fourthly, almost all irregularities or ambiguities relate to the breakdown of shares within a cluster of related households (that is, households whose heads are descended from a single proximate ancestor). While this last factor makes it tempting to give all households within a household cluster equal shares, this would ignore such factors as unequal inheritance through adoption, purchase of new land and so on.

The most likely source of error in the figures is in the case of households which are in the transitional stage of breaking away from another household, or where households are separate but, because the household head is a part time resident, land has not yet been transferred.

In the absence of specific evidence that land has been legally or *de facto* allocated to them, they are treated as having no land. A related situation is that of a landless Bishnoi who has legally transferred all land to his sons and is now nominally landless. The sons are heads of separate households, although the household cluster operates fairly cooperatively. The landless household category is, thus, something of a false category as it essentially comprises people who would normally own land.

I have focused on landholdings per household rather than on landholdings per household cluster despite the fact that more reliable figures could be calculated for household clusters. I have done this because the household is fundamentally more important as a focus of economic activity. The household cluster is simply not a corporate unit, especially in terms of landholding, despite the fact that members often work cooperatively together and sometimes hold land in trust for other members. To analyse landholdings on the basis of household clusters would be to impose a function on to a social category to which it has no relevance. Further, as household clusters are immensely variable in size and composition, the resulting figures would be of little value for comparing economic status.

The analysis of Hinganiya landholdings which follows needs to be qualified in one other respect. I have based my figures on an analysis of the land records for Hinganiya. A significant amount of land within the administrative boundaries of the village is held by people who are not resident. Some of these people are 'part-time residents'. A person is a part-time resident if he is a member of a household which is normally resident in the village, but spends most of his time living and working elsewhere. (The category is explained more fully in Chapter 9.) This is quite different from people who have economic interests in the village (including land ownership) but who are members of and live with a household resident elsewhere. I call these people absentees. Absentees who have landholdings in Hinganiya include close relatives (siblings or sons) of householders presently resident in Hinganiya. Others are resident in nearby villages.

The main difficulty with all of this is that, given the considerable share of village land held by non-residents, it is clear that residents may also hold land outside of Hinganiya. In fact I am explicitly aware of only a single Rajput who does own land elsewhere and he was rather confidential and secretive about it. I simply do not have any other data on outside landholdings. In order to find other landholdings held by people from Hinganiya it would be necessary to examine the records from all villages. Obviously this is impossible. The only way that the Patwari can assure that an individual's holdings in other villages do not cumulatively exceed the land ceiling is by liaison with other Patwaris. There is considerable margin of error in this, and consequently there is some potential for cheating on the land ceiling laws. This fact, plus the fact that all 'absentee' landholders who hold land in Hinganiya are from higher castes, tends to suggest that absentee land-ownership is more likely with larger landholders. The distortion is in the direction of under reporting of larger holdings.

Class Models of Rural Peasant Societies

The working hypothesis in my analysis of landholdings is that there is a close nexus between land and wealth. Thus, I will initially be treating economic status as purely an outcome of the size of a household's landholding. I am, of course, aware from the beginning that this is not the case. In fact, even if the quality of land is fairly constant, factors such as household size and alternative income are important factors in economic status. Nevertheless, the size of landholdings makes a useful starting point for discussion. My purpose in approaching the data from the point of view of the land-wealth nexus is to identify the points at which the nexus breaks down.

I must stress that I am concerned with variations of economic status *within* the peasant sector of the society of western Rajasthan, not with the broader class structures. While it might be argued that 'class' ought to be used only for categories of people who are identifiable by fundamentally different relationships with the means of production, I believe it is useful to use the term as a gloss for sub-categories within the broader category 'peasant'. I use the term class in this way because my aim is not to discuss the subtleties of class theory, but to examine sub-categories of peasant farmers which identify qualitatively different levels of economic self-sufficiency or dependence.

Before examining the land-wealth nexus in Hinganiya, I will, in this section, establish a typology of economic strata within which households can be ranked. This presents some preliminary theoretical and practical problems.

Agrarian households can be ranked using a variety of different principles of ranking. It is possible to plot households hierarchically using various single factor criteria such as size of landholding or average annual cash income. Alternatively it is possible to use multi-dimensional criteria, such as a formula which takes account of landholding, agricultural production, non-farm income and the number of consumers in the household. However, continuous scales produced by numerical ranking alone are of limited value for analysis. Some method of classification is needed to define categories of households into classes with some basic economic characteristics in common. Simply breaking numerical rankings into deciles or quartiles or other numerically defined ranges is not particularly helpful unless the ranges coincide with some sort of qualitative differences. This is not to say that the qualitative characteristics need to have fixed boundaries coinciding with the numerical ones, but at least the characteristics need to form a cluster approximately related to the range.

Thus, there are two problems: (1) on what numerical criteria can households be ranked? and (2) what method can best be used to group ranked households into economically distinct and meaningful categories?

Athreya *et al.* (1986), in an analysis of a rural class system in southern India, adopt a 'surplus criterion of class'. Depending on complex calculations of surplus production, particular farms are placed on a continuous scale. A number of points on the scale are treated as modal points roughly identifying particular 'reproductive levels'. The 'reproductive levels' coincide with differing capacities of the income of a farm to enable the farm to reproduce itself and the household without non-farm income. The first reproductive level comprised poor peasants 'whose farms do not yield enough to provide the household even with its grain requirement' (p. 4). The second and third levels, comprising lower middle and middle peasants, are able to meet household grain requirements, but require non-farm income to meet 'cash costs for production' and 'the needs for non-grain consumption'. Reproductive level four comprises the 'notional middle peasant' whose farm is 'a fully reproductive farm where non-farm sources of income are not necessary for the reproduction of the family and the farm' (p. 4). Reproductive level five includes the 'surplus appropriators' who may be of several types: 'rich peasants, capitalist farmers, big capitalist farmers, cultivating landlords, and pure landlords' (p. 4).

A merit of this approach is that the 'classes' are defined in terms of various levels of farm self-sufficiency. The qualitative characteristics suggest economically significant categories. Before they can be used, however, there is a major problem to be resolved: the whole approach depends too much on a very complex formula for defining where a farm (or household) fits on the continuous scale.

The formula for defining the surplus requires data in order to establish variables on 'gross income from marketing of farm produce', 'grain requirement of the household', 'cash costs for production', 'cash required to meet non-grain consumption needs', 'wage equivalent of family labour days' etc. I am very suspicious of attempts to obtain good data for any of these variables. Data could be obtained either by watching a very small number of households for a full annual cycle or through very detailed interview data for each household. The first approach might provide accurate data for the households actually observed, but would not help for other households (and would not help where conditions varied drastically from year to year). The second approach makes all sorts of assumptions about the cooperativeness of household heads, their detailed knowledge of all facets of the economic affairs of the household, their ability to quantify inputs and outputs and, unless interviews are very regular, their ability to remember inputs and outputs over a period of time. As Hill (1984) shows, none of these assumptions can easily be made and data based on such assumptions are likely to be very dubious. Even if satisfactory data could be collected in a given year, the problems of using this sort of formula would be multiplied in an environment where 'normal' conditions rarely apply.

My view is that complex formulae based on dubious data are unlikely to produce anything more useful than classification made on the basis of *relatively* simple criteria. However, even if this is accepted there are alternative approaches each with strong arguments for and against their adoption. Ranking in terms of the single criterion of land ownership per household has seductive appeal due to its very simplicity. However, where farm production is directed at subsistence as a first priority and surplus is a secondary concern, there is some argument for including some allowance for the subsistence requirements of particular households. This can be done either by simply dividing land area by the number of people in a household or by dividing landholding by the number of consumption units (a measure which provides a differential weighting for adults and children). Ranking would thus be in terms of land available per person or per consumption unit.

There are problems involved in rankings which take account of subsistence requirements. Firstly, the subsistence requirements of a particular household vary over time as people are born, grow older, marry outside the household and die. Ranking households to take account of such factors produces rather ephemeral results: people go up and down the 'class system' according to the part of the household development cycle they have reached. If people can move in and out of particular classes so easily, we have moved away from a concept of a class as a ranked status group whose members *tend* to pass on their status to their descendants. A class is usually thought of as a ranked status group which tends to reproduce itself.

There is another problem with a ranking which takes account of household size. One relationship which I wish to examine is the relationship between landholding and household size. If this relationship is to be tested then the two variables need to be kept separate.

This leaves us with something of a dilemma. On the one hand simple ranking in terms of the size of landholding alone, tends to obscure variations in the self-sufficiency of the farming unit due to differing subsistence requirements. On the other hand including some measure of variable subsistence requirements tends to overemphasise the ephemeral changes of economic status due to the life cycle stages of particular households.

It seems to me that the latter is perhaps a larger problem. I will proceed with an analysis of rankings based on landholdings alone. This brings me back to the second problem of ranking: what method can best be used to group ranked households into economically distinct and meaningful categories?

I have pointed out that the numerical formula used by Athreya *et al.* is so complex as to be of dubious value as a basis for ranking. However, the characteristics of the various reproductive levels indicate substantive differences in what the authors describe as the differing capacities of the farm to reproduce itself and the household without non-farm income. These reproductive levels are perhaps better described as levels of self-sufficiency.

I propose a slightly simplified series of agricultural classes for Hinganiya and the surrounding villages, based on a similar model. The system does not take account of non-farm income, or of income from pastoralism, being based purely on land ownership.

The categories are as follows:

Category 1:

Very poor peasant owning less than two hectares of land. As explained below two hectares is a threshold below which grain production will be inadequate for an average household's consumption even in a good year. Peasants in this category are heavily dependent on non-farm income. (Non-farm income refers to income earned otherwise than from the household's own land.)

Category 2

Poor peasant owning two or more but less than five hectares. Households in this category will be self-sufficient in grain for household consumption in a good year, but would not to be able to meet consumption needs in a poor year. Households would be substantially dependent on non-farm income.

Category 3

Lower middle peasant owning five or more but less than ten hectares. Households in this category would produce enough grain to meet household consumption needs under most circumstances. Surplus grain produced in good years allows the household to survive in most poorer years. Farm income needs to be supplemented by paid labour to obtain cash for non-grain needs and to enable needs to be met in a bad sequence of years.

Category 4

Middle peasant owning at least ten but less than twenty hectares. Households in this Category produce enough income from agriculture to meet all normal household requirements even in poor years and can be regarded as self-sufficient.

Category 5

Rich peasant or capitalist farmer, owning more than twenty hectares. Capitalist farmers are differentiated from rich peasants by virtue of carrying out capital intensive agriculture, by the use of tractors, investment in irrigation etc.

A key issue in this typology is the categorisation of households in terms of their tendency to hire labour or to work as hired labourers. The importance of income from wage labour is a crucial indicator of the qualitative differences between households in terms of self-sufficiency/independence. The poorest category of householders rarely, if ever, hire labour. People from households in categories 4 and 5 rarely, if ever, work as hired labourers, although individuals may earn income from military or other career occupations. Households in categories 2 and 3 may both employ labour and provide wage labour to other households. This is because some agricultural tasks require large inputs of labour for a short time. The general trend, however, is for households in category 2 to be substantially dependent on wage-income (they are net suppliers of labour) whereas those in category 3 have substantially less dependence on wage income and may even be net employers of labour, although only slightly so. Those in categories 4 and 5 are net employers of labour.

The use of specific landholding sizes as numerical thresholds for each category is obviously arbitrary. The numerical ranking is useful only to the extent that it is a tool which helps to identify qualitatively different categories. However there is a logical basis for selecting the thresholds and the results are quite consistent with various observations made during fieldwork.

Firstly, there is the question of the logical basis. The average household size in Hinganiya in 1985 was 4.8 consumption units. The average has been calculated using both full-time and part-time population. A consumption unit is based on the rather arbitrary assumption that adults consume about equal amounts and that children consume about half the amounts of food and other resources as adults do. In practice in the field it did not prove practical to obtain data on the ages of all offspring and, in fact, I am unable to differentiate consistently between infants, young children and adolescents from my census and genealogical data. So I have treated each married adult or unmarried person judged to be seventeen or older as a consumption unit and everyone else as a half unit. I assume that infants will balance adolescents. The concept does not differentiate between the food requirements of an adult man and the requirements of an adult woman. Nor does it allow for increased energy requirements during peak work periods. The notion of consumption unit has, therefore, only a very general indicative value, but it is a more refined basis for estimate than simple household numbers.

According to estimates by informants, an average adult male requires between twenty and twenty-four kilograms of millet per month. This is quite consistent with my own observations and estimates, although I did not carry out test weighings. I would stress, however, that villagers are acutely aware of such matters as the weight of grain and many households routinely weigh production after harvest. Loans of grain (for household consumption) are also weighed. It is reasonable to assume, then, that villagers' estimates are fairly accurate. One qualification about the average is that poorer people have much less varied diets and may eat somewhat more millet than those in wealthier households. The ration of grain provided by the government as famine relief was twenty-two kilograms per month, which is close to the other estimates discussed above. Accepting this figure as a working estimate, then the requirement for an average household (of 4.8 consumption units) for a year is 1267 Kg of millet.

In converting these figures into expected outcomes for small landholders there are some qualifications. It is a common practice to leave land fallow occasionally. Smaller holders tend to be unable to carry out this practice as regularly as larger holders. Very small holders also tend to place emphasis on millet production only. For these reasons lower productivity from smaller holdings might be expected as land deteriorates. This would suggest that a landholder with twelve bighas (about two hectares) would produce somewhere between 1200 and 1800 Kg of grain in a good year, probably something closer to the lower figure than the higher one. (See Chapter 6.) In a good year this would meet household grain requirements and possibly provide a slight surplus for storage, sale or barter. Where there is reduced production due to drought a grain deficit would be inevitable.

Households with five hectares would be able to produce somewhere around 3000 Kg in a good year, allowing for some land remaining fallow or being placed under mixed crops. Assuming one good year in four, two years with about 50% production and one year with little or no production, the average annual production over a four year period would be 1500 Kg, enough to meet average grain requirements. An average 50% production is, in fact, very optimistic (see Chapter 6). Households with five hectares would have some years of serious deficit. The further landholdings are above the five hectare threshold, the more likely the household is to be self-sufficient.

Of course these thresholds are arbitrary, but I would suggest that they approximately indicate points at which qualitative differences in the level of self-sufficiency begin to appear. Observational data on the extent to which households are self-sufficient is generally consistent with these thresholds and tends to confirm that they represent qualitative differences. Firstly, my census of Hinganiya of December 1985-January 1986 shows a close association between landholdings owning less than five hectares (categories 1 and 2) and emigrant labour. Of eleven people identified as part-time emigrant labourers nine were from households which were landless or in categories 1 and 2, one was from a household in category three and one was from a household in category 4. The emigrant labourer in category 3 was from a household holding only a fraction of a hectare above the threshold.

The case of the household above the ten hectare limit (in category 4) is also barely above the appropriate threshold. It is the case of a Bishnoi household of four (household head, wife, widowed adult son and the female daughter of the household head) in which the son worked fairly regularly in Jodhpur and the household head himself very occasionally did the same. (Only the son has been counted as a part-time resident.) I have no knowledge of any particular factors which might explain the need for additional cash. It may be that it is all simply a matter of economic opportunism - taking the opportunity to collect some extra cash. The household is part of a cluster which includes three other households headed by the other three sons of the household head. This is one of the cases where household and household cluster have somewhat blurred boundaries. Three of the four households live in the same *dhani*, although each is regarded as a separate household. Presumably the close proximity of the households, with the opportunities for cooperation in labour it provides, frees some members of the household cluster to work in Jodhpur. The young man's widower status suggests that he may work in Jodhpur as much for some sense of independence as for anything else.

The second way in which observations support the validity of the thresholds relates to observations about wage labour (and famine relief labour) in the village itself. I do not have comprehensive data on this, but my field notes contain frequent references to the composition of work parties. I have no evidence of people from households in categories four or five working as wage labourers. On the other hand people from most households in category 3 were sometimes observed doing wage labour, although these households may have been net employers of labour. There were only two households in category 3 from which I have no record of individuals doing wage labour. One is the case of a Rajput household (just under the ten hectare threshold) from which two members were in 'service' in Jodhpur. People in categories 1 and 2 were frequently observed working for wages.

It is important to stress that references to wage labour above refer to agricultural labour, paid labour on domestic projects or famine work. Work at *adolas* (voluntary working parties - discussed in Chapter 6) or other voluntary or cooperative work is not included, even if food was provided.

All of this observational evidence supports the view that the thresholds I have used coincide fairly closely with points at which qualitative differences in the capacity of households for self-sufficiency emerge. Obviously some cases will occur where households do not easily fit into categories, but the thresholds are surprisingly reliable indicators of agricultural self-sufficiency. I cannot stress the importance of this too much. My objective was to develop meaningful categories. I attempted to develop a numerical basis for placing individual households. Essentially it works. However, the fact that a numerical scale is used should not obscure the qualitative/structural basis for the classification. The coincidence of qualitative and numerical ranking occurs, despite my concerns about using a ranking system which does not take account of consumption requirements. I suspect that this may be because household size is relatively uniform and relatively small at the lower end of the scale of landholding sizes. In fact, of the total of 37 households owning less than five hectares, only three households have more than seven members. Thus, the households with small landholdings rarely exceed the average of 4.8 consumption units per household. (I will further discuss the relationship between household size and landholding in Chapter 8.)

The threshold of twenty hectares for rich peasants and capitalist farmers is quite arbitrary. The main basis for selecting twenty hectares is that the land ceiling on unirrigated land in the Bhopalgarh Tehsil is 135 bighas (21.6 hectares). Thus twenty hectares seems to represent a major departure from the normal situation. The cases in which the land ceiling are exceeded are all apparently explained in terms of increases to the ceiling to allow for large households.

The category 'capitalist farmer' is virtually an empty category in Hinganiya itself. At first sight it may appear odd that little investment in capital intensive projects has occurred, particularly given that there are four households owning holdings over twenty hectares. The answer lies in the fact that opportunities for capital investment are limited. Athreya *et al.* (1986) analysed class differences in farming in south India, examining both wet and dry areas. Wet, in this case, refers to canal-irrigated land. The dry area depends on rainfall for water. They found that opportunities for capital investment on dry land were comparatively limited, private irrigation works providing the main opportunity. For this reason capitalist farming was proportionately less common (in comparison to middle peasantry) in dry areas than in wet areas. These generalisations would be equally true of my field area. In adjoining villages several individuals have invested in private wells and pumps and have flourishing land as a result. However, in Hinganiya, the depth of the water table, and the salinity of the existing wells, means that this option is not viable. The opportunities for capitalist investment in agriculture are very limited.

Only one household could be said to have made any capital investments of any significance and that on a small scale. This household, the largest in size and the one with the largest landholdings, owned half-share in a tractor, which the household used on its own land and for hire. The tractor was purchased in 1983. By 1987 it had been sold. The use of tractors to intensify farming has limited use. No tractor owner with only unirrigated land would be able to use his tractor enough to justify the Rs 70,000 cost, so there is a heavy dependence on hiring tractors to other farmers. The main uses for a tractor, besides occasional use as transport for people to fairs and so forth, are for ploughing, for crushing crops prior to threshing and for carrying harvested crops (or water, in a bad year). These activities are limited by the fact that there is only one crop per year. Thus a tractor will be of economic value mainly for a few operations in peak periods of high demand *within* a five month agricultural season. In bad years there is even less potential for use.

The potential for hiring out a tractor is further limited by the fact that smaller farmers usually cannot afford to hire a tractor and, in any case, find the use of a bullock or camel drawn plough quite adequate for their relatively small plots. Unirrigated land is usually only ploughed once, in any case.

A tractor, then, is used relatively intensively for a few peak periods within the growing season. Occasionally tractors might be hired from another village if the local tractor happens to be occupied, but generally a single tractor meets most of the needs of the village. Capital investment in a second tractor is not likely to be particularly helpful for self-cultivation or as a source of additional income from hire.

In this section I have developed a typology of economic categories based on the assumption that there is a land-wealth nexus. One disadvantage of this typology is that it does not allow for the ranking of pastoralists. Within Hinganiya, however, there are no full-time pastoralists, and only two or three households whose income from pastoralism probably exceeds income from agriculture. In one of these cases pastoralism apparently became possible because the householder has a source of income from outside the pastoral sector. I will be showing the role of non-agricultural inputs in determining economic status later. For the present, however, the typology will suffice.

An Analysis of Landholdings in Hinganiya

(a) Overview

The administratively defined boundaries of Hinganiya encompass a total of 735.3 ha. Table 5.1 gives a breakdown of this into major categories. (Although the present tense is used I am referring to the situation according to the land register in January 1986.)

The total amount of land held by people not normally resident is a significant proportion of the total land available for private purposes (34.47%). Most of this land is held by people resident in nearby, usually adjoining, villages. There is no evidence of urban dwellers owning land, except in the case of a few people who are immediately linked with resident households and who are likely to re-settle. In these cases landholdings are small. I have already pointed out that residents of Hinganiya may own land in other villages. While I know of only one such case, it is reasonable to assume that the pattern of absentee ownership of land in Hinganiya is similar to the pattern of Hinganiya residents owning land elsewhere. In Hinganiya some land is held by Brahmans and Goswamis. These people are descendants of temple priests (*pujaris*) who had access to 'temple land' prior to land reform. These aside, most of the absentee ownership involves Bishnois, Jats and Rajputs, castes which generally held relatively large amounts of land. (Table 5.2 gives a breakdown of absentee landholdings in Hinganiya by caste). It is probably reasonable to assume that those residents of Hinganiya who hold outside land are from similar categories. Thus, the figures for the poorer (usually lower caste) farmers in Hinganiya are likely to be more reliable than those for the wealthier (usually upper caste) farmers.

Table 5.1

Summary of Hinganiya landholdings

Identified resident landholders, including part-time residents		451.47 ha
Absentee (landholders permanently resident outside village)*		237.47 ha
Total private land		688.94 ha
Panchayat (common) land		46.36 ha
	Total	*735.3 ha*

* Includes 5.85 ha held in name of person allegedly from Hinganiya (according to land records and the Patwari) but unknown to me.

Table 5.2

Absentee ownership of land in Hinganiya, by caste

Caste	Ha.
Rajput*	42.1
Bishnoi	122.15
Jat	48.81
Nayak	8.26
Brahman/Goswami	16.15
Total	*237.47*

* Includes 5.85 ha held in name of person allegedly from Hinganiya (according to land records and the Patwari) but unknown to me.

The following analysis excludes the element of absentee landownership (unless it is clearly indicated otherwise) both in terms of outsiders owning land in Hinganiya and in terms of Hinganiya residents owning land elsewhere.

Taking the 451.47 ha owned by people normally resident in Hinganiya (this includes part-time residents) the average landholding per household is 6.74 ha. The average per individual is 1.04 ha. These averages are quite high by an all-India standard, but it must be remembered that the land is of poor quality, being very sandy and also being entirely unirrigated.

On the basis of the typology of rural 'classes' developed in the previous section, I have ranked all sixty-two landholding resident (full-time and part-time) households in Table 5.3. Note that there are also five households which are effectively landless. There are some irregularities about each of these. Three of the household heads are part-time residents, either in the army or working in Jodhpur. They hold no land in a *de jure* sense, and are not regarded as being landholders in a *de facto* sense. In each case future partitions of land may change their status. Of the other two landless households, one is the household of an old man who has already distributed all of his land to his sons, while being regarded as the head of his own separate household. His household could be regarded as dependent on others in the household cluster. The final case is that of a household which is apparently in a transitional stage: it is regarded as separate, but no land has yet been transferred. For the purposes of Table 5.3, I have excluded the five landless households as being, each in some way, anomalous.

Table 5.3

Landed households. Average size of holding by class and percentage of total land by class

Class/ category (ha)	Holding range	No. of house- holds	% age of total house- holds	Average size (ha)	Total land (ha)	% age of land (ha)
5	20+	4	6.45	28.2	112.80	24.99
4	10-<20	16	25.81	12.39	198.26	43.91
3	5-<10	10	16.13	7.24	72.36	16.03
2	2-<5	15	24.19	3.17	47.52	10.53
1	0-<2	17	27.42	1.2	20.53	4.55
	Total	62	100	7.28	451.47	100.01*

* - Error due to rounding

The first thing to note is that only twenty households (32% of the total) fall within the top two classes, that is, the classes which can be described as agriculturally self-sufficient. Sixty-eight per cent of households (the lower three classes) are to some extent dependent on income from sources other than their own land. In the case of the seventeen households (27.4%) owning less than two hectares, other sources of income are very important.

The average size of holdings within each category and the percentage of total land held by that category are also set out. The distribution is quite uneven in these terms. The four households in Category 5 (6.45% of all landed households) own 24.99% of the land. At the other end of the scale, the seventeen households in Category 1 (27.42% of landed households) own only 4.55% of the land. The twenty households in categories 4 and 5 (32.26% of landed households) own 68.9% of the land. The 42 households in the lowest three categories (67.74% of landed households) own only 31.11% of the land.

(b) Landholdings and Caste

The association between landholding and caste is very marked, but presents some important irregularities. Table 5.4 gives the average landholdings per household and per head of population by caste. The averages suggest an association between caste status and economic status.

Nevertheless there is a large variation in the range of landholding sizes within castes. This is evident in Table 5.5. The Rajputs have the largest average holdings on both a per person and a per household basis. While all four households in Category 5 (the largest landholding class) are Rajputs, the Rajputs are represented in all categories. They are even present, for what it is worth, considering the anomalies discussed above, in the landless category. In fact there are more Rajput households in Category 1 than there are in category 5 and the total number in categories 4 and 5 (ten) is only greater than the total number in categories 1 and 2 (nine) by one. This means that the Rajputs cover the entire range of landholding size categories, being the only caste to do so. The Bishnois are confined to the three middle landed categories and are not represented at all in either of the extreme categories. The single Jat household also falls in the centre. The landed Meghwals all fall in categories 2 and 3. The Meghwal household in Category 3 is, in fact, right on the threshold between the categories. All Nayak households fall within the two lowest landed categories.

Table 5.4

Landholdings by caste

Caste	Total land	No. of households	Average land/ household	No. of persons	Average land/ person
Rajput	222.51	23	9.67	155	1.43
Bishnoi	176.03	21	8.38	142	1.24
Jat	7.84	1	7.84	7	1.12
Meghwal	15.25	5	3.05	25	0.61
Nayak	29.84	17	1.75	104	0.29
Total	451.57	67	6.74	433	1.04

Table 5.5

Range of sizes of landholdings by numbers of households and by caste

Class/ Category	Ha	Total No. households	Rajputs	Bishnoi	Jat	Nayak	Meghwal
5	20+	4	4	-	-	-	-
4	10-<20	16	6	10	-	-	-
3	5-<10	10	2	6	1	-	1
2	2-<5	15	4	3	-	5	3
1	0>-<5	17	5	-	-	12	-
	nil	5	2	2	-	-	1
	Total	67	23	21	1	17	5

There is a clear relationship between caste and landholding in all castes except the Rajputs. This raises two important questions:

- Why do caste differences in landholding still appear so striking, despite land reform?
- Why do the Rajputs diverge from the pattern of a close relationship between caste and landholding?

A look at the effects of land reform in Hinganiya will help to answer these questions.

(c) The Effects of Land Reform in Hinganiya

Earlier I suggested that the most important indicator of the effectiveness of land reform is the gross distribution of land. Clearly land reform in Hinganiya did not achieve a great deal in this respect as my analysis of the various tables showing the variations in the size of landholdings and the distribution of land by caste has shown. It is particularly clear that, whatever the effects of land reform, the lower ranked castes (that is, the scheduled tribes and castes) are still relatively poorly off in terms of land. In this section I want to examine the land records to ascertain to what extent the balance has changed, given the fact that it is pretty obviously skewed.

Fortunately there is a record of the rights which existed in Hinganiya not long before land reform. A land settlement was made in 1947. The papers are available in Jodhpur and I was able to transcribe the details. Using these records, it is possible to ascertain some indications of the shifts in land ownership between castes and it is sometimes possible to trace the broad outlines of what happened to particular households. There are some limitations in interpretation, however.

- It is not possible, from the data I have, to ascertain whether proprietorial rights or tenancy of particular plots of land were transferred sometime between 1947 and the period of land reform or after land reform. The 1947 situation simply has to be taken as the point of comparison because I have no intermediate data.
- It is sometimes possible to trace the movement of individual plots of land because both the 1947 land register and the 1986 land register give plot numbers. However plots are sometimes split and renumbered. From the continuity of plot numbers in the possession of identifiable individuals and their descendants (in some cases the same individuals actually appear as landowners in both 1947 and 1986) any renumbering appears to have been minimal, but there is no way of confirming this. I was unable to obtain a usable copy of either the 1947 or 1986 maps which indicate plot location and numbers.
- There are a number of people on the 1947 register who I was unable to match with people on genealogies even after questioning older informants. In some cases these people were absentee landholders or tenants. In some cases individuals seem to be identified by reference to a father whose name differs from the name given in the genealogies. This may be the result of different names being given to the same person in the construction of my genealogies and on the land register, or it may result from the fact that a person was an adopted son of a person who simply does not appear on my genealogies.

In 1947 Hinganiya was under a joint *jagir*, consisting of a resident Rajput of the Bhati clan and an absentee Rajput of the Tanwar clan. The latter was resident in Jodhpur. Each of the joint Thakurs held a half share. A number of relatives of the Bhati Thakur also held smaller grants of *jagir* land. For convenience I will describe these as sub-*jagirdars*. The sub-*jagir* lands were often held jointly by several Rajputs and the resulting shares were often quite small. Close relatives of the Thakur, described in the register as the Thakur's brothers, held larger shares than more distant relatives. Both the joint Thakurs and the sub-*jagirdars* held some land for self-cultivation and let the rest to tenants. In the case of the smaller joint holders of sub-*jagirs* the land was sometimes held by one combination of sets of siblings and let out to tenants in another combination of sets of siblings. Individual Rajputs may have held a share of a particular plot as sub-*jagir* holders and been part-tenants of the same plot. In these situations calculation of the rights of a particular individual are dazzlingly complex.

Besides the land used by Rajputs for self-cultivation, and a small amount of temple land for self-cultivation by the *pujaris*, the only land not let to tenants was the land held for public purposes, including land for wells, roads, the cremation ground and the village residential area (*abadi*). Table 5.6 presents a summary of all land in Hinganiya in 1947, identified (apart from public or temple land) by the caste of the person *using* the land. The category of Rajput land-users includes land used for self-cultivation by Rajputs and land used by Rajput tenants. The 1947 figures are compared to the 1986 figures for land ownership. Thus the principles of classification shift from land user (including both persons holding rights as proprietor and tenants) in 1947 to persons holding proprietorial rights only in 1986.

These figures do not separate non-residents and residents. While it is possible to do so for 1986, it is impossible to do so for 1947. As most absentees came from nearby villages in 1986 and the situation was presumably similar in 1947 (tenants, almost by definition, are likely to live nearby) the figures are comparable.

The table demonstrates one point conclusively: while the basis under which people in various castes gained access to land in 1947 and 1986 was different, there were only minor shifts in the distribution of access by caste. Very small variations to areas used for temples and public lands can possibly be explained by a resurvey or resurveys since 1947 coming up with slightly different areas for different plots. There are, however, some genuine changes which should be examined.

Firstly, the Daroga tenant of 1947 has disappeared from consideration. He was certainly an absentee tenant, presumably from a nearby village, since all of my informants are adamant that no Daroga has ever lived in Hinganiya. The plot number held against his name now appears as the property of a Rajput living just outside the village boundaries, although the area has approximately been halved, which suggests a division since 1947.

In general a small decrease in the land available to Rajputs has allowed increases to land available to the Bishnois, Meghwals and Nayaks and a very small increase to Jats.

Table 5.6

**The effects of land reform.
Shift in land access by caste - 1947-86**

Caste	1947 (ha)	1986 (ha)	% age change
Rajput			
Jagir (self-cult)	38.1		
Jagir's relatives (self-cult)	15.44		
Jagir's brothers (self-cult)	172.76		
Rajput tenants	57.51		
Total Rajput	*283.81*	*264.6*	*-6.77*
Tenants (1947)			
Bishnoi	278.44	298.18	+ 7.09
Jat	55.25	56.65	+ 2.53
Meghwal	7.95	15.25	+91.82
Nayak	33.77	38.1	+12.82
Daroga	6.96		-100.00
Other			
Temple	15.97	16.15	+1.13
Public	46.15	46.36	+0.45
Total	*728.3*	*735.3*	*+0.96*

Note: The discrepancy in totals is presumably due to a resurvey done since 1947

While the percentage increase to Meghwals is considerable, the actual amount of land is not, since they hold so little land anyhow. In fact the entire difference is accounted for by the transfer of a single plot, held by the joint Thakurs for self-cultivation in 1947. All other plots used by the Meghwals as tenants in 1947 are now held by Meghwals. During my 1985-86 fieldwork there was a legal dispute over the single transferred plot, which had been purchased by some Meghwals from one of the former Thakurs, in fact the Bhati Thakur. The descendants of the now deceased co-Thakur (of the Tanwar clan) had claimed that their father had never been paid by the Bhati Thakur for his share of the sale. I was unable to find out when the sale occurred, but it was presumably since land reform.

In the case of the Nayaks, all plots for which there were Nayak tenants in 1947 are held by the descendants of the particular Nayak tenants, with the exception of a single batch of three plots (totalling just under four hectares) apparently purchased since land reform.

The fact that a large proportion of the land previously used by rent paying tenants is now used by people holding proprietory rights is an important change given that tenancy before land reform was insecure and rent was high. On the other hand the reform has been less than revolutionary because there has been very limited change in terms of the distribution of access to land on a caste basis. Assuming the land wealth nexus, there has been no major change in the relative economic status of various castes. The tenant castes (Bishnois and Jats) are now middle peasants. The village service castes are now poor peasants. The places of castes in the hierarchical structure have not changed.

The reason why the caste-based structure of the rural hierarchy didn't change with land reform is straightforward. The main emphasis of land reform legislation was in *transferring title to land to those who were already using it.* The question of transferring surplus land to the scheduled castes and tribes applied only to surplus land used by *jagirdars* for self cultivation, not surplus land used by tenants. The tenants themselves got that land. In a small village like Hinganiya, which was a petty *jagir* anyhow, and where quite a lot of land had been granted to various Rajput relatives of the Bhati Thakur, there simply wasn't much available land. It is also quite likely that surplus land held by the *jagirdar* for self-cultivation was given to other Rajputs as tenants when the possibility of land reform looked imminent. Such land would be transferred under land reform legislation to the Rajput tenant, not treated as surplus land for transfer to scheduled castes and tribes. There is some evidence that this may have occurred.

If we examine the land held by the joint Thakurs for self-cultivation in 1947 we find that, in 1986, only three plots were no longer held by the adopted son of the Bhati Thakur or the sons of the Tanwar Thakur. Of these, one plot is the one sold to the Meghwals and currently under dispute. The other two plots were still held by Rajputs in 1986. I do not know when the transfers from Thakur to other Rajputs occurred, but the land was apparently never treated as surplus land for the purposes of transfer to scheduled castes or tribes. It therefore seems likely that land reform may have been to some extent bypassed by the simple expedient of obtaining Rajput tenants rather than leaving land as surplus. This would not have avoided the loss to the landholder, but would have kept the land within the Rajput caste. This is, of course, supposition, but it is plausible and at least explains how land remained Rajput land. There is no reason, of course, why favoured Bishnoi or Jat households might not have received land in the same way.

There are certain other ways in which certain Rajputs, closely linked with the *jagirdar* or his descendants, have maintained large holdings. I have already mentioned that there are four households in category 5, that is with land in excess of twenty hectares. In fact each of these households owns land in excess of the nominal land ceiling of 135 bighas (21.6 ha). In each case, however, the household size is in excess of the standard size of five for which the ceiling is calculated. On a pro rata basis each household technically owns land within the limit for its household size.

Case 1. Holding 35.8 ha.

This household has the largest landholding in the village and is also the largest household. There are seventeen members (one of whom is in the army and is therefore a part-time resident). The land is registered in three names: the household head (14.59 ha), his brother who is in the army (15.34 ha) and their mother (5.85 ha). As the amounts of land owned individually by the brothers are less than the land ceiling, there is no direct connection between household size and the need to beat the ceiling by maintaining a large household. The joint family structure is apparently largely determined by the exigencies of looking after the military brother's large and young family. A third brother heads a separate household. He recently joined the Rajasthan Armed Constabulary and has a young child. While he is the youngest brother he heads a separate household because he has received his land (14.9 ha) through adoption from his father's brother, whose wife is still the registered landholder. The household is emphatically regarded as separate, but is, in fact co-resident. The effects of the adoption are to keep the land owned by the previous generation intact within the household cluster.

Case 2. Holding 30.24 ha.

The household head, whom I will call Nahar Singh (not his correct name), is the brother of the previous Thakur (and the genitor of the current Thakur). Figure 5.1 shows the household and its place in the Bhati Thakur lineage. With a household consisting of nine members (including one part-time member), Nahar Singh is not in breach of the land ceiling. However, he has had to juggle two different requirements. On the one hand there is the need to have a household large enough to enable the land ceiling to be raised so as to avoid loss of land. On the other hand there is the need to minimise the number of heirs who will obtain full shares when the land is partitioned.

In all there were originally five sons and six daughters. All of the daughters are now married or deceased. At present two married sons and their wives and children are household members (one son is a part-time

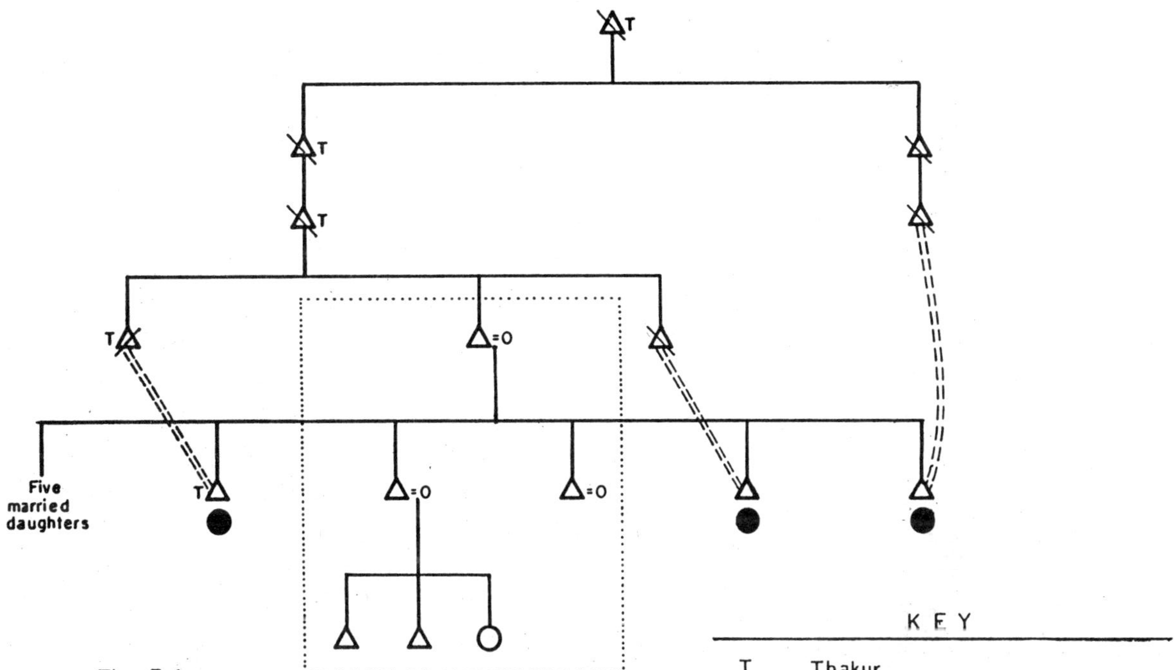

Fig. 5.1

The lineage of the Bhati Thakurs, indicating the household of Nahar Singh.

member). All of the household head's other sons inherited land by adoption from other Rajputs. By maintaining a joint household comprising the wives and children of two of his sons, Nahar Singh has maintained the household numbers required to meet the land ceiling exemption requirements. He has managed to avoid having too many heirs by having his sons adopted to kinsmen without sons so that they will no longer inherit from him. It is, of course, rather fortunate that so many of his male kin (including two brothers) died without male offspring. Nevertheless, the fact that a strategy depends on some luck doesn't stop it from being a good strategy. The sons left in his own household will inherit a sizable holding after his death. Further, the land held by deceased ancestors has been held within the lineage, at least for the current generation. I do not wish to suggest that Nahar Singh had a large family in order to achieve these aims. However, he has responded to the situation by manipulating household size to delay partition of his landholdings.

Case 3. Holding 25.26 ha.

This household has seven members.The eldest son (who is classified as a part-time resident) is married. The household head has four sons and five daughters. All of the daughters are married. Again it is clear that having a large family has advantages in allowing a household to own in excess of the land ceiling. In the next generation, however, the land will be split four ways.

Case 4. 21.51 ha.

The household head is the current Thakur, adopted son of the previous Thakur and son of the Rajput in Case 2. There are six members of the household.

It seems to me to be significant that all of the households which exceed the 21.6 ha bigha limit have household sizes sufficient to enable them to fall within the adjusted limits for large households. Further, each household has a joint family structure, and in two cases siblings of the household head, or sons of the household head, have received land through adoption. In one case the household head himself was adopted. In the only case where adoption was not a factor the household head has several daughters, now married. It seems to me that large joint households and large numbers of children provide the flexibility which allows household size to be built up to a size adequate to maintain land ceiling requirements. Some of the implications of this will be followed up later.

A final question which remains to be answered is why the distribution of land within the Rajput caste is so skewed. The current distribution is comparatively easily explained. Apart from those who have managed to purchase land since 1947 and those who have sold or lost surplus land through land reform, Rajput landownership today is a result of the inheritance of land for which user's rights were held before land reform. The question, then, is not to explain the current distribution, but to explain why rights were so unevenly distributed *before* land reform.

The above discussion shows that the Rajputs most closely related to the *jagirdars* were the ones who held the most land. Other Rajputs were comparatively disadvantaged. But why should they have been worse off than the tenant castes, the Bishnois and the Jats? Nowadays it is from the poorer Rajput households that most people go into military service. Presumably the same applied in the period before land reform. It has been suggested to me (Neil Maclean, pers. comm.) that the answer may be asssociated with the need for the Thakur to maintain a pool of potential soldiers. Too generous a distribution of land amongst Rajputs would certainly have made it difficult for a *jagirdar* to meet his obligations for the provision of troops when the *rekh* was assessed in terms of military obligations. Even in the later 'feudal' period, when the *jagirdar* had no such obligations, those Rajputs who chose a military career would have been unable to farm large landholdings and would not have needed them for their support. There is a clear tendency for those Rajputs with little land to be associated with a tradition of military service. Case 1 in Chapter 9 involves a lineage, with relatively little land in 1947, which has a tradition of at least three successive generations of military service.

(d) Tenancy

There are some ways of defeating the limits to household staple production imposed by land ownership. Legally, land tenancy is restricted in Rajasthan. Except in the cases of nominated categories (such as widows, minors or servicemen), landholders are not permitted to enter into long-term tenancy agreements. The maximum permitted period of tenancy (except when the owner is in an exempt category) is five years.

Details of existing tenancies are very hard to obtain, largely because most tenancy agreements are outside the provisions of the legislation. Consequently, people are reluctant to discuss them. Even when a particular tenancy is legal (when the legal owner is a widow, for example) there is a great reluctance to register agreements. However, despite the difficulty in obtaining systematic information, tenancy appears to be relatively common.

Hissar, the most common form of tenancy, requires the tenant to pay a fixed proportion of the crop to the landowner. The proportion varies: sometimes it is one third, sometimes it is fifty percent. In *hissar* the tenant provides all seeds and labour, but has to pay the landowner only on the basis of actual production. In another form of tenancy (*harsal*) a fixed fee is paid before sowing. The risk, therefore is entirely for the tenant. This latter form does not, apparently, exist in Hinganiya. Given the risk of crops failing it would have little to offer to a tenant.

I have information on only four tenancy arrangements. In all cases the landowners are Rajputs. Three of the tenants are also Rajputs, while one is a Meghwal. This is, however, not a complete list of all arrangements in Hinganiya and the apparent predominance of Rajputs as tenants almost certainly reflects the fact that one or two Rajput informants were forthcoming on the subject.

Interestingly, one of the Rajput tenants himself owned about seventy bighas (over 10 ha). He farmed an additional twelve bighas (2 ha) on the tenancy arrangement, leaving about twenty bighas of his own land fallow. This raises an important point. Apart from the obvious advantages of larger landholdings, there are advantages in terms of flexibility. Large landholders are able to rotate their crops and keep some land fallow. On the other hand, small landowners tend to limit their crops to millet, which is the staple, and to exploit all their land. In the long term this means that smaller landholdings would be expected to become less productive. Small landowners may be able to leave land fallow if they are able to obtain a tenancy agreement.

The ultimate limit to the number of tenancy arrangements is the amount of land available which is surplus to the needs of the owner. In fact, this is relatively limited and would generally belong only to landowners in landholding categories 4 and 5, although I know of one case of a category 3 landowner who has a tenant.

What are the advantages of a tenancy arrangement? To a landowner they are obvious. In a good year he obtains a substantial share of crop without any increased inputs. In a bad year he loses nothing. In fact he gains because any preliminary work or seed costs for which he might otherwise have been responsible are borne by the tenant. There are no risks for the landowner.

From the point of view of the tenant the position varies. It may be a means of increasing flexibility, as in the case I mentioned above, or it may be a means of increasing overall production beyond potential produce from one's own land.

Discussion

In this chapter I have examined the pattern of distribution of landholdings in Hinganiya. The main conclusions are as follows:

- The distribution of landholdings by size is very uneven.
- There are significant differences in landholdings by caste, both in terms of averages per household and in terms of averages per head of population. The average landholdings increase as the relative ranking of the caste increases.
- In the cases of all castes except the Rajputs the range of landholding sizes per household are limited to two or three adjacent categories. The spread of landholding sizes is, thus, relatively consistent for each of these castes.
- The range of landholdings sizes for Rajputs covers all five categories, although the caste averages (per household and per head) remain higher than those of any other caste. The diversity of landholdings among Rajputs probably derives from the fact that the Rajputs have always had a sub-class of people not closely related to the *jagirdar* who tended to join the military.
- In terms of the total amounts of land available for the *use* of each caste, there have been very few changes since land reform took place, although the proprietorial rights to land have changed from almost total Rajput domination (the exception was land held as temple land for self-cultivation by *pujaris*) in 1947 to a distribution of proprietorial rights amongst the *users* in 1986.
- Land reform in Hinganiya did not lead to a significant redistribution of land. This may be a result of the fact that, in what was a small *jagir* anyhow, land had been effectively distributed to a number of Rajput sub-*jagirs* before land reform.

As far as the relationship between castes and landholding is concerned, the greatest problem of interpretation lies with the Rajputs, who cover the entire range of landholding sizes. This range is a striking feature of the economic status of the Rajputs in Hinganiya. But there is a second striking feature: to a much greater extent than any other caste the Rajputs have permanent attachments to non-agricultural sources of income. While men from other castes obtain income from migrant labour, permanent salaried income (particularly in the army) is almost a monopoly of Rajputs. The Rajputs in the lower landholding categories, including the nominally landless category, tend to be in 'service' or to be returned military men. In terms of their overall economic position land ownership is not an accurate indicator of the wealth of these Rajputs.

The land-wealth nexus seems to work for the other castes, but falls down in the case of Rajputs. The cases of landless Rajputs and of landless Bishnois highlights this fact. The two landless Rajputs both have salaried jobs in Jodhpur. The two landless Bishnois, on the other hand, are landless by virtue of life cycle factors: one has already settled land on his sons and the other is a new household head who has not yet received his share of land. Both cases are irregularities which are nevertheless consistent with the assumption that wealth is based on land.

This chapter has examined the 'agrarian hierarchy' in terms of the working assumption that land equals wealth. That, while useful as a working assumption, is inadequate in two respects. Firstly, it ignores the importance of pastoralism as a source of income. While there is a link between pastoralism and land ownership it is quite possible for small landowners to make substantial income from livestock and there are, in any case, nomadic and semi-nomadic herders who make considerable income from pastoralism without any need to own land. I will consider this in Chapter 6. Secondly it ignores income from outside sources.

In Chapter 9 I will be pursuing the second of these inadequacies. In particular I will be continuing the argument (commenced in Chapter 4) that the Rajput caste has certain characteristics which can be turned into economic advantages.

Chapter 6

Agriculture, Pastoralism and Household Economy

Introduction

Vincze (1980) has discussed the features of economies which he refers to as 'agro-pastoral peasant economies'. The term can usefully be applied to the economy of Hinganiya and its surrounding villages. It is a peasant economy in the sense that it is concerned with subsistence, while being oriented towards markets for the sale of surpluses. It is agro-pastoral because the economy combines agriculture and herding.

This chapter describes agricultural and pastoral production in Hinganiya. It then goes on to describe subsistence activities, placing emphasis on the annual work cycles associated with both agriculture and pastoralism. A major aim is to identify priorities for production and any points of conflict between the requirements of the various subsistence activities.

It is important to emphasise that the production of both agricultural and pastoral products is aimed primarily at subsistence and, only secondarily, at cash income.

Agricultural and Pastoral Production

(a) Agricultural Products

The main crop grown is *bajra* (pearl millet). Bread made from millet is the staple of village diet in much of western Rajasthan. The 1981 Census of India names millet and wheat as the staples of all four villages in the cluster (Census of India 1981a), but this is simply incorrect. Wheat is only occasionally eaten and is regarded as something of a luxury. Wealthier families provide chapatis made of wheat to honoured guests, but, even given the high prestige value of wheat, some individuals express a personal preference for *hogra* (chapatis made of millet). I believe this is a genuine preference, not one motivated by any defensiveness about the fact that wheat is rarely available. Wheat is provided by the government at rationed prices in famine periods, but this hardly makes it a staple.

Other major crops are the pulses *moth* and *moong*, both sources of lentils used for making *dal* and *jowar* (sorghum) which is a secondary grain crop for human consumption. *Guar* (cluster bean) is used as fodder. The stalks from millet and sorghum are stored for dry season fodder. Vegetables are grown on a few irrigated plots in Kur, but as there is no irrigation in any of the other villages, most vegetables in the diet are from further afield. Sometimes vegetables are available in the shops in Kur or Kukunda. Malis (gardeners) from other irrigated villages frequently pass through Hinganiya selling vegetables from camel or bullock carts. (Table 6.1 summarises crops grown in Hinganiya and identifies them by botanical names.)

Table 6.1

Major crops grown in Hinganiya

Common Name	Local Name	Botanical Name	Use
pearl millet	bajra	*Pennisetum typhoides*	staple cereal
sorghum	jowar	*Ardropogen sorghum*	secondary cereal
moth bean	moth	*Phaseolus aconitifolius*	vegetable (dal)
moong bean	moong	*Phaseolus aureus*	vegetable (dal)
cluster bean	guar	*Cyamopsis psoralioides*	fodder & vegetable

Note: Botanical names taken from Jodha and Vyas, 1969

The first use of all locally grown crops is subsistence. Surpluses are sold as cash crops in Jodhpur and Pipar City. Occasionally bags of surplus millet may be exchanged directly (one for one by weight) for bags of wheat from wheat producing villages.

Bajra is by far the most important crop. It is favoured by farmers because it is highly drought-resistant. High yielding varieties (HYVs) have been introduced, although adoption has been relatively limited (see later discussion). *Bajra* is sometimes grown on its own, and sometimes intercropped, particularly with *moth*.

It is a monsoon crop, planted as soon as the rains commence. Productivity varies immensely, depending on the success or failure of the monsoons and on the quality of land. Local estimates for production from one bigha vary from 100 to 300 kg for a good year, although the upper figure almost certainly refers to HYVs. In 1983, I recorded production for sown areas as reported by two farmers, giving averages of 172 kg/bigha and 162 kg/bigha. 1983 was an exceptionally good year, so the yields were atypical. Nevertheless, these figures suggest a higher level of productivity than usually reported. Bapna (1976) gives the hectare yield for Jodhpur District as 166 kg, which translates to 25.56 kg/bigha. This, however, is an average figure, apparently covering a twenty year period (this is not absolutely clear) and also covering production from all land in the district, including the worst as well as the best land. The coefficient of variability of production reported by Bapna was 82.5%, indicating a very high range of variation from the average. Sardar Singh (1896), referring to Marwar, says that the average yield is two maunds (about 75 kg) per bigha, a figure which matches a rough estimate by Jodha (pers. comm.).

Given that the figures that I recorded refer to a good year, and given that the majority of land in Hinganiya is classified in the higher quality categories of unirrigated land (Hinganiya is in the relatively fertile eastern half of Jodhpur District), and given that informants consistently estimated yields in the order of 150-200 kg per bigha, I am inclined to accept that a figure somewhere between 100 and 150 kg per bigha is a reasonable outcome for good land during a good year, although higher figures are certainly possible in some circumstances. This translates to 625 to 940 kg per hectare.

To put this into perspective, there were eight years of declared famine in the ten year period 1978-1987 in Hinganiya and its environs. There was one good year (1983) and one year regarded by farmers as satisfactory (1984). In 1985 local estimates of production were in the order of 30% of good year production. In 1987, production was negligible. As an order of magnitude guess, something like a 20-30% average over the ten year period is probably realistic, given the number of drought years, the fact that 1985 was not a particularly bad drought and the fact that fields are either fallow, or not planted with *bajra* in some years. This amounts to 30-45 kg per bigha per year (about 187-280 kg per hectare per year). This is slightly above the Jodhpur District average mentioned above and therefore is consistent with the slightly better average quality of land in the eastern parts of the district

Productivity for high yielding varieties (HYVs) is usually reported as being about double that of ordinary *desi* (local) seed. I will discuss HYVs later in this chapter.

Market prices for *bajra* in Jodhpur vary immensely, depending on availability. For example, in December 1983, after most of the good harvest had been collected, the price was Rs 1-50 per kg. Informants estimated that it would rise to Rs 2 per kg a few months later. In the midst of the drought of late 1985 it was Rs 2-50 per kg.

Because other crops are usually grown in intercropped fields, productivity is not easy to estimate accurately. In an experimental treatment in which *moong* and *guar* were used as controls, Shankarnarayan *et al.* (1987) give per/ha yield for *moong* as 640 kg/ha and for *guar* as 320 kg/ha. These figures refer to 1983, and thus refer to the same good season as my figures for *bajra*. The figure for *guar* is consistent with reported output for a four bigha plot of *guar* in Hinganiya for the same year. Reported production was 200 kg, which converts to 312.5 kg/ha.

(b) Livestock Production

Livestock production involves a variety of species. Domestic animals raised in the region are camels, cattle, buffalo, sheep and goats.

All the cattle in the district are of the humped Brahman variety (*Bos indicus*). Cows are highly valued for milk, both for domestic consumption and for sale in Jodhpur. At the time of my fieldwork few milk producers in Hinganiya itself owned enough cattle to become substantially involved in the sale of surplus milk. However, small amounts of milk surplus to household requirements (as little as a litre at a time), were sometimes taken to Kukunda and sold to middlemen who, in turn, transported it to urban outlets.

Bullocks are used as work animals, either for pulling carts or for ploughing. Bulls are of no economic value apart from breeding, and are occasionally seen wandering wild. In fact very few bulls or bullocks are found in the area. Most young males are castrated and bullocks are often sold because they are of relatively limited value in an area where there is only one agricultural season and where there is a proportionately small need for ploughing. Camels are preferred as work animals because they can haul bigger loads by cart and can also haul ploughs. Unlike ploughing, cart transportation has year round application.

In 1985/6 I carried out a livestock survey, obtaining data for animals owned by all households. Of 125 adult cattle, 116 were cows, two were bulls and there were seven bullocks. Table 6.2 sets out the figures for all cattle, by sex and age category.

Surplus bulls and bullocks are often sold at cattle fairs (such as the Pushkar Mela or the Jajiwal Mela). Buyers tend to come from areas (in other states, or in eastern Rajasthan) where plough animals are of greater use. This, essentially, means areas where two crops (the winter or *rabi* and the summer/monsoonal *kharif*) are grown each year.[1]

Buffalo are highly valued as milk animals. Apart from breeding, male buffalo have no economic value. Table 6.3 gives the sex/age breakdown of buffalo in Hinganiya.

Table 6.2

Cattle in Hinganiya 1985/6, by sex and age category

Adult Male	2		
Adult Female	116		
Bullock	7	Total Adult	125
Young Male	39		
Young Female	60	Total Young	99

Table 6.3

Buffalo in Hinganiya 1985/6, by sex and age category

Adult Male	1		
Adult Female	12	Total Adult	13
Young Male	8		
Young Female	6	Total Young	14

Table 6.4

Camels in Hinganiya 1985/6, by sex and age category

Adult Male	4		
Adult Female	21	Total Adult	25
Young Male	4		
Young Female	6	Total Young	10

Note: 'Young' refers to cattle, buffalo and camels under three years old

1 Lodrick (1984) argues that livestock markets in western Rajasthan act to circulate livestock out of the drought area in bad seasons and that they particularly remove zebu bulls and bullocks, but rarely milk producing females. Thus a situation *approaching* a desired balance is achieved within the strictures of the sacred cow complex. The ratios of male to female cattle in Hinganiya were explicitly explained to me by a villager with reference to the selling of bulls and bullocks to areas where they are needed for ploughing.

Male camels are used as work animals, usually for pulling carts or for ploughing. Female camels are sometimes used for lighter tasks, such as carrying water bags or for riding. Generally, in this region riding tends to be a supplementary use for camels kept primarily for other purposes. There is considerable income to be made in raising camels for sale. In Hinganiya, however, the only people who own more than one camel are Bishnois. Table 6.4 gives the numbers and age/sex breakdown of camels in Hinganiya.

Goats are raised both for their milk (for domestic consumption) and for sale as meat. Young male animals are sold to travelling buyers who then sell them in cities such as Jodhpur. Most people in the village are non-vegetarian, but this is a statement of their willingness to eat meat rather than of common practice. Animals are rarely butchered for domestic consumption. The only meat I saw in Hinganiya was deer meat (obtained by hunting) or mutton (goat meat) purchased in Jodhpur. The reluctance to slaughter animals in the village clearly relates to their cash value - about 150 to 200 rupees for sheep or goats.

Table 6.5

Goats in Hinganiya 1985/6, by sex and age category

Adult Male	17		
Adult Female	261	Total Adult	278
Young Male	42		
Young Female	55		
Young Unspecified	41	Total Young	138

Table 6.6

Sheep in Hinganiya 1985/6, by sex and age category

Adult Male	14		
Adult Female	226	Total Adult	240
Young Male	5		
Young Female	10		
Young Unspecified	85	Total Young	100

Note: 'Young' refers to kids and lambs under one year old

Sheep are raised almost entirely for commercial purposes - for wool and (less often) for meat. They are occasionally milked for household consumption. Tables 6.5 and 6.6 give the age and sex distribution for goats and sheep respectively. I have included the figures for young animals (animals under a year old), but must stress that these figures are not very useful for several reasons. Firstly, informants did not always know the sex ratios of the 'young' components of their flocks. Secondly, the numbers were sometimes approximate. Thirdly, the survey took several weeks to complete. During this period a number of animals were sold to butchers and new births were occurring all the time.

It is useful to compare the patterns of ownership of sheep and goats. The survey of 1985/6 reported a total of 278 adult goats and 240 adult sheep. Forty-one households owned goats making an average of 6.8 per goat owning household. Only fourteen households owned sheep, an average of 17.1 per sheep-owning household. In other words fewer people own sheep than goats, but those who own sheep tend to own more. This is because quite large numbers of sheep are required to justify involvement in production of wool, whereas even a small number of goats provides good returns, at least at a basic subsistence level. Wool production tends to be a specialist activity. This conclusion is supported by the fact that specialist sheep herders exist in the region, whereas there are no specialist goat herders.

The cash value of sheep and goats is important, although the two types of animals have a distinctly different economic role. One thing they have in common is a potentially prodigious rate of herd growth. Both sheep and goats breed twice in a year; multiple births are common. Dahl and Hjort (1976) have modelled, on a computer, the growth rate of flocks with average age and sex distribution, based on conditions in semi-arid parts of Africa. While, as Dahl and Hjort readily admit, models based on dubious assumptions about average conditions are suspect, they do suggest the order of magnitude of herd growth potential.

Regarding goats, Dahl and Hjort's figures show that flock size can increase between double and triple in three years, depending on basic flock age and sex structure. My own calculations reinforce this notion. Given a breeding population of ten female goats (and access to a male for breeding purposes), assuming a 75% fertility rate (and no multiple births), two breeding seasons would produce fifteen young animals per year. Of these an average of 7.5 would be male. Allowing a high rate of 33% mortality, five male kids would be available for sale. The base number of female stock would also increase by 7.5. Even allowing 40% overall female mortality, the base flock of ten females would be preserved. In other words a stable flock could be maintained and still produce males for culling each year equivalent to 50% of the number of breeding females.

Dahl and Hjort calculate that, if an entire population (adult male, adult female and young animals) is included, 32% of the *whole* flock can be culled each year. This is close to my figure which relates to 50% of the base breeding population.

All this assumes herd stability. In fact a lower female mortality rate means that herd size can increase while allowing culling to continue. As female numbers increase so does the annual number of young males available for culling. Of course, high mortality due to very serious drought or epidemic would invalidate the assumptions. Lower fertility during drought conditions is another factor which would act to reduce productivity. Nevertheless the argument demonstrates the high potential productivity of goat flocks.

These figures apply to goats, though similar arguments could be made for sheep. The other thing that applies in each case, is the importance of maintaining breeding stock so that the flock can reproduce itself rapidly. In Rajasthan the sale of young males of both species for meat is acceptable, but females of both species are not eaten or sold to butchers. This has a ritual aspect, but is also pragmatic.

The sale price of a six or seven month old goat was approximately Rs 150 at the time of my fieldwork. Even a small owner, with ten breeding goats could sell approximately five male kids in a year, at Rs 750. Even two or three goats are valuable, providing milk for domestic consumption and the odd male kid for sale.

The economics of sheep production is more complex. Male animals are sold for meat, rates being much the same as for goats. Sheep are usually shorn twice a year, the yield varying and the price per kilogram varying according to quality. The most highly regarded breed of sheep is the Bikaneri, producing 1-1.5 kg of wool per shearing, twice each year, around April and October. In 1985 each kilogram of Bikaneri wool was worth between Rs 15 and Rs 18. The three other important breeds (in decreasing order of desirability) each produce about one kilogram per shearing and are the Jaisalmeri (Rs 12-15 per kg), the Marwari (Rs 8 per kg) and the Mewari (Rs 6-8 per kg).

In a good year, a flock of fifty breeding Bikaneri sheep would earn up to Rs 1500 per year for wool, plus Rs 3750 for the sale of twenty-five male lambs at Rs 150 each. The total, less costs for medicines etc (sheep are very disease prone) represents a considerable income.[2] Nevertheless, sheep raising is risky. In 1985/86 the herds of two of the four sheep

2 For a herd of 100 sheep, Salzman (1986) estimates an annual income of Rs 10-15000. His calculations include sale of milk products and dung. No one in Hinganiya counts his sheep in multiples of 100, but the estimate is comparable.

specialists in Hinganiya were decimated by disease. (This occurred after my livestock census.)

(c) Utilisation of Trees, Shrubs and Natural grasses

An essential aspect of both the ecology and economy is the role of trees, shrubs and natural grasses. All of these natural resources are used primarily for fodder (*chara*). Apart from natural grasses, small bushes are major sources of naturally growing fodder for grazing and browsing animals. In winter and summer, *shinnia*, a small bush sometimes woven into rope, is a major source of fodder for all types of livestock. *Shinnia* grows in the winter. *Bhivna*, a bush which grows in the monsoon, is eaten by sheep and goats. As it dries out the branches become a rich source of fuel which burns quickly and with great heat. It provides a major source of fuel during winter. In good seasons the growth of these and other bushes and grasses is prolific.

Several species of trees are valued by villagers. Of these the most significant are the *khejri* (*Prosopis cineria*) and the *ber* (*Zizyphus nummularia*). Both of these species are valuable fodder species and the *ber* also produces a popular fruit.[3] Quite apart from its fodder value, the *khejri* is considered to have beneficial effects on crop production, since it helps maintain soil moisture and soil conditions (Shankarnarayan *et al.* 1987).

There are a surprising number of trees in the vicinity of Hinganiya and Khokhariya in particular, although the whole region around Pipar (in eastern Jodhpur District) is generally fairly well wooded. In a rough experiment, I counted trees on a sample plot of farm land in Hinganiya and found twenty-three trees over shoulder height in an area I estimated to be about 1.25 ha. This amounts to a density of 18.4 shoulder height trees per hectare. While this was by no means a precise measurement,[4] it does indicate, as an order of magnitude, just how common trees are. The selected plot was fairly typical, in my subjective judgement, of the surrounding area.

Trees on farm-land are generally not planted, but result from natural regeneration. The fact that smaller trees are present indicates that they are protected to some extent from grazing animals, and pruning, while

---

3 Bhandari (1977), who identifies twenty-three species of edible plants in the Rajasthan Desert, says that the leaves, shoots and even the bark of the *Khejri* are edible.

4 The survey was very 'unscientific', simply because it was done as something of an afterthought during my very short visit to Hinganiya in 1987. I had previously recognised the importance of trees, but had not thought to count them systematically. Seven months working on a forestry project in Nepal immediately prior to my visit had sharpened my recognition of the importance of trees.

severe, always leaves enough growth to enable regeneration. In addition to trees on farmland, trees on common land are protected from pruning by a prohibition backed by sanctions. I have seen no evidence of illicit pruning of such trees. Although I have not carried out any study to support this argument, I suspect that the common stereotype of the desert loosing tree cover at an astounding rate is not accurate, at least in this part of the Thar Desert. There is every sign that trees are valued and protected and the evidence of regeneration is a healthy sign.

Villagers also plant trees in the village, protecting them from goats with a cover of thorny bushes. Seedlings are available from the Central Arid Zone Research Institute in Jodhpur.

The Agricultural Cycle

I have already mentioned the monsoonal basis for the agricultural cycle. I will now expand this and then show some aspects of the relationships between agricultural and herding activities. It is essential to remember that annual work cycles vary according to the success or failure of the monsoon. Thus, the preliminary description is of an ideal situation, that is a year of good monsoon rain.

The wet season, when it comes, usually arrives in early to mid July and lasts until late August or early September. If the monsoon does occur, there is a season of agricultural activity lasting through the monsoon and into the winter. The final phase (threshing and winnowing) runs into early January in a good year.

Throughout the agricultural cycle priority is given to *bajra*. It is planted first and harvested when it is ready. Everything else fits around the *bajra* crop. Other crops are only planted after no essential tasks related to *bajra* are outstanding. The slightly longer period of growth for other crops (*bajra* only takes about seventy days) allows them to be planted after *bajra* and to be left until the essential work related to *bajra* is completed. This is fortuitous, since it minimises competing priorities, but it should not be allowed to obscure the priority. If the rains fail later during the monsoon, then the other crops are expendable, but *bajra*, as the staple, is not. Thus, the reason for the order of planting does not relate to later conditions being better for other crops, but to the need to minimise risks to the staple crop.

The agricultural year can be divided into a number of stages.

(a) Ploughing and Planting

Ploughing and planting usually take place in July. The actual timing depends on whether rain has fallen. Planting does not take place until after the first rain has fallen. Similarly, there is normally no ploughing unless some rain has fallen. Once the first rain falls the fields are ploughed and seed is sown.

At the beginning of the monsoon farmers make an assessment of the probability of good rain. During the 1985 season the monsoon came slightly late, some good rain followed and then the monsoon petered out, virtually no rain falling in the latter part of the monsoon. From my arrival in mid-August there was no rain in Hinganiya (apart from mild sprinkling) until early October, by which time the poor harvest had already been brought in. One Nayak had only sowed half of his meagre fields, despite the fact that his landholding was barely adequate to provide a year's supply of *bajra* for his family, even in a good year. He told me he had done this because the early rains were very poor. Apparently he was confident enough of his forecast to not risk wasting the effort required to sow all of his land. He may also have decided to make the best of a bad situation by leaving the land fallow.

Ploughing is done either by use of bullock or camel-drawn ploughs, or occasionally by tractors. Those farmers who do not own camels or bullocks have to hire or borrow them, or they may hire a tractor. For *bajra*, the land is ploughed only once. For other crops it is ploughed about three times.

Sowing is done by means of a funnel-shaped tube (*bijni*), or a pair of such tubes, attached to a single or double pronged plough. For local varieties of *bajra* approximately one kilogram of seed is required per bigha. Normally the seed is simply left over from the previous year. HYV seeds are purchased.

Mixed cropping, intercropping, fallowing and alternating crops are important aspects of the agricultural cycle. I have already pointed out that the first priority in agriculture is guaranteeing, as far as possible, the production of the staple crop. Within this context the production of secondary crops, including cash crops, is pursued enthusiastically. Generally speaking, poorer farmers rarely devote significant proportions of their land to crops other than *bajra*, although they often favour mixed cropping of other crops with *bajra*. Larger farmers, or those with alternative sources of income, may devote considerable areas to other crops.

Farmers recognise the value of leaving fields fallow, but the opportunity to do so is obviously greater in the case of farmers owning relatively large amounts of land. Among the cases of sharecropping arrangements I recorded are two cases of farmers using someone else's land on a sharecropping basis and leaving their own land fallow ('for the goats').

Overall, fallow fields comprise only a small proportion of total cultivable fields. According to Jodha (1977), more than 80% of private holdings 'in most districts' were actually cultivated in 1970-71. This is consistent with my experience.

The disadvantageous effects of poor farmers having to plant wherever possible are probably reduced to some extent by enforced fallow periods during drought. This factor, plus the unpredictability it involves make me very dubious of attempts to describe crop rotation patterns as if they were regular cycles. Agarwal (1979), for example, lists common cycles for unirrigated land, such as *bajra*-fallow-wheat and *bajra*-fallow-*moong*-fallow. Nothing works that regularly.

The value of alternating *bajra* with pulses is recognised, but circumstances do not always permit this. Again, larger farmers have the advantage. Mixed cropping and intercropping are ways of obtaining some of the benefits of alternating crops.[5] As some crops do not compete it may be possible to maximise production of both. Intercropping of *moth* or *moong* or *guar* and *moth* is quite common. Intercropping *bajra* and pulses is reported as being common (Agarwal 1979), and I have seen *bajra*-*moth*-oilseed and *bajra-moth-jowar* combinations. Although intercropping does occur it is often the case that, where *bajra* is grown in the same field as pulses, the pulses tend to be kept in a separate section of the field. This is not intercropping in the normal sense. A field, however legally registered, may be sub-divided amongst several owners, so there is nothing surprising about having different crops, or combinations of crops, in different sections.

(b) Hoeing and Weeding

Throughout the period of crop growth there is a fairly heavy and consistent work-load involved in hoeing and weeding, particularly of fields of *moth* and *moong*. While this work is sometimes carried out on the level of the individual household, it is often a large chore and many farmers, especially those with bigger holdings, hire labour to do the task. The work groups are sometimes quite large (ten or twelve are common) and are of mixed caste and sex. There are two qualifications regarding the mixed nature of the groups. Firstly, while married women of other castes often work, it is unusual for married Rajput women to work in such groups. Unmarried Rajput women will do so. Secondly, while Rajput men will work side by side with men of other castes, in practice this usually occurs only in fields owned by Rajputs. The fact that Rajputs

5 Mixed cropping involves growing two or more crops on the same field or part of a field at the same time. Intercropping is defined by Ruthenberg (1980) as a system in which 'two or more crops. . . are grown on different but proximate rows' (p.133).

rarely work for Nayaks or Meghwals probably reflects the fact that members of these castes, having small amounts of land, do not require very large work groups. The prestige of working for, as opposed to with, other castes, may also be a factor. Thirdly, Bishnois do not often work in work groups for other castes. Work-groups on Bishnoi fields tend to be made up largely, but not exclusively, of Bishnois.

The work groups operate in lines, which work their way up and down the fields. Men and women work in separate lines, but there is no caste segregation within the male and female sub-groups.

Some farmers prefer to do the hoeing themselves. In such cases it tends to be a regular chore. I timed a working party of twelve people hoeing an eight bigha plot of *moth*. They completed the job in somewhat less than a single eight hour day. For a single farmer to do the same task would, presumably, have taken about ten days.

(c) Harvesting

The first crop harvested by any particular farmer is usually *bajra*, although the harvesting of various crops does overlap, in that some large *bajra* crops are still being harvested after other farmers have completed their *bajra* harvest and moved on to other crops. If the monsoon is good, harvesting can take several months. It is usually finished by the end of November. In 1983 the *bajra* harvest began in early September and was nearly finished by the end of that month. Other crops were still being harvested into December. In 1985, which was a poor year, virtually all crops of all species were harvested before late September.

Bajra is harvested with the use of a small hand held knife with a curved blade (*dantla*). The stem is cut just below the head. The worker wears a piece of cloth folded and tied so that it hangs as a bag around his or her back. The heads of the *bajra* are placed in the bag until it is full. It is then emptied onto a blanket placed on a cleared patch of sand near the section of the field being worked. When the pile of heads on the blanket is large enough, the four corners of the blanket are tied together and it is lifted onto the head of one of the male workers. He then carries it to a central cleared area and empties it onto the sand. Later the pile is covered with *bajra* stalks to protect it from birds (mainly pigeons and the ever-present peacocks).

Work groups are sometimes limited to the field-owner's household. On other occasions hired agricultural labour is used. Composition of work groups follows the pattern described for hoeing/weeding parties. Some specialization occurs, two or three men being responsible for carrying the blanket, sweeping up loose grain detached while the *bajra* is being transported and gathering stalks to ensure protection of the harvested grain. Where the field owner is a Rajput he usually co-ordinates this activity and also prepares tea and ensures that a steady supply of drinking water is available. Food for the workers is usually prepared by the women of the household and carried to the field from the village. I have not observed the arrangements made for food for clean caste people working in fields for people from unclean castes because, as I pointed out above, this rarely occurs. In other non-agricultural situations (such as the making of mud-bricks), Rajputs working for Nayaks or Meghwals prepare their own food.

Where the owner of a field owns several dispersed fields, the harvest from each is later transferred to a single cleared area which will be used as a threshing floor. (This is done after the harvest of a particular field is completed or, after the entire *bajra* harvest is completed.) *Bajra* is carried to the threshing floor by camel or bullock cart (usually hired, because few people own carts).

A great deal of care is taken at all stages of the harvest, including transporting the crop, to sweep up loose grains of *bajra* and to ensure that nothing is lost.

Harvesting *jowar* is a similar process, although the quantities grown are much less and large working parties are not necessary.

Once a land-owner has harvested his *bajra*, the other crops are harvested, if ready. In the case of *moth* there is a fairly brief optimum period for harvest and large amounts of labour are necessary to bring in the harvest quickly. A common method of obtaining this labour is to hold an *adola*. Unlike other types of agricultural working parties, there is no cash payment for working at an *adola*. The owner provides tea, *bidis* (local cigarettes) and a meal. In return, depending on the prestige of the person who holds the *adola*, people may come from miles around to participate.

The work of harvesting *moth* is extremely arduous and unpleasant. The men (only men participate in the actual harvest in this case) squat on their heels and pull up the plants (small thorny bushes up to about fifty centimetres high) by the roots. Working in a line, the workers, each waddling rather like a duck, move up and down the field still on their heels. This action is very uncomfortable and the small thorns at the base of the plant make the whole process quite unpleasant.

Despite this the whole atmosphere of an *adola* tends to be festive. While the work proceeds a chant inevitably starts up. This chant consists of endless repetitions of a single line: *'O bolo bayi Ram hey ho'* (O speak brother god). It was the only line I ever heard chanted on these occasions.

The exuberance which characterises attendance at an *adola* was typified by the behaviour at the first *adola* I ever attended. It was held by Gooman Singh, a highly respected Rajput from a nearby village. I counted about fifty people at this *adola* (the continual coming and going makes it difficult to keep an accurate count), including people from several nearby villages and Rajputs, Nayaks and Meghwals from Hinganiya. In addition there was the usual party of women from Gooman Singh's household preparing food and tea in a field adjoining the field where the work was going on. Harvesting started at about 11am. There were breaks for water and bidis, and sometimes for tea. The meal was served in the mid afternoon. It consisted of a dish made of *hogra* (millet chapatis), *gur* (molasses) and large quantities of *ghi*. The workers, eating from trays shared with caste fellows, ground up the *hogra* and mixed them with the other ingredients before eating. After this dish, which was regarded as a treat, *dal* and *haldi-subzee* (vegetable in tumeric) were brought. This menu was duplicated at every *adola* I attended and the expensive ingredients were a large part of the attractiveness of an *adola*.

In the late afternoon it became clear that a lot of work needed to be done quickly. Despite the heat and effects of a long day doing arduous work the villagers from Hinganiya accelerated and started to work at a furious pace, racing with the other groups in an extraordinary display of friendly competition. The work finished at about 6.30 pm, when it was quite dark.

Why do people attend an *adola*? Firstly, there is the fun aspect. *Adolas* only occur when good harvests of *moth* are to be had. In the excellent 1983 season they were held frequently. When the rains fail, as they did in 1985, *moth* is not likely to be a successful crop, and, in fact, there were no *adolas* in 1985. The coincidence of a well catered festive occasion with the general buoyancy of mood which goes with a year of generally good harvests seems to be a major reason for attending. Secondly, the food provided is generally lavish in terms of the value of food provided. On one occasion I attended an *adola* held by a poorer Rajput. He had purchased poor quality local *ghi*. One of the Meghwals who attended was very critical of this. At first he said the Rajput was a 'bad man'. He corrected himself saying that he was not really bad, 'just poor'. Clearly, however, there is a strong expectation that workers are to be rewarded with good food.

Other reasons for attending are related to reciprocity and respect for the holder. People express the view that reciprocal attendance is desirable, but an analysis of attendance does not strongly support this. Table 6.7 shows reciprocal attendance at five *adolas* held in November 1983. The table only refers to attendance by people who had held *adolas* themselves, not the many others who attended. All five people referred to in the table are Rajputs. My records are incomplete, but it is clear that simple reciprocity does not apply. Rajput E, for example, did not attend any of the other *adolas*, but other *adola* holders attended his. The fact that he had a serious operation several years ago might be seen as a justification for his not doing too much heavy work, yet in other contexts, he did quite heavy work. Whatever the reasons for his non-attendance, he is held in great respect and his *adola* was attended by members of all castes.

Table 6.7

Reciprocal attendance at *adolas* 1983

	Holder of *adola*				
Attendance at *adola*	A	B	C	D	E
A	x	o	x	x	x
B	x	x	x	x	x
C	x	x	x	x	o
D	x	x	-	x	o
E	o	o	o	o	x

Key: x - present o - absent - not recorded

The prestige of the person giving an *adola* is obviously one reason for attendance. People tend to go to *adolas* held by people they respect, but failure to attend is not necessarily regarded as an insult. Sometimes people have other obligations (including urgent work in their own fields.

(d) Threshing and Winnowing

When the full harvest has been gathered threshing begins. *Bajra* is usually threshed first, but the process can be delayed if other crops are ready for harvest. I have already described how all of the crop is transferred to a threshing floor. Each household normally has a separate threshing floor. The pile of *bajra* heads is first levelled to cover the whole floor and then a crushing operation takes place. A tractor is hired to drive over the pile until the bigger pieces of *bajra* are broken up and the grain is loosened. Where a crop is small and/or the farmer is poor, the process can be carried out by bullocks walking repeatedly over the *bajra* to break it up. Occasionally the crushing is done by hand, using a *lathi* (a heavy wooden staff). Even poorer farmers sometimes hire a tractor, which does the entire task quickly and efficiently. The winnowing operation is carried out by household labour, sometimes supplemented by the use of one or two hired labourers.

(e) Harvesting and Gathering Fodder

A final stage in the harvest is the harvesting of the stalks of *bajra*, *jowar* and *guar* for use as fodder. Again larger fields are harvested by mixed (by caste and sex) work groups, often of paid labourers. The stalks are collected into bundles and stored for use as animal fodder in bad seasons, or as a dietary supplement at other times.

Previously harvested batches of *bajra* stalks are cut into chaff and stored. In late 1985, this was done with the use of a hired tractor with an attached chaff-cutter. The work requires several men to feed the stalks into the cutter (which works very quickly). The overall task takes only a short time even for people with large amounts of fodder to process and the labour (all male) is voluntary.

The timing of all these stages varies somewhat (within the general parameters of the monsoon period) according to the quality of the crop, the amount of land sowed, and the types of crops grown by a particular farmer. In 1985 the entire cycle was compressed due to the poor production. All harvesting was completed before the end of September and farmers estimated that only about twenty to thirty per cent of the desired *bajra* harvest was collected.

The late 1985 season was marked by quite intensive activity revolving around the gathering of fodder from non-crop sources. This emphasised the state of siege atmosphere resulting from the failure of the crops. The atmosphere was in marked contrast to the same period in 1983, when there was a feeling of satisfaction and optimism about the following year. In 1985 new components of agricultural work became prominent after the routine processing of fodder discussed above was completed. Faced with at least seven lean months before the next possibility of monsoon rain, villagers began to gather fodder (*chara*) from any possible source.

Following the routine harvesting of crop leftovers for fodder (routine but carried out comparatively early in the post-monsoon period of 1985) the first task is the gathering of *palo* (leaf fodder) from various naturally occurring bushes including the *ber* in bush form. These are cut off at ground level by means of an angled blade of heavy metal attached to a handle (a *jarbar*). The bushes are then gathered into piles where they are beaten with a *lathi*. The edible fodder (the leaves) is gathered and stored. The branches are kept as firewood.

A second task is the cropping of *khejri* trees. Branches are lopped off and the same process of separation of edible material and firewood occurs. The trees themselves are not cut down, although the pruning is very severe. A small amount of green growth is always left and the trees are said to rejuvenate very quickly. Small trees are not cut. The trees apparently regenerate very quickly. According to one informant this takes only about four months, although I assume that this would depend very much on conditions.

An estimated 10 kg of *loong* (edible leaves) can be cut from each tree. In the case of a particularly big tree, about 40-50 kg of branches and leaves are cut, of which about 10-15 kg is *loong*. The rest is used, and sometimes sold, as firewood.

This gathering of fodder occurs only on private land. Labour can either be household labour, or, where large amounts of land are involved, hired labour is used. The work groups tend to be small and the cropping of *khejri* in particular is often done on an *ad hoc* basis. For example a woman or child from a household will simply go and cut a small amount from a tree to meet immediate needs.

The Herding Cycle

Herding, unlike farming, is a year round activity. Nevertheless, the nature of herding activity changes with the agricultural cycle.

Village land falls into two types in terms of ownership/access. The first category is Panchayat land, effectively common land available to all villagers for grazing throughout the year. According to local rules, fodder cannot be collected for storage from village common land, although animals are allowed to graze freely on grass, bushes or branches. Theoretically, sanctions can be imposed by a village assembly, but this rarely, if ever, occurs, perhaps largely because the rules are not often broken. The village assembly supposedly meets twice yearly, although it certainly never met at any time when I was in Hinganiya. The sanctions which can be imposed are beatings and fines.

The second category is privately owned land. In the agricultural season land-owners control grazing on their land. Agricultural workers may bring a cow, goat or camel and tether it to bushes at the edge of a field while they work, or the land-owner's livestock may be carefully grazed on stubble, under close supervision to prevent wandering into unharvested crops. Until harvesting is completed (and this includes the harvesting of stalks for off-season or emergency fodder), great care is taken to protect the rights of land-owners from grazing animals. Once the entire process of harvesting has been completed there is no reason why other herdsmen cannot graze their herds on private land, although care must be taken to protect *khejri* trees which are regarded strictly as private property.

Jodha (1985) describes off-season access to farming land as seasonal common property. This implies that seasonal open-access is a recognised right. In my opinion it is not so much a formal right as an activity tolerated because it is advantageous to the landowner. The amount of fodder available (particularly once the stubble from crops has been consumed) is negligible. From the owner's point of view the benefits from manure outweigh the loss of potential fodder. Very little artificial fertiliser is used, so manure is a major contribution to soil fertility. In fact, visits by large flocks from outside the village are welcomed and fees are, according to some informants, sometimes paid to migrating herdsmen in return for the manure resulting. The payment of fees by the landowner, reinforces the view that the land is regarded as private, even in the off-season.

Vincze (1980) suggested that agro-pastoral economies include some factors which promote integration and some factors which work against it. Integrative factors include the opportunity to exploit marginal lands and the use of manure to fertilize fields. Among the anti-integrative features are conflicting labour requirements. Conflicting labour requirements certainly complicate the integration of agriculture and pastoralism in western Rajasthan.

The agricultural season has a number of implications to the labour requirements of herding. Firstly, during the agricultural season, requirements for herd supervision are increased. The main reason for the high labour requirement is that different types of livestock need to be grazed separately. Sheep and goats are grazed together, but cattle, buffalo and camels have different fodder needs. These larger animals are often tethered and hand fed, but the collection of fodder or the carrying of fodder from storage both require significant labour. Secondly, most men (and, often, women) are involved in agricultural work, either as landowners or as paid agricultural labourers. This means that herding duties fall on children between six and twelve years old. In the case of the Rajputs girls do most of the work, because most Rajput boys go to school. The boys look after livestock after school and on holidays. Among the Nayaks and Meghwals, on the other hand, it is common for boys to carry out this task, as school attendance is rare for either sex among these two castes.

In the agricultural off-season labour requirements and practices differ. Men usually have considerable time available (unless they are involved in government sponsored famine relief projects) and they may become involved in herding themselves. Supervision of herds tends to be easier, since there is no worry about damaging crops. In fact cattle and buffalo are often allowed to roam freely. They return home at night and there are no large predators. Sheep and goats, on the other hand, require supervision since they do not have a homing instinct and are subject to predators.[6] Camels, which often wander long distances are either tied to a tree or hobbled while grazing. They, therefore, require fairly constant, but not onerous, supervision. All livestock are kept in stalls at night (or, in the case of larger animals, at least tethered) in all seasons. In winter, temporary shelters are sometimes provided for cows.

The relationships between the annual cycles of agricultural and pastoral activity described above depends on there being a monsoon. When the monsoon fails the situation is different. Obviously increased labour requirements due to the need to protect crops do not apply. On the other hand herd migration may occur.

Herd Migration

There is no *regular* pattern of herd migration in Rajasthan. Migrations, even quite extensive migrations, occur frequently, but the extent of migration, direction of migration, and even whether migration occurs in a given year, depend on the particular conditions which apply in a given time or place. Migrations are much more extensive during droughts and animals from Jodhpur District may migrate as far east as Delhi, or as far south as Gujarat. In good years migrations may, if they occur at all, be of very limited extent.

In the early winter of 1983, following a good monsoon, some Raikas (a caste of specialist herdsmen) were migrating through Hinganiya with flocks of sheep and goats. I interviewed one such herdsman from a village a few kilometres away. His migration was in the form of a circle of only thirty or forty kilometres diameter. It seemed to be necessary simply because of the number of animals (about 400 sheep and 25-30 goats). The herdsman was accompanied by a few male kinsmen. Their families had remained in their village. In a good season small domestic flocks can graze locally, but larger flocks (such as those owned by specialist herdsmen) need to move around somewhat. Even for these larger herds migrations are not necessarily extensive.

The situation in late 1983 was in extreme contrast to the situation a few months earlier, before the monsoon and following several years of drought. At that time I found few specialist herdsmen in either Jaisalmer or Jodhpur Districts because most of the livestock had been taken away. In late 1985 and early 1986 a similarly extensive migration was beginning. Herds of all species were passing through the vicinity of

---

6 The main predator is called a *chali-nahar*, which is apparently a caracal or a desert cat, although few people have seen one and there is something of a mythical air about it. Some sort of small predator does undoubtedly exist and I have seen a cat-like track in the sand which was described as a *chali-nahar* track. There are also foxes and jackals.

Hinganiya, particularly from Jaisalmer and Barmer Districts which had been very severely affected by the drought. I saw herds of up to several thousand sheep and goats and other herds of fifty to one hundred camels. Unlike the situation in post-monsoon 1983, the herdsmen were not all Raikas. Sindhis, Mussalman and Rajputs were all involved as the drought had forced all people with livestock in the affected areas to migrate. In late January 1986 I spoke briefly to a group of Rajputs from Jaisalmer who were heading east in the vanguard of a party with camels, sheep, goats, donkeys and cattle. They were, like my hosts from Hinganiya, Bhati Rajputs of the Bera Dasot lineage. Even with the momentary excitement caused by the meeting of 'brothers', they were in too much of a hurry to stop for more than a few moments before following the rest of the party. There were no women or children with the party - they had remained in their village.

In my 1985-86 survey of households in Hinganiya, I asked whether any households would be migrating with their herds as conditions became worse. Only one household head (a Rajput) said he would be doing so and he intended only to take his sheep a few kilometres to the east. He was, in fact, the owner of the biggest flock of sheep in Hinganiya. As it turned out, his flock was decimated by an epidemic in January 1986, and the trip would not have been necessary.

In Hinganiya there are no people engaged purely in pastoralism. In fact the herds, while important, are comparatively small. At least while supplies of fodder remain, migration is not necessary. Further, given the extent of the 1985-86 drought, short migrations are no real solution and there is a natural reluctance to take very small numbers of livestock to other states. I suspect, however, that a longer drought (like the one that ended with the 1983 monsoon) will lead to migrations by even small owners.

I have pointed out the importance of migration as a response to drought and/or season variations in grazing conditions. One of the implications of the dual agro-pastoral economy is that it is not always convenient for a livestock owner with *relatively* small herds to migrate with them himself, particularly as his labour will be necessary for planting when, and if, the next monsoon comes. For this reason specialist herdsmen (usually Raikas) are sometimes used to look after animals on such migrations.

Migrations aside, even within the village grazing lands it is not always practical to allocate household labour to look after a relatively small number of animals. One herdsmen can certainly look after larger flocks than the ten or twelve goats or sheep owned by many villagers (although, as I have shown, mixed herds are a different proposition). The most common solution is simply to amalgamate herds. A number of related households may put all of their animals in the hands of one or two herders. A second solution is to place animals in the hands of a paid shepherd for the purpose of day to day herding. In Hinganiya, where there are no resident Raikas, this herdsmen can be from any of the castes. However, in all of the cases I am aware of, the hired shepherds were Nayaks or Meghwals who looked after livestock owned by Rajputs and herded them with their own animals. Payment was more likely to be gifts of clothing or food than cash. In fact, the arrangement resembled patronage, a subject which I will turn to in Chapter 9.

Intensification of Agriculture and Risk Management

According to Maclachlan (1983) one solution to the risk of drought is intensification of agriculture.

The agricultural cycle described above has not been subject to major innovations. High yielding varieties of various crops, including millet are available, but are rarely used in Hinganiya. The potential increase of *bajra* production through the use of HYVs is impressive. Villagers' estimates for the yield of *hybrid* (as HYVs are collectively called locally) in a good year were 250-300 kg per bigha, representing a 50 to 100% increase on production using *desi* seed. This is consistent with Murty's estimate for improved management of *bajra* 'particularly with hybrids' (1976: 46). Despite this increased potential, few farmers report using *hybrid*.

Hybrid seed is relatively expensive, costing (in 1987) Rs 30 per kg, or Rs 60 for three kg. Informants certainly describe it as expensive. In comparison, *desi* seed is easily obtainable from the previous year's crop. Yet, in absolute terms, the seed cost of *hybrid* is not prohibitive. It also needs fertiliser (urea), whereas fertiliser is rarely added to *desi bajra* under rainfed conditions, the main source of nutrients being manure from grazing animals. The cost is a bar, but probably only a minor one, except to poor farmers.

The main disadvantages are that HYV seed is relatively subject to disease and requires a comparatively large amount of water. In contrast, *desi* seed is highly drought resistant and relatively disease resistant. The selection of millet in the first place, is primarily a result of its high degree of natural drought resistance.

Those farmers who use *hybrid* tend to be relatively wealthy, although one smaller farmer (Category 2) claimed to use it. Even those who do use *hybrid* tend not to use it all the time. One large farmer in Kur, who had irrigated land as well, used both types. The reason for non-adoption is clearly related to the increased risk associated with HYVs. Following the safety-first principle (Scott 1976), poor farmers are unwilling to take the risk, and even larger farmers hedge their bets. There is, of course, nothing new in this pattern of HYVs being rejected by small farmers on the basis of higher risks.

One form of intensification of agriculture is the increased use of marginal land for cultivation. This is an important trend in Rajasthan (Jodha 1980), but it appears not to have occurred in Hinganiya. In Chapter 5, I showed that land classified as agricultural land changed little in Hinganiya between 1947 and 1986. This was largely because almost all available land was identified as agricultural land in 1947.

Jodha identifies another form of intensification. He points out that during the period of the *jagirdari* system 'the peasants could satisfy their increased demand for cropland only through reduction in the extent of long fallow' (1985:257). In a situation where the absolute amount of land available is limited, a similar form of intensification could operate. This suggests the possibility that, while the amount of agricultural land in Hinganiya has not changed much since 1947, it may be used more. This may have occurred, although I have no evidence to support it. However, given my reservations about regularity of fallow, the effects, either in terms of increased production or increased damage to soil, would be marginal.

Superficially, the most obvious opportunity for intensified inputs is through irrigation. As there are no naturally flowing streams or rivers in Hinganiya or in nearby villages, riverfed irrigation is not an option. Further, the land is relatively flat, so water from rainfall collection areas cannot be carried far in canals. There are several other possibilities.

Rainwater harvesting techniques (Pacey and Cullis 1986) can allow farmers to collect water when it rains. The techniques include the construction of underground tanks and the collection of water on contoured surfaces, sometimes behind artificially constructed bunds. This latter technique is used in Rajasthan, where the area behind the bund is known as a *khadin* (Pacey and Cullis 1986:135-36). The *khadin* requires land which is not too flat. The main water harvesting effect of bunds in Hinganiya seems to be to trap moisture in the soil for the benefit of sections of crops grown near the bunds themselves, rather than to trap water to be re-channeled over a field. As I was never able to see how fresh rainfall was distributed within the fields (I didn't see rain fall very often during my fieldwork), I do not have much data on relevant practices.

There are other methods of collecting and storing rainwater, although they are of little value for agriculture. One artificially constructed earthen pond or lake (*nadi*), for the collection and storage of rainwater exists in Hinganiya and such *nadis* are relatively common in the region. The main value of *nadis* is for watering livestock after the monsoon, but evaporation is rapid. Building *nadis* is one of the most common forms of drought relief projects, since the process is essentially one of digging a large hole and since it requires only readily available tools and little supervision.

Underground tanks are sometimes built in the fields or in the *abadi*. They can be filled from a mobile tank, but also have a dishlike catchment area of up to twenty metres diameter, shaped around them. They are, however, expensive since they need to be lined and covered to avoid evaporation. (Minimum costs for lining and covering are in the order of Rs 2-3000.) Those that exist are mostly privately owned, and are mainly used as a supplementary supply of private drinking water. However, two large tanks on Panchayat land were built in the past, at least one for a famine relief project. The water for these is used both for human and livestock needs. One of the tanks is connected to the pipeline.

Machlachlan describes the digging of private wells as the most productive form of agricultural intensification in Yaahvahalli, the village in south India where he worked. Most irrigation in Jodhpur District is by well or tube-well. However, in Hinganiya, saline water makes this option unviable. The only attempt to dig a private well of which I am aware led to the expected result that the water was unusable. (The water from that well is now used for making bricks.)

All this sounds rather hopeless; surely something is possible as a means of improving production?

The main local solution, as applied to agriculture, is in terms of risk management. This works in a number of ways, many of which were mentioned by McAlpin (1983). The first technique open to landowners is plot scattering. Farmers prefer to own plots separated from their other plots. Microclimatic variations can damage crops in one area, leaving plots elsewhere in the village unaffected. One common cause of this is high wind. Although the region is not hilly, there are mild undulations, and plots facing different directions limit the risk of losing all crops due to a single heavy wind or prevailing winds. Even rainfall can differ in patches within a village. In 1987, while very little rain fell at all, there were some patches where scanty rain fell, particularly on the eastern side of the village. Most of the village crops failed completely, but there was some small *bajra* production in these scattered patches.

Plot scattering is of little relevance to poor farmers who own a single plot. Further, as land transfers are rare, most farmers have little ability to change the position of their plots. Fortunately, in the past, tenants apparently had use of scattered plots and this situation has continued into present landholding patterns. One way of getting around the inflexibility of current plot location is through a tenancy (or sharecropping) arrangement.

Another simple strategy for risk management is diversifying crops. Certain combinations are quite common in Hinganiya. The chances of losing two different types of crop to a disease at the same time are considerably less than the chances of losing a single crop. Further, the secondary crops are usually crops like *moong* or *moth* which are valuable supplementary foods and which have high market value if there happens to be a good crop.

However, the single most important aspect of risk management is involvement in a mixed agro-pastoral economy. One of the major aims in this chapter has been to show that the activities of agriculture and pastoralism are rarely in direct conflict in the area under discussion. On the contrary, they generally complement each other, particularly in that pastoralism provides essential fertiliser and agricultural crop residues provide fodder.[7] Labour demands are the main area for conflict, and this is limited. There is a peak in labour demands for both activities during the agricultural season, but most of the tasks of pastoralism can be performed by children who don't work much with crops anyhow.

The advantages of involvement in pastoralism far outweigh the disadvantages. Firstly, it provides milk, a basic subsistence need. Secondly, production from pastoralism is not so susceptible to drought. It is argued (CAZRI 1983, quoted in Robinson 1985) that, while crop production on rainfed lands in a drought year can be less than 10% of the production in a good year, milk and wool remain above 50% of good year levels. Thirdly, pastoralism can provide a useful cash income, even when crops fail. Providing the basic reproductive animals are not sold or lost to the drought, livestock herds can regenerate. The rate of regeneration of goats and sheep is much greater than that of the larger (and more expensive) livestock, thus making them better as an insurance against risk and making them a particularly attractive option for poorer farmers.

The value of small livestock is enhanced by the fact that prices for sheep and goats are not badly affected by decreased prices during droughts. For example, in 1983 and early 1984 male goats sold in Hinganiya for Rs 100-150. The price was similar in 1985, although conditions were much worse. This price stability is probably due to a relatively stable supply and demand for goats for meat. The supply will tend to remain much the same until breeding stock die off (or until prolonged drought reduces their fertility), because most young male goats are sold for meat anyhow. Once breeding stock die off supply of young males will drop, presumably forcing prices up rather than down. Demand, which is largely for urban consumption, will tend to remain constant.

7 Singh cites a saying by a renowned Raja '. . . which means that whoever has a couple of Khejiri trees on his land and a camel and goat will not die of starvation' (1943: 10).

Given the obvious advantages of small livestock, including their potential herd growth, the relatively low labour demands and stability of prices, it is somewhat surprising that more small farmers do not develop a greater reliance on them. I remain uncertain as to why this is so, although I suspect that the frequency of drought leads small farmers to sell their breeding stock.

While small livestock are particularly good as insurance, the emergency sale of large livestock also has a role during droughts, although prices are naturally depressed as supply increases. Large livestock are sold at a market called a *mela*. The famous Pushkar Mela is the best known of these, although there are many others.

The sale of valuables to provide cash in years of poor income is one way of coping with bad years (McAlpin 1983). Morris (1975) has argued that the sale of assets is not an indicator of crisis, but, rather, that it is a routine mechanism for coping with drought. However, Jodha (1975) counters that the sale of assets is, in fact, an indicator of economic distress due to drought. It occurs only after cut-backs in consumption have occurred and is a sign that the situation is getting serious. Jodha differentiates betwen sale of valuables, such as household goods and jewellery, and sale of reproductive assets, that is assets which provide for the reproduction of an economic level (such as land, female livestock, a tractor). Sale of valuables (non-reproductive assets) is preferred as an early response ahead of the sale of reproductive assets.

In essence, this is a sound differentiation in terms of the relative merits of various sales. Sale is a common adaptive mechanism. Even poor Rajasthani women have some gold or silver. Richer women (and men) sometimes have huge amounts. (I photographed a Brahman couple in Kur, when they were wearing what I estimated to be Rs 100,000 in jewellery, mostly gold.) However the sale of jewellery is not undertaken lightly. Jewellery functions as an insurance mechanism, but it also has high prestige value. Sale of jewellery is a sign of distress, although a less serious one than the sale of land. Further, once jewellery has been sold the next step (if bad conditions continue) will be the sale of land, female livestock, or, occasionally, valuable male livestock (such as working camels). However, unless a long string of bad years occurs it is often possible to reinvest in jewellery (as a future buffer) before selling productive assets. The poorer farmers, of course, do not have as a many non-productive assets and must cut into their productive base much earlier. A long series of droughts would probably have no long-term effect on richer farmers, but may push poorer farmers off the land.

In 1983, one Nayak owned a camel and a cart, from which he earned considerable income during the good 1983 season (about Rs 50 per day when working). By the time I began my second period of fieldwork in

1985 he had sold the camel and cart, but purchased a new and younger camel. The sale had been forced by circumstances (limited work during two bad seasons). Although forced to sell his first camel and cart, he attempted to maintain a hold on the future by buying a young camel for future use. In the worsening conditions after the 1985 monsoon failure he tried to avoid selling his new camel for as long as possible, but was forced to do so and went off to look for work in Jodhpur. Yet, even during the 1985 harvest season (such as it was) he had attempted to get money together to buy jewellery for his wife. In other words, even in the midst of a drought, he was concerned with maintaining his productive base and building as much of a buffer (in the form of jewellery) as possible, in anticipation of further lean years.

The camel was sold at a *mela*. The camel, a young bull, had been purchased two years earlier for Rs 2100. The Nayak expected to be able to sell it for Rs 3-3500, but ultimately settled for Rs 2750.

The buyers for livestock at *melas* often come very long distances, including from other states. The *melas* in 1985-86 were particularly busy as villagers sold livestock off at reduced prices to buyers eager for bargains. For all this, one villager took advantage of the prices, selling a buffalo and buying a camel and cart at reduced prices. While the sale of valuable livestock at less than optimum prices can be interpreted as a sign of desperation, it can also be argued that purchasing the livestock in the first place is an insurance strategy.

A theme that keeps recurring in this analysis is the notion that poorer farmers are consistently less able to take advantage of risk managment options than better-off farmers. At this point I would like to analyse a 'notional' household budget for a small farmer to indicate just how inadequate on-farm income can be. (For this purpose on-farm income refers to income either from the personal landholdings or, through wage-labour, from the farms of other farmers.)

Balancing the Household Budget

The household is the basic economic unit. To make sense of differing responses to drought it is most useful to start with the household. In Chapter 5, I discussed my use of the term consumption unit (c.u.). While the term has, of course, only a very general indicative or notional value, it gives a reasonable order of magnitude for considering subsistence demand and provides a basis for comparison between households.

Table 6.8 provides an estimate of monthly cash requirements for an average household of 3.5 consumption units. The estimates of monthly requirements for various goods were provided by an informant in 1983. Interestingly the prices in January 1986 were the same for all major items. Staples (essentially millet, but including milk and other subsistence products) are excluded, because I am initially concerned with cash requrements.

Table 6.8

Estimate of monthly cash requirements

(Household of 3.5 Consumption Units)

Item		*Price (Rupees)*
Tea	1/2 kg	20
Salt		3
Sugar	5 kg	30
Oil	1 kg	18
Matches	6-7 boxes	1/50
Kerosene	1 litre	3
Bidis	6 Pkts	4/50
Tumeric, Ghi, Chillies, Vegetables		20
	Total	*100*

My calculations suggest tha Rs100 would meet the monthly 'grocery' bill - tea, salt, sugar, kerosene, spices, vegetables. This is not a generous budget, but conforms fairly closely to the likely needs of an average sized houshold. Obviously poorer people could economise slightly on some items. (In fact people buy 50 gm packets of tea for Rs 2, or buy poorer quality tea and drink less tea). To an annual grocery bill of Rs 1200, I would add a further Rs 300 per year for clothes, buckets, ropes and other miscellaneous items. This is very spartan, but fits the expenditure of poorer households. The total annual requirement is about Rs 1500.

So much for minimum expenditure. What about income? If we take a small household in landholding category 1 (owning under 2 ha) it quickly becomes apparent that the situation is very tight, even in a good year. I will take as an example a household of 3.5 c.u. owning 10 bighas (1.6.ha) of land. Allowing a rate of production per bigha of 175 kg, which is probably a little on the high side, the total production would be 1750 kg, in a very good year. Allowing twenty-two kilogram per month per c.u. a household of 3.5 c.u. would need 924 kg for a years supply, giving a balance of about 800 kg. Following the 1983 agricultural season this would have had a cash value of Rs 1400 (Rs 1-75 per kg). Of course, for a poor farmer, selling would be a very drastic step, because it would leave no reserve for a bad year. In drought years purchase of the same amount of grain would cost considerably more. Assuming 50% production over a four year period the household would produce only 3500 kg, barely enough to meet domestic needs. In fact 1983 was preceeded by four drought years and followed by one satisfactory year and then by several more drought years. In any case 50% production is very optimistic: I have suggested that an average 20-30% of optimum production is more likely over a lengthy period.

We can, however, for purposes of discussion, talk in terms of potential cash income from land, *in a good year*, of Rs 1400, bearing these constraints in mind.

Working as a labourer, either on drought relief projects before a drought broke (at Rs 7 per day) and as an agricultural labourer (at shifting rates) for a notional 100 days (most informants report less paid working days) would probably amount to another Rs 700 (plus one meal per day in farm work). Sale of about five male goats per year from a herd of ten female goats would provide another Rs 750.

In all, the potential cash income (excluding extra-village income) in a good year amounts to Rs 2850, which is in excess of the Rs 1500 cash requirement. But it must be remembered that the income projections are very much on the generous side, and they refer to a good year only. On-farm labour opportunities in a poor year are less and pay is less (because the supply of labour enables employers to employ labourers at cheaper rates).

In a bad year, or when a series of bad years are strung together on-farm income (from the farmers own land and from paid labour on other farms) would be much less. Obviously there must be substantial deficit for a small landowner.

These figures are deliberately based on generous estimates of income and conservative estimates of costs. The purpose of the exercise is to show that, even on the most optimistic estimates, the net income of small landholders simply cannot meet needs except in good seasons and that, in terms of income and expenditure, they must be in net deficit over a period with a statistically average range of conditions. The implications of this will be explored in Chapter 9.

Chapter 7

Population Growth, Famine and Economic Growth

Introduction

The aim of this chapter is to examine briefly some aspects of the demography of my field area. This discussion will lead into the focus of the next chapter, which aims to examine the organisation of production and labour, paying particular attention to the relationship between labour demand and household size and structure.

The concern with demography is relevant to this study for at least two reasons. On *a priori* grounds it would seem that susceptibility to famine is likely to increase with increased population. I have already discussed the high rate of population increase in Rajasthan generally, so this question needs to be considered. It is, however, interesting that, as the population of Rajasthan has increased since the last century, the drastic human consequences of famine have been less evident, so it may be that the *a priori* assumption is incorrect. It was just this sort of contradiction that stimulated an impressive study by Maclachlan (1983). In studying the organisation of agriculture in a south Indian village called Yaavahalli, he was struck by the fact that a drought related famine in 1877-78 caused very high mortality, whereas a very serious (although less serious) drought in 1965 caused much less suffering and no deaths directly related to famine in Yaavahalli itself. The puzzling thing was that the population in 1965 was much higher than in 1877-78. I will return to Maclachlan's argument in the next chapter. For the present the main point is that the *a priori* assumption that increasing population increases susceptibility to famine is not as certain as it appears.

A second reason for including consideration of demography is the connection between population growth and the apparent decline in the quality of natural resources, through desertification, in western Rajasthan. To the extent that there is an environmental crisis then the increased use of marginal land and overgrazing to meet the needs of increasing population are relevant.

Village Census Methodology

The most recent information on village population for Hinganiya comes from a village census of Hinganiya which I carried out in December 1985 and January 1986. The census was carried out as a series of semi-structured interviews, using a check list of questions. Information on population was compiled in the form of genealogical charts covering all residents of Hinganiya. I interviewed at least one member of each household (not necessarily the household head), or a member of a closely related household, in order to obtain data on population by sex and by age category. I use the term 'age category' because the actual age of children and youths in years was often simply unknown. I was forced to classify people in fairly broad categories based on 'social age' rather than on chronological age. The definitions used are as follows:

'Adult' - A person is counted as an adult when he or she fulfills either one of the following criteria:

- Married or previously married. For the purposes of this definition a child-marriage is not regarded as a marriage until the *mukhlawa* (the final ceremony before co-habitation) has taken place.

- Known to be (or thought by informants to be) over seventeen years old.

'Child' - A person is counted as a child if he or she has not completed all stages of the marriage process and is under seventeen years old.

'Full-time Resident' - A person is treated as a full-time resident when he or she is normally resident in the village.

'Part-time resident' - A person is treated as a part-time resident if he (the category, in practice, only includes males) is a member of a household resident in the village, but normally spends a substantial amount of time living and working elsewhere (in Jodhpur, in the Army, at school etc.).

Where a man owns land or property in the village, and perhaps visits occasionally, but is normally resident elsewhere with wife and children, he is not included in my census. I refer to such people as 'absentees'.

The census was taken over a rather lengthy period and is not intended to represent actual residence on a particular day. Rather, it represents *de jure* residents, those people who would normally be resident, wherever they might have been at the end of January 1986. (Although the census was collected over a period of approximately two months, it was amended as changes occurred in order to represent the situation at the end of January.) Middle-term visitors (such as married daughters returning to spend a few weeks or months with parents) are, thus, not included. On the other hand, married women normally resident in Hinganiya but absent at the time of my census visiting their parents or kin in their village of origin, are included.

The Growth of Village Populations

In Chapter 2, I discussed the general trend of a high rate of increasing population for Rajasthan in general and for western Rajasthan in particular. Within this general trend there were severe fluctuations connected with major famines. The same general pattern is evident in village level census figures, from 1891 to 1981.

The populations of the four villages from 1891 to 1981 are set out in Table 7.1. (I have, unfortunately been unable to obtain village populations for 1951.[1]) An overall increase from 1891 to 1981 occurred in all four villages. In fact the overall increases are about threefold, ranging from two and a half times to four times increases for the various villages. This is consistent with a statement by Malhotra and Saha (1985) that population in the Thar Desert increased threefold between 1901 and 1981.

Table 7.1

Village populations according to censuses 1891-1981

	Village			
	Hinganiya	Kur	Knokhariya	Kukunda
1891	163	405	158	370
1901	98	315	124	304
1911	49	402	105	280
1921	67	282	73	245
1931	102	422	114	281
1941	140	534	189	397
1961	196	674	334	697
1971	229	1014	490	768
1981	409	1312	653	1084

Note: Population figures are based on decennial censuses of Marwar State (1891-1941) and of India (1961-81). Figures from 1891 to 1931 were extracted from a retrospective summary in Census of Marwar, 1931; figures from 1941 are from Census of Marwar, 1941 and subsequent figures are from Census of India 1961b, 1971 and 1981a.

1 I have been unable to locate the relevant volumes in any of the collections I have searched. I suspect village level data was not published at all for the ex-Princely States in the turmoil of transition which was occurring in the early 1950s.

In addition to the general trends the fluctuations in population are interesting. In each village there were decreases from 1891 to 1901, coinciding with a general decrease of 23.4% for Marwar in the same period and with the serious famines in the second half of the decade. Yet between 1901 and 1911 one village (Kur) experienced an increase, while the others experienced decreases. This occurred in the context of a general increase of population for Marwar of 6.3%. Further, from 1911 to 1921 Hinganiya experienced an increase, the other three experiencing decreases in the context of an overall 10.5% decrease for Marwar in the same period. (Trends for Marwar from 1891-1901, 1901-1911 and 1911-1921 have been calculated from figures in the Census of Marwar 1931b.) The occurrence of decreases in population is usually related to death or migration due to drought. But, why is it that a decrease occurred in some villages, while an increase occurred elsewhere in the same period? The point of mentioning this is to emphasise that general demographic changes occur in the context of significant local variations. For example, the anomalous increase in Hinganiya from 1911 to 1921 is probably related to the arrival of the ancestors of the present Soda Rajput inhabitants, who are reported to have settled about sixty years ago. Other factors, such as the failure of a well, may lead to a crisis situation when everything is normal elsewhere.

The decreases in population, either at a village level or at the level of Marwar State (or, now, Jodhpur District) do not necessarily indicate high mortality, although the major sequence of famines from 1896 to 1900 caused high mortality in western Rajasthan (Kachhawaha 1985). During that famine the brothers of the ancestor of all the Meghwals in Hinganiya left due to the drought and went to live in Mewar (now Udaipur District), leaving a single household of Meghwals in the village. That this sort of permanent crisis migration was fairly common among the other castes is evident in the 70% reduction in Hinganiya's population from 1891 to 1911. It was only in the 1930s and 1940s that the populations of the four villages recovered to the 1891 levels. From this point population seems to have expanded rapidly, despite the occurrence of famines.

The huge increase in Hinganiya from 1971 to 1981 is highly suspect. The decadal percentage increase for 1971-1981 was 78.6%, whereas comparison of the 1981 figure with my 1986 figure (433) represents a five year increase of 5.87%. Obviously a natural increase of 79% in ten years is impossible, and there is no local account of major immigration during that period. I have no explanation for the discrepancy, although I assume that it must relate to an error in the 1971 census, as the 1981 census is fairly consistent with my 1986 findings.

The major pattern here is that this century has been characterised by a huge overall increase, despite setbacks due to famine in the first decades of the century. Interestingly, it is at about the time of the incorporation of the State of Marwar into modern India that the population increase becomes consistent. It is possible that it may have been the implementation of land reform, combined with improved economic conditions under the Indian Republic, that took the brakes off population control. I will return to this point later in this chapter.

The other important point arising from these figures is the importance of migration in adjusting population. The role of shorter term migrants is highlighted in a breakdown of village population, which specifically identifies part-time residents. The details are in Table 7.2. Just under 26% of all adult males are part-time residents, including nearly half the Nayak men and nearly a third of Rajputs. This pattern, in which village populations include a number of people (almost always males) who have an ambiguous residential status, is a common one in western Rajasthan. I have described these people as part-time residents, although they could also be described as having dual residence.[2] I will examine this form of migration further in Chapter 9 and show how it is connected with drought.

Discussion

I have very briefly outlined some of the demographic characteristics of my field area, with particular reference to Hinganiya. In terms of overall population trends the main point is the occurrence of an apparent acceleration of growth rate some time after the 1941 Census. Essentially this amounts to stabilisation of the death rate, which had previously fluctuated widely due to famines. This brings us to a debate about the relationship between economic development and population growth.

D'Souza discusses the common assumption in demography 'that there is a negative correlation between economic development and population growth' (1986:77). In other words as an economy develops the rate of population growth declines. According to D'Souza's summary, the argument works in four stages:

- Prior to economic development a country has high birth and death rates resulting in a net slow rate of population growth.
- Sustained economic growth brings down the death rate leading to a faster rate of population growth, as the birth rate remains static.
- Population pressure leads to a fall in the birth rate, 'narrowing the gap between birth and death rates' (p.77).
- The birth and death rates again establish a balance, but this time at a lower level.

2 Rosin (1968) deals with what I call part-time residents in terms of a differentiation between actual population and total possible population.

Table 7.2

Population of Hinganiya January 1986 by caste*

Caste	Full-Time Adult M	Full-Time Adult F	Full-Time Child M	Full-Time Child F	Full-Time Total	Part-Time Adult Male	Part-Time Child Male	Part-Time Total	Overall Total
Rajput	28	39	36	39	142	11	2	13	155
Bishnoi	33	35	29	39	136	5	1	6	142
Jat	1	1	3	2	7	0	0	0	7
Meghwal	5	5	7	6	23	2	0	2	25
Nayak	11	24	36	24	95	9	0	9	104
Total	78	104	111	110	403	27	3	30	433

* = excluding absentes

This assumed process has, according to D'Souza, often been explained in terms of an economic decision making model which treats children as 'durable consumer goods for their parents' (p. 78). In other words, people in underdeveloped economies have large numbers of children because they provide labour and support to parents in their old age. With economic development, according to the economic decision making model, the value of children to their parents becomes less. On this model, rural western Rajasthan would be on the second step.

D'Souza claims that the economic decision-making model which is alleged to explain 'the negative relationship between economic development and population growth has not been systematically tested' (p. 78). He presents his own study of three villages in the Indian Punjab as evidence that there is no necessary relationship between economic development and population growth. He concludes that, in fact, economic development sometimes actually *encourages* the development of large families, by providing alternative economic opportunities. His own analytical model is

> that parents, rather than regarding children as consumer durables, are anxious about the career prospects of their children. If the parents try to restrict the size of their families it is not so much because they do not derive much economic benefits (sic) from their children but because thereby they hope to improve the career prospects of their children. (D'Souza 1986: 92-3)

The point I wish to emphasise is that the relationship between economic prosperity and family size is arguable. Economic prosperity is usually seen as being a stimulus for smaller families, but it can be seen as a stimulus for larger ones, at least in some circumstances.

In order to see whether there is any relationship between economic prosperity and family size in Hinganiya, I have attempted to make a comparison of numbers of children in different landholding groups. I adopted the strategy of looking at the surviving offspring of wives of present household heads (and women who are themselves household heads), because I wished to exclude very young married women and to get a figure as close as possible to the fertility of women who have had all or most of the children they are likely to have. Focusing on wives of household heads is a way of focusing on mature women. Recently married women are not likely to show much about lifelong fertility. For this reason it seemed useful to *minimise* the distortion caused by life-cycle factors by excluding the wives of junior members of joint households. This does not entirely solve the problem because nuclear family households, with relatively young women as wives of household heads do exist. Nevertheless, focusing on wives of household heads reduces the distortion.

In order to examine the relationship between fertility and landholdings, I have ranked all households into the landownership categories developed in Chapter 5. Taking the average number of surviving offspring of the wives of household heads for each of these landholding categories, there is a tendency for those with more land to have more children (see Table 7.3).

Although the differences between any one category and another are not statistically significant,[3] the overall pattern of trends for the five categories remains suggestive. There were no landholding categories which fell outside the overall pattern of average numbers of living offspring increasing with landholding size. Assuming that the *pattern* may be significant, analysis of fertility patterns (the basis of population growth) in Hinganiya lends some support to D'Souza's claim of a direct positive relationship between prosperity and the development of large families. However, the analysis of the implications of differences in prosperity in Hinganiya really is dealing with small differences within a generally economically depressed population. Any direct relationship may well be a result of the greater health disadvantages of the poor rather than of increased economic opportunities of the less poor. In a situation where the general mortality rate has fallen without compensatory declines

3 A test was carried out using the Scheffe procedure (a very conservative test), which showed no significant differences between any two categories at the .050 confidence level.

Table 7.3

Number of surviving offspring of wives of household head or female household head by landholding size category

Category (land - ha)	*Average living offspring*	*Range*
5 (>20)	5.75	2-10
4 (10-<20)	4.87*	1-10
3 (5- <10)	4.8	1-7
2 (2-<5)	3.47	0-6
1 (<2)	3.53	0-7
Nil	2.6	1-5

* - One household head has two wives and one of these is not normally resident. If she is counted (no offspring) the average for category 2 becomes 4.59.

in the birth rate, the mortality rates (particularly child mortality rates) of the poorer people may have dropped less.[4] Rather than prosperity leading to increased fertility, we may have a case of greater poverty contributing to higher mortality. In other words, it is not so much a case of wealthy people having more children, but of the children of poor families surviving less often.

A further theme of debate is the relationship between population growth and labour requirements or labour inputs: does population increase because of increased need for labour, or do labour inputs increase because population has increased?

Boserup (1965) argued that the intensification of agriculture is a response to population increase. Geertz (1963), arguing along similar lines, concluded that the population increase in Java in the early nineteenth century resulted in a massive degree of intensification of agriculture. These writers treat agricultural labour as a dependent variable and population as the independent variable in the relationship between population and agricultural intensification. The population changes, so agricultural inputs, including labour, increase. Increasing population in Java was frequently seen as being the result of improved economic conditions under Dutch colonialism.

4 Unfortunately, it is impossible to compare meaningfully the crude birth and death rates (number of births or deaths per thousand per year) for separate castes or landholding categories, because the populations are so small. Further, in the case of crucial factors such as infant mortality, it is impossible to obtain reliable data, largely because people are reluctant to talk about them.

Other writers have disagreed with the view that population growth is the independent variable. Bronson (1972), for example, argues that population increase occurs *in response to* increased labour demand. This labour demand model has been suggested as an alternative explanation of what happened in Java. White (1973) argues that increased labour demands resulting from the Dutch system of forced production led to increased population. Thus, population becomes the dependent variable.

Alexander, in a review of the debate in respect of Java, argues that the historical evidence for a vast increase in labour demands in the nineteenth century is far stronger than the evidence that population increased as a result of the benign effects of Dutch rule. He argues that Geertz's (1973)

> . . .claim that Dutch labour demands could be met by rearranging work patterns is based on a substantial underestimate of the extent of labour expropriation by the Dutch. (Alexander 1984:364)

The possibility of increasing population in Rajasthan being a result of the large demands of the *jagirdars* is enticing. Unfortunately for this argument, the sudden surge in population growth in Rajasthan occurred in the 1940s to 1960s, at a time when the *jagirdari* system was breaking down. Land reform in the 1950s, in fact, saw the end of the system.

This suggests an alternative possibility: perhaps it was the labour demands of newly acquired land that led to the change. Again, I think this is unlikely, at least as far as the villages in my field area are concerned. The area under cultivation in Hinganiya changed little after land reform. In Chapter 5, I concluded that land reform, in Hinganiya, mostly changed the status of the people who were farming land, rather than transferring use rights on a large scale. If this is correct, then people were essentially farming what they farmed before and, possible reduced fallow periods aside, demands on labour would probably not have increased significantly. On the contrary, freed of the need to give a substantial proportion of production to landlords, the new landholders would have had far more to feed themselves with, without any increase in work, had the population remained constant.

The relationship between land reform and population growth has not been explored in detail. Jodha suggests that the introduction of land reform was one of the factors which 'unleashed the forces of population growth' (1985:258), but he does not explore the mechanism behind the relationship. From the context in which his statement is made, the implicit argument is that the results of land reform became part of a general improvement in economic conditions, which lead to population increase.

In the light of this sort of argument, I am forced to return to a fairly conventional view of population growth. As economic growth, connected with incorporation into India (at first merely in terms of incorporation into the economy of British India and later into the Indian state) occurred in the 1940s to 1960s, mortality rates decreased without a comparative reduction in birthrates. An important factor in declining mortality was probably the increased capacity of the state to deal with drought and famine.

Labour demand is rejected as an explanation for population growth in this chapter. However, this does not mean that increased labour demand, or increased labour inputs, could not have developed as a consequence of, or a response to, population growth. This possibility will be explored in the next chapter.

Chapter 8

Labour Demands and the Household

Introduction

Coming to grips with the organisation of labour is crucial to understanding the workings of any agrarian system. In this chapter I wish to examine the organisation of labour in Hinganiya paying particular attention to the ways it is related to reducing the risks of drought.

Maclachlan (1983) has suggested that one response to population growth in a high famine-risk environment is agricultural intensification and argues that one way to intensify labour inputs is through the organisation of the household to maximise the availability of male labour. This chapter will explore the situation in Hinganiya to see whether a similar argument applies there. In fact, I will argue that analysis of labour demand does not support an argument for intensification based on large households and maximising male membership. On the contrary, large households, while being of value during peak labour periods, present a problem for subsistence for the rest of the year, and throughout bad years. Large households, where they exist, have other functions, particularly in terms of delaying partition of land.

As I am rejecting Maclachlan's model as not being applicable to Hinganiya (and as Maclachlan would make no claims that it should be), there is some risk that I am taking a straw man approach in discussing it in some detail and in using it to frame this chapter. That is not my intention. Given the high population and the existence of some large households which tend to have large landholdings (and thus are likely to need considerable labour), there are substantial reasons for taking the possible applicability of the model seriously. The analysis enables us to identify the alternative functions of large households.

In his study of the organisation of agriculture in Yaavahalli, Maclachlan, following Boserup, sees agricultural intensification as a response to population growth. He does not present a detailed argument about the causes of population growth. As far as his major argument is concerned population growth is seen as a given, as part of the problem to be dealt with rather than as part of the solution. Reorganising households to maximise male labour is a way of intensifying labour in the context of high population. There is no sense in which the solution is seen as a permanent one. The current levels of high population are a new phenomenon and the situation will change.

Maclachlan modified Boserup's approach to intensification in insisting that it should be defined as 'energetic output per worker per unit of time' (p. 201) rather than simply as increased labour per unit of time. This change of emphasis accommodates his concern with the differing application of male labour and female labour: labour 'is organized in such a way as to exploit the greater physical strength of adult males' (p. 93) because men are, on average, stronger in terms of 'isometric muscular strength and aerobic work capacity'. Maclachlan argues that the organisation of labour inputs into production takes account of the relative advantages of male strength in specific types of work. It is not that women cannot do particular tasks, it is just that (according to Maclachlan) they cannot do them as quickly as men. As agriculture becomes intensified the time factor becomes most crucial.

Maclachlan's main concern is with the ways in which the intensification of agriculture is organised within the household. He argues that the joint family household is locally regarded as an ideal and that its value is explained by the 'elders' in terms of the advantages held by joint families in organising efficient and intensive agriculture. Maclachlan claims that this indigenous theory is supported by his own data and analysis. He also argues (following his arguments about the differences between male and female labour) that it is particularly important to have at least one adult male in a household.

It is not my intention to assess the validity of Maclachlan's analysis of his own data in any detail. I must say, however, that I find it fairly convincing in most respects.[1] I am interested in examining the extent to which Maclachlan's view of the importance of the joint family and male labour is of value in understanding the organisation of labour and the structure of households in Hinganiya.

In the rest of this chapter I will be attempting to answer the following question: how are household size and structure related to the demand for labour, if at all? The procedure will be to begin with an analysis of

---

1 Maclachlan goes to quite a lot of trouble to defend his view of the part the sexual division of labour plays in his analysis, presumably because it is rather controversial. Much of the defence seems to be unnecessary. Maclachlan does not claim that the sexual division of labour is based on fundamental differences in the genetic basis of behaviour. He is simply arguing that much of the sexual division of labour derives from the pragmatic allocation of labour resources in terms of different capacities for 'isometric muscular strength and aerobic work capacity' (p.83) arising from sexual dimorphism. Far from being a rationalisation for sexual inequality, the study explains how the sexual division of labour may have developed, without resorting to genetic determinism.

statistics on household size and structure, on the assumption that larger landholdings are likely to require more labour. I will examine the relationships between landholding and household size and structure (particularly adult male numbers). This analysis will show that there is, on average, a direct relationship between landholding size and household size. This, however, is largely due to a small number of large households distorting average household size upwards for larger landholdings. I will then examine labour demands to see how they influence household size.

Household Size and Structure

Household size and structure in Hinganiya do not conform to any expectations of large joint households which are raised by Maclachlan's study. Very large households are quite rare and only about 40% of households are composite households. Few of these are complex joint families.

Taking household size first, Table 8.1 sets out the frequency distribution of households of various sizes. Two sets of figures are provided: one shows household size including both full-time and part-time resident members, while the second shows household size counting full-time residents only. In this discussion I will concentrate on the figures which include both full-time and part-time resident members.

The average household size is 6.46 and, in fact, households with six members are most common. Six also represents the median size, since there are exactly as many households with less than six members as there are with more than six members (twenty-six of each). There are only two households which could be described as very large, and only three households have more than ten members. On the other hand, four households have only two members and fifteen have four or less. Thus, while household sizes cover a fairly broad range, very large households are less common than very small ones.

Table 8.2 gives a breakdown of the frequency distribution of household sizes by caste. The crucial point is that almost all large households are Rajput or Bishnoi households.

Table 8.1

Frequency distribution of households by numbers of members

	No. of Households	
	(a)	(b)
No. of members	both Full-time and Part-time	Full-time only
17	1	-
16	1	2
15	-	-
14	-	-
13	-	-
12	1	-
11	-	-
10	5	4
9	6	5
8	4	5
7	8	6
6	15	12
5	11	17
4	10	4
3	1	7
2	4	5
Total households	67	67
Average No. of members per household	6.46	6.01

Table 8.2

Distribution of household sizes by number of households and caste

(both full-time and part-time members)

Size of Household	*No. of Households*					*Total*
	Rajputs	Bishnois	Jat	Meghwal	Nayak	
17	1	-	-	-	-	1
16	-	1	-	-	-	1
12	-	1	-	-	-	1
10	3	1	-	-	1	5
9	3	3	-	-	-	6
8	-	2	-	-	2	4
7	4	-	1	-	3	8
6	3	3	-	2	7	15
5	2	7	-	1	1	11
4	5	1	-	2	2	10
3	1	-	-	-	-	1
2	1	2	-	-	1	4
Total No. Households	23	21	1	5	17	67

Turning to household structure we find that forty of the sixty-seven households (60% of the total) consist either of a nuclear family only, or of a single parent and his or her children only. The other twenty-seven households (40% of the total) are some form of composite household. In Table 8.3, which gives a breakdown of household *types* by frequency and caste, I have presented composite households as two types: (A) nuclear families or families consisting of a single parent and offspring plus only one other person (such as the wife of the son of the household head or the mother of a household head) and (B) either nuclear or single parent families with two or more other people. It should be noted that ten of the composite households are of type A.

Table 8.3

Household type by caste

Type	Bhati	Soda	Total Rajput	Bishnoi	Jat	Meghwal	Nayak	Total
Single parent with offspring	0	1*	1	2*	0	0	1	4
Nuclear	8	2	10	12	1	5	8	36
Composite A	6	0	6	0	0	0	4	10
Composite B	5	1	6	7	0	0	4	17
Total	19	4	23	21	1	5	17	67

* = One household head is female

Definitions:

Single parent with offspring: Household consists of single parent (as household head) and his/her offspring only.

Nuclear: Household consists of married couple and their children only.

Composite A: One of above types plus one other person.

Composite B: One of above types plus two or more other persons

Thus, most households are households with a single parent, nuclear family households or near nuclear family households. Further, some of the larger composite households (type B) consist of nuclear families with a combination of two or more widowed mothers or grandmothers or unmarried siblings of the household head. The concern, in these cases, is with looking after people who have no place in a nuclear family, rather than with maintaining a labour supply. Households consisting of complex joint families (i.e., those including two or more married couples) are relatively rare, even within the composite type B.

A further point to notice about larger households and households with a joint family structure is that both of these features tend to be associated with caste. Table 8.2 shows that most of the larger households are Rajput or Bishnoi households: the three largest households are Rajput or Bishnoi and only one of the fourteen households with more than eight members comes from a caste other than Rajput or Bishnoi. Unlike the other castes, whose household sizes tend to the lower half of the range, Rajput and Bishnoi households range from the smallest to the largest.

The presence of the few large households among the Rajputs and Bishnois influences the average size of households by caste (as set out in

Table 8.4). The higher average for Jats is of no importance, there being only a single household. I would also be rather wary of making too much of the small average size of Meghwal households. One household has recently split from a parent household and the low average is, thus, partly a result of life cycle factors and of the small numbers of households involved. If the recent split had not occurred the average household size for the Meghwals would be 6.25. All of this means that there is little that can be done with a comparison of the average household size between castes. What is important and what needs to be explained is the fact that *the few large households* (barely enough to affect the averages) *are restricted to two castes.*

I will now explore household size and structure on another dimension: how are they related to the size of landholding? The most obvious point is that larger landholdings tend to be related to larger average household size. In Table 8.5, the relationship is summarised. The range of household sizes is indicated for each category. In order to identify situations in which the upper end of the range is represented by a single household I have also indicated the size of the second largest household. In Category 1 the second largest household is eight, the same as the upper limit of the range. This indicates that there are two households with eight members in Category 1.

These figures show that there is a positive relationship between household size and landholding. There are, however, inconsistencies in the pattern: Category 4 landholders have slightly smaller households, on average, than Category 3 landholders. The two largest households (seventeen in Category 5 and sixteen in Category 3) have a strong distorting effect. If the largest household in each of categories 5, 4 and 3 is not considered the averages drop to 7.33, 6.67 and 6.89 respectively. The differences within those three categories are really not very important. The difference between these three categories and the nil landholding category and Categories 1 and 2 are, however, important. What seems to be happening is that small landholdings discourage the formation of large households, but there seems to be no necessary relationship between large landholdings and large households. If large landholdings do not *necessarily* require large households, then what is the relationship between household size and structure and agricultural labour demands?

Table 8.4

Hinganiya - Average household size and average landholding by caste

(including both full-time and part-time members)

Caste	Population	No. of Households	Average size of Household	Average land-holding per Household (ha)
Rajput	155	23	6.74	9.67
Bishnoi	143	21	6.76	8.38
Jat	7	1	7	7.84
Meghwal	25	5	5	3.04
Nayak	104	17	6.12	1.75
Total	433	67	6.46	

Table 8.5

Landholding category and household size

(including both full-time and part-time members)

Category	Area	No. of Households	Average Size	Range of Sizes	Second Largest Household
5	20+	4	9.75	6-17	9
4	10-<20	16	7	2-12	10
3	5-<20	10	7.8	2-16	10
2	2-<5	15	5.6	2-10	7
1	<2	17	5.53	2-8	8
Nil	0	5	5.2	4-9	5
	Total	67	6.46		

Average for categories 2-5 omitting largest holdings

[5] 7.33 [4] 6.67 [3] 6.89 [2] 5.29

I will now turn briefly to consideration of the numbers of adult men per household. This is important in terms of Maclachlan's argument that, in Yaavahalli, the major problem of household organisation is to provide adequate male labour for the heavy work involved in farming.

Sixty-two of the sixty-seven households in Hinganiya have two or less full-time adult male members. Only five households have more. Of these, two households are Rajputs (each with three) and the other three households are Bishnoi households (see Table 8.6). The three biggest Bishnoi households, in terms of adult males, have three, four and five members.

Table 8.6

Hinganiya - Full-time adult males per household, by caste

No of F/T Adult Males	Bhati	Soda	Total Rajput	No. of Households Bishnoi	Jat	Meghwal	Nayak	Total House-holds
Nil	3	2	5	1	0	1	7	14
1	9	1	10	13	1	3	9	36
2	6	0	6	4	0	1	1	12
3	1	1	2	1	0	0	0	3
4	0	0	0	1	0	0	0	1
5	0	0	0	1	0	0	0	1
Total	19	4	23	21	1	5	17	67

Table 8.7(A) sets out the number of full-time adult males per household by landholding category. There are, in fact, fourteen households with no full-time adult males at all, and thirty-six households have only one full-time adult male. Only five households have more than two full-time adult males. The occurrence of households with large numbers of adult males tends to be uncommon in landholding categories 1 and 2 and to be more common in categories 3, 4 and 5.

If seasonal labour heavily influences the number of males then the number of part time males should also be considered. Table 8.7(B) gives the number of all males (full-time and part-time) per household by landholding category. Even when part-time males are counted there are still two households with no adult males at all and thiry-nine households have only one male.

Table 8.7(A)

Number of households in various landholding categories by number of full-time adult males

Category	Ha.	Nil	No. full-time adult male members 1	2	3	4	5	Total
5	20+	-	1	3	-	-	-	4
4	10-<20	2	8	4	1	-	1	16
3	5-<10	-	6	2	1	1	-	10
2	2-<5	3	11	-	1	-	-	15
1	<2	7	8	2	-	-	-	17
	Nil	2	2	1	-	-	-	5
Total No. of Households		14	36	12	3	1	1	67

Table 8.7(B)

Number of households in various landholding categories by number of adult males

(both full-time and part-time)

Category	Ha.	Nil	No. adult male members 1	2	3	4	5	Total
5	20+	-	-	2	2	-	-	4
4	10-<20	1	6	6	2	-	1	16
3	5-<10	-	5	1	3	1	-	10
2	2-<5	1	12	1	-	1	-	15
1	<2	-	14	2	1	-	-	17
	Nil	-	2	3	-	-	-	5
Total No. of Households		2	39	15	8	2	1	67

When we examine the number of adult males (full-time and part-time) and the number of adult females it is clear that households in Category 3 or above tend to have more adults of both sexes (Table 8.8), whereas the lower landholding categories have less adults generally, but noticeably less full-time males. Below landholdings of five hectares, full-time adult male labour seems to be inessential, or at least to have lower priority than alternative income. Nevertheless, despite the higher averages for full-time males in categories 3,4 and 5, it is important to note that there are two households with no full-time men in those categories. Further, not all of the men who appear in the tables are capable of doing physical labour anyhow. For example, in the the largest household and the household with the most land in Hinganiya, there are two full-time adult men and one part-time (in the army). One of the full-time men is, however, very old and does no work at all.

Table 8.8

Average numbers of adults per household by landholding category

	Average Numbers			
		Adult Males		Females
Category	Full-time	Part-time	Total	Total
5	1.75	0.75	2.5	2.75
4	1.5	0.31	1.81	1.69
3	1.7	0.3	2	1.9
2	0.93	0.27	1.2	1.2
1	0.7	0.53	1.23	1.35
Nil	0.8	0.6	1.4	1.2

So far, I have been analysing the size and structure of households in Hinganiya in terms of data on the distribution of features by landholding size and caste. The main patterns are summarised below.

- Sixty percent of all households are single parent or nuclear family households. Various forms of composite household make up the other forty percent. Very large households are rare.

- Larger households and composite households are most common among the Bishnois and Rajputs.
- Average household size tends to increase with the size of landholdings. However the distribution of households of various sizes *within* the landholding categories suggests not that larger landholdings encourage the development of larger households so much as that smaller landholdings hinder the development of larger households.
- The presence of full-time adult males is not a *sine qua non* for the existence of a household. While there is a tendency for households with large numbers of men to be more common in the higher landholding categories, there are also households with few or no adult men in the larger landholding categories.

I will now move away from statistics into somewhat more descriptive ethnography[2] informed by the following questions:

- How do labour demands affect household size and structure?
- As large households are not always related to large landholdings, why do large composite households sometimes develop?
- What other factors affect household size and structure?

Labour Demands Related to Agro-pastoralism

(a) Labour Demands of Agriculture

The pattern of seasonal activities was discussed in Chapter 6. The most obvious characteristic of labour requirements is that they are highly seasonal and highly variable between good and bad years. The only time when the demand for agricultural labour is likely to approach, equal or, perhaps, outstrip supply is for a few weeks during the harvest season. Labour requirements for planting and ploughing are also concentrated into a brief period, but, overall, less labour is required than during the harvest. Weeding is carried out occasionally, but can always be deferred if labour is not immediately available. It is not a continuous activity in the period between planting and harvest. In fact, before the *bajra* harvest there is often a lull in activity.

2 Although much of this discussion depends on rather detailed consideration of statistics from a single small village, I do not claim that it is a rigorous statistical analysis. Rather, my intention is to present a descriptive analysis, supported by statistics.

It seems unlikely that people would respond to the labour demands of a few peak weeks by forming large households which would be otherwise unnecessary, unless there was no other way to obtain labour. How are labour needs met?

For the poor farmers it is a fairly simple matter. Harvesting *bajra* from a few hectares can be done in a few days using household labour. Both women and men are involved in cutting the *bajra*, and it is only the task of carrying heavy head loads of cut stalks which is almost invariably done by men. The time frame within which the harvest must be carried out is wide enough to enable the small landholder to work for others in the meantime. Cooperative labour involving other households in a household cluster is another option. The advantages of using this sort of labour rather than forming larger households is that labour needs can be met without creating extra mouths to feed during the busy times of the year.

Larger farmers have more of a problem obtaining the labour needed to bring in the harvest within the appropriate time frame. Depending on the availability of work on a given day, reported wages varied from Rs 4 to Rs 10 per day during my fieldwork. While I am acutely aware that what people say they pay or are paid is highly unreliable (often the wages reported by employers and employees are inconsistent), there is no doubt that the levels of pay vary according to demand. Both men and women are hired.

If, for a specific brief period, labour becomes short there are two ways to get around the shortage. Firstly, it is possible to start earlier (work parties usually do not start until at least 10 a.m.) or to work later. Working into the night is not really an option in harvesting *bajra* (a job which needs to be done when there is daylight), but related tasks such as transporting or storing *bajra* can be done at night. A second option is hiring outside labour. As the timing of the harvest varies according to micro-environmental conditions it is quite possible for a peak period of demand in one village to coincide with a slacker period elsewhere.

In terms of the specific demand for male labour, there are comparatively few jobs in agriculture which women and men do not both do. However, there are some specifically male tasks and these, as in the case of the village studied by Maclachlan, tend to be tasks which are perceived to require considerable strength. Men do the ploughing, carry the heavy head loads of harvested heads of *bajra* and do the work associated with heavy transportation. (Harvesting *bajra* stalks tends to be done by men, since it is heavy work, whereas harvesting the crop itself is done by both males and females.) The work of carrying harvested *bajra* does not require a large male work force. A working party of six or seven could work during harvesting with only one or two men to do the male-specialist tasks. There is no reason why the rest should not be women and it is quite common for working parties to consist predominantly of women. As their wages are less and they work just as quickly as men at cutting, this is hardly surprising.

Labour demands in the agricultural season can be met by domestic labour (for smaller landholders) and by hired labour (for larger landholders). While paid work is readily available during a good harvest, the long slack periods and the uncertainty of the harvest do not constitute a stable level of demand for labour.

I will return to the question of the specific demand for male labour after discussing the labour demands of pastoralism.

(b) Labour Demands of Pastoralism

While agricultural labour demands alone do not encourage high population growth or the formation of large households, the economy is an agro-pastoral one, so I will now discuss the implications of the labour needs associated with livestock management to household size.

Management of large livestock (that is, of camels, cattle and buffalo) presents a continuous and fairly intensive labour demand throughout the year, particularly in terms of feeding and watering. The demand is somewhat reduced in the agricultural off-season, when large animals may be allowed to wander. While work associated with large livestock may be done by men when they are free (mostly outside of the farming season), it is done by women, older men or children at other times. Stall feeding is common, and often relieves the need for labour to be set aside for herding. The task of collecting fodder for stall feeding is easier during the agricultural season, because of the luxuriant growth of various sources of fodder. Having more than one or two large animals requires a considerable commitment of labour.

Small livestock management (sheep and goats) requires more or less continuous labour during the day, although the animals are penned at night. The labour requirement for herding is, however, not for heavy or specialist labour. Small children can look after flocks and one or two shepherds can manage the joint flocks of several households. Stall feeding of small livestock is generally restricted to young or sick animals. Only in the case of people with no more than one or two fully grown sheep or goats is it practical to stall-feed. Larger numbers need to be herded. Small livestock are not allowed to wander unprotected, because of the risk from predators, their lack of homing instincts and, I assume the risk of theft. Labour demands related to small livestock are generally greater in the rainy (agricultural) season because supervision needs are greater.[3] (Stall feeding of larger livestock is actually easier during the rainy season.)

If livestock ownership has large labour demands this could be reflected in a tendency for households with large numbers of livestock to be large ones. However, before this can be explored it is useful to see whether landholdings are related to livestock ownership.

Analysis of the numbers of livestock of the two types (large livestock and small livestock) owned by people in the various landholding categories shows separate patterns for large and small livestock (see Table 8.9). The average number of big livestock tends to decline with the decreasing size of landholdings, while the numbers of small livestock seem to be basically unaffected, fluctuating in an apparently haphazard manner.

Table 8.9

Average numbers of large livestock and small livestock per household classified in landholding categories

Category	Large Livestock	Small Livestock*
5	9.5	9.75
4	7.69	1.44
3	5.8	11.3
2	2.13	8.67
1	1.24	12.47
Nil	2.8	0.2

* excluding animals under one year

Large Livestock	*Small Livestock*
cattle, buffalo, camels	goats, sheep

3 This discussion leaves aside the question of labour associated with herd migration in time of drought. I have already explained (Chapter 6) that this is usually done by hired shepherds or in combined co-operatively shepherded herds. It would, therefore have little bearing on demand for household labour in the village. In any case, when migration to escape drought is necessary, little agricultural labour is likely to be needed.

The pattern regarding big livestock is fairly easily explained. Large animals are quite expensive and require quite large amounts of fodder. Not only does landholding size affect the financial capacity to purchase livestock, but fodder largely comes from agricultural by-products, particularly during periods of drought. Thus, while grazing land is not *directly* an issue (since grazing is unrestricted outside of the agricultural season) land ownership greatly facilitates ownership of large livestock, because agricultural land is a major source of fodder for stall-feeding.

On the other hand there is no clear relationship between the numbers of small livestock and landholding. In Table 8.9 the figures for categories 1,2,3, and 5 do not demonstrate any particular pattern. Variations are caused by the distribution of a small number of people who own particularly large flocks. The very small numbers of small livestock in Category 4 seems quite anomalous, but there is a simple explanation for this: ten of the sixteen households in the category are Bishnois and Bishnois have a religious prohibition against raising sheep or goats (although one Bishnoi household owns one sheep). This distorts the average drastically. The five landless households own only a single goat between them. Again, this appears anomalous as part of the overall pattern, but the fact that three of the households are small households with part-time household heads and that the other two households are Bishnois explains the distribution.

Ownership of land is not a major factor in managing/owning small livestock. During much of the year grazing on farming land is quite unrestricted, since no crops are in danger. Further, grazing provides manure so farmers are quite happy to have their land grazed by flocks owned by other households. During the agricultural season grazing occurs on common land and fallow fields. If there has been enough rain to make crops grow then there will be ample fodder on these available fields.

Within the context of a relationship between wealth (landholding) and large livestock owning, labour demand affects the ability of a given household to look after animals. Adult male labour is not essential, but it is useful. While younger children can handle some of the work, handling cattle tends to require the experience of adults or adolescents (male or female), particularly when animals are being tethered and so on.

The fact that large households find it easier to manage large numbers of big livestock is apparent from case by case comparison of big livestock numbers and household size. Large households do not necessarily own large numbers of big livestock, but those households with large numbers of big livestock are almost invariably larger households. Only one household with less than eight members owns ten or more big livestock. This household, with four members, owns fourteen big livestock, including eleven cattle and three camels. The household is part of a particularly coherent and cooperative household cluster, consisting of four Bishnoi households living in a single *dhani.* In this situation cooperative labour is readily available.

Thus, labour demands are a factor in managing big livestock, although membership of a cooperative household cluster may allow smaller households to meet labour needs. On the other hand the labour demands in managing small livestock are a less evident constraint.

The main problem with the agricultural season is that flocks need to be supervised more closely, although even in the off-season small livestock are not allowed to wander in the same way that big livestock are allowed to wander. While small livestock require constant supervision, the herding is not labour intensive, since one shepherd can look after fifty or sixty animals with ease. In fact no single household in the village owned a flock large enough to require more than one shepherd. Households can amalgamate flocks. In any case, the work is often done by small children, who tend to amalgamate flocks so they can play together. Among the Rajputs, the shepherds are usually small girls, since many Rajput boys go to school. In other castes, where school attendance is not particularly common, even for boys, either girls or boys can do the work.

Small livestock are penned at night. Consequently, for goats, the main labour demand comes from the relatively small demands related to herding flocks during the day. Milking of goats is not done systematically. If milk is required (and cow milk is unavailable) a lactating goat is simply milked on the spot. (Working parties are often accompanied by a tethered goat, which is milked whenever tea is to be made.) No one with large numbers of goats would systematically milk all of them twice a day.

Sheep, on the other hand, present a workload quite separate from the moderate demands of herding. Firstly, they are comparatively susceptible to diseases, so providing adequate shelter and tending sick sheep requires considerable time. Secondly, they are shorn twice a year and this again is time consuming. Large scale sheep raising tends to be a specialist activity. Of the total of 240 adult sheep (1985/86) 198 were owned by four households, whereas the 278 goats were spread far more evenly amongst all non-Bishnoi households. The largest sheep owner owned 80 animals, the largest goat owner only 33. The explanation for the focusing of sheep ownership in a comparatively small number of households is related to specialist labour requirements.

Adult male labour is not necessary for herding sheep. However, expertise is very much necessary for other aspects of tending sheep. and the work cannot be left to children. Consequently it is often just as easy for the men to do everything, including herding, themselves. Women, whose domestic responsibilities are not incompatible with agricultural work, are not able to spend a whole day in the fields with livestock. Of the four households owning more than 25 adult sheep, all are nuclear family households. In all except one case, the male labour for shepherding is provided from within the household. In the case of a Nayak sheep owner, his sheep are looked after by another Nayak when he is in Jodhpur. Interestingly, all the four households are relatively small landholders: one household owns just over 5 ha, one owns 2.5 ha and the other two own less than 2 ha of agricultural land.

(c) Labour Demands and Household Size and Structure

In summary, the main points about labour demand are the following:

- Labour demand for agriculture is highly seasonal and variable between years as crops often fail.
- Demand specifically for male labour is comparatively limited. Most jobs can be done equally easily by men or women.
- Large livestock ownership requires some fairly large labour inputs, particularly during the agricultural season.
- Goat ownership is not demanding on adult time, since the work can be done by young children and cooperative herding is common.
- Sheep raising tends to be a specialist activity, requiring fairly continuous attention and expertise. While the work is not heavy, the consistent demands tend to rule out women from involvement, since they compete with domestic work. Nevertheless, the work can be done by a single man from a nuclear family household.

In order to examine the subtleties of labour demand it is useful to use the landholding categories as a framework, starting from categories 1 and 2. In defining these categories (Chapter 5), I used 2 and 5 ha of land respectively as thresholds. I also stated that those within the two categories depended on income earned outside their own landholdings. In this chapter I have suggested that labour requirements from such small landholdings can generally be met by domestic labour, leaving time for employment in someone else's fields. In practice, people in these categories will almost always accept employment, finding time for their own domestic requirements somewhere. Households in these categories do not require a full-time adult male member for all of the year (or, at least, they can do without one). During the agricultural season men may return from working in Jodhpur to work their land for a few months. Alternatively, they may simply return for a few brief periods of holiday. Some cooperation occurs between households in terms of small livestock herding and some members of a household cluster may even work land on behalf of other households within the cluster.

In the case of sheep-raising, male labour is quite important and sheep-raising tends to be a full-time occupation. However, there are only four households engaged in comparatively extensive sheep-raising.

People in categories 1 and 2 are the main sources of agricultural labour within the village. The small average size of households is a result of the inability of landholdings to provide adequate income to support large households. The numbers of full-time adult males are small, this being directly a result of the generally small size of households.

In categories 3 and 4 the households are more or less self-sufficient in agriculture. Some quite large households occur, bringing up the average size. There are advantages in having large households, since they allow reduced dependence on hired labour and assist in large livestock raising. The importance of self-sufficiency in labour is evident in the fact that most of the households with three or more adult males fall into these categories. However, there are also disadvantages in having large households in that the members must be supported during the non-agricultural season and bad years.

If we turn to Category 5, we have four households which are high level employers of wage labour. Although all of these households have more than one adult male, old age, infirmity or military service mean that each household has only one effective full-time adult male resident available. In each case, while the households have labour resources for herding and most other requirements, the needs of the harvest season can only be met with the hire of labour. Thus, *in the very households with the largest labour demands, adult male labour is not available from within the household.*

In my opinion labour demand is simply not an adequate explanation for landholders in these categories having large households. There are several reasons for thinking this.

- The extra labour may be an asset during the agricultural season, but it is not necessary during the off-season and, in fact, becomes a liability because of the increased subsistence requirements.
- Many large landholders operate quite effectively without large households or large numbers of males.
- There are other ways besides large households to get around the problems of labour shortage. Hired labour is one possibility. While it is expensive it is less expensive than supporting unproductive household numbers during the long non-agricultural off season. Other possibilities are cooperative labour with other households.

There are peaks in agricultural activity and, at such times, landholders may find it difficult to meet labour demands. However, given that these peaks are few and brief, it is not surprising that permanent joint households have not been the organisational response. The situation calls for a flexible response. Relatively small households with close ties to other households are a viable way to meet requirements. This is where the household cluster comes in. Household clusters are based on lineage connections. Within the cluster individual households operate rather atomistically, particularly in terms of consumption and expenditure. However, like atoms, they have connections to other units. The ties are most commonly used for the purposes of cooperative labour.

Cooperative labour can involve short term agricultural working parties. It can also involve relatively permanent arrangements, such as joint herding of small livestock under a single herdsman. Sometimes one household head will take responsibility for managing the agricultural affairs of the absent head of another household. One such case involved a resident household head (a Rajput) who takes responsibility for most of the day to day running of the affairs of a brother and son employed in Jodhpur. However, while this arrangement was relatively permanent and superficially looked like a supra-household economic unit, income and expenditure were not systematically pooled. Several household clusters of Bishnois, consisting of linked households resident in particular *dhanis*, involved similar routine cooperation in labour, while maintaining distinct household based ownership of land and livestock. This type of organisation, based on relatively small households with genealogical links to other households, is a highly flexible arrangment able to cope with short term labour needs.

In addition to this relatively formal lineage based cooperation, there are more routine and informal types of cooperation, which can be described as generalised reciprocity, or perhaps just as neighbourliness. It is common for someone passing by a field where work is going on to stop and help for a while. I have seen this occur between members of both high and low castes. On one occasion a party of people hoeing in one Rajput's field finished the work early and went off to work in the field of another worker (also a Rajput). Apparently no additional pay was involved and, more to the point, the Rajput employer saw it as 'mutuality' (using the English word).

The *adola* functions as a way of obtaining large amounts of labour for a short time. It is also possible to sub-let land to tenants, thus obtaining return, in the form of crops, without costs in the form of labour input.

(d) Large Households and Partitioning of Land

From the discussion so far, it does not seem at all likely to me that household size is a response to labour requirements. The issue becomes one of demography and in particular of the demographic effects of the life cycles of household growth and development. Large households will usually have to split in future. In fact, the existence of some smaller households within these categories reflects previous splits. Presumably, in the next generation, the small households will grow and, in turn, split, sharing their land in smaller holdings. In that generation the new households will fall into a lower landholding category.

As suggested in Chapter 5, I believe that the difference in the sizes of landholdings *partly* reflects the extent to which individuals have delayed, or not delayed, the partitioning of land. Some households have already done so and exist as households within household clusters, holding smaller shares of land than they originally held. Other household heads have simply maintained the size of their holding by delaying partition. Thus, household size within categories 3 and 4 is partly a matter of life cycles and the present household sizes represent a statistical snapshot, made at a particular point in time.

There is one point I wish to emphasise very strongly here. Large households and the delaying of partition are not a permanent solution to the problem of land partition. In fact, for most farmers, the problem did not exist before land reform because they did not own land. Prior to land reform the problem was almost solely a problem for the *jagirdars*, who got around it by the rule of primogeniture. Land reform occurred quite recently. Current landholders may, in fact, have been tenants or landholders before land reform. It seems likely that those who have already partitioned land were originally larger holders, who felt that the smaller sub-divided shares would still be viable. Those who have held on foresee even smaller shares in the next generation. What we have is a situation in which individual household heads are attempting to cope with the particular circumstances of their own households at a particular point in history (less than 40 years after land reform). Their individual household circumstances depend on many factors, including the land gained through land reform, the number of male siblings in their own, their fathers' and their children's generations, and so on.

The elaborate juggling of household numbers in the case of Nahar Singh (Case 2, Chapter 5), is an extreme case of a household head balancing the need to keep household numbers up (so as to meet land ceiling requirements) with the need to keep numbers of heirs down.

Is there a way out of this continuing cycle of partition? (It must be recognised that while there is a cycle of household development ending in partition, the division of landholdings is unidirectional, not cyclical.) One way is to develop alternatives to a dependence on land. I will return to this in Chapter 9. The size of some of the households is possibly related to the desire to beat the land ceilings. It should be noted, however, that once land has been partitioned similar strategies will not work again.

Conclusion

In this chapter I have been examining the relationships between labour demand and household size and structure. One reason for doing so has been to consider whether Machlaclan's model (intensification of agriculture, associated with large joint househholds, as a response to the risk of drought) applies to Hinganiya.

In fact, the model does not apply. If it did we would expect household size to closely correlate with landholdings (because more land requires more work). In fact, this happens in terms of average household size in each landholding category, but the variations in household size amongst the largest landholders and the relatively low degree of variation amongst the smallest, suggest an alternative explanation. I have suggested that small landholdings *restrict* household size, while larger landholdings *permit* larger households to form. Analysis of labour shows that labour demand is high only for very short periods and I have argued that the short term advantages of large households would barely justify the cost of supporting them during the long slack periods.

The purpose of this chapter has not only been to demonstrate that Maclachlan's model does not apply. If that was the case then the exercise would have been rather pointless. The value of the comparative analysis is that it has helped to identify important differences between the two situations and thus helped in developing an understanding of the dynamics of labour demand, household organisation and agricultural intensification. In fact, rather than refuting a Yaavahalli type situation in Hinganiya, the evidence suggests that almost the opposite argument applies. Labour demands are so episodic that there can be no particular advantage in having large joint households from the point of view of organising labour. Relatively atomistic small household units with lineage connections are at something of an advantage in these conditions. Short term cooperative labour, either on a lineage basis or through the institution of *adolas*, are ways of dealing with occasional peaks in labour demand. Large households may be able to take advantage of the situation at times of peak labour demands, but they actually form for other reasons. Among larger landholders the reasons are often connected with avoiding partition of land. Among poorer landholders, where they occur, composite households are frequently the result of a large mortality rate leaving people without support.

Nothing in this argument implies that Maclachlan got it wrong in Yaavahalli. There are apparent similarities in the situations of Hinganiya and Yaavahalli. In each case there are two major factors present: the risk of drought due to inconsistent rainfall, and an increasing population which somehow seems to survive when smaller populations were devastated by droughts in the past. There are also major differences.

Yaavahalli is an area of moderate average rainfall, although rainfall is inconsistent. In Yaavahalli the opportunity for intensified agriculture is provided by a water table which allows exploitation of underground water. The costs, in terms of labour, are high, but the opportunity exists. The result is that more than one crop a year can be grown and that failure of the monsoon does not lead to total failure of the crop. In Hinganiya the water table is too deep to be, under current conditions, economically exploited. Consequently, a fundamental precondition for the type of intensification which occured in Yaavahalli is missing.

In other villages near Hinganiya irrigation is possible and a process similar to that at Yaavahalli may have already started. At this stage, however, intensified labour seems not to be the key even in these cases. The water table is so deep that tube wells, rather than manually excavated wells, are viable. Intensification is a question of capital in such circumstances, not of increased and more efficient labour. In Kur, the ex-Thakur owns land with a well about 35 metres deep. In 1985-86 it enabled him to harvest crops, but by 1987 it had become virtually useless. The water table had dropped and the machinery to dig tube wells was not readily available and was very expensive. This farmer, unlike any in Hinganiya, could be classified as a capitalist farmer. If he, in more favourable conditions (the water table in Kur is higher than Hinganiya), could not obtain water, the poorer farmers in Hinganiya had no chance.

The argument I have presented about household organisation and labour demand is not intended to apply to parts of western Rajasthan where well irrigation is common. Rosin (1968) suggests that the relatively large size of Jat families (he uses 'family' the same way I use 'household'), in his field area, is important for labour supply. His work deals with an area on the edges of the Aravalli mountains, where well irrigation is a major factor. The similarities between my field area and his are important, but this difference is crucial.

For Hinganiya the answer to the question 'Why they did not starve?' is not in terms of intensified agriculture. In the next chapter I will attempt to answer the question for Hinganiya.

Chapter 9

Adapting to Drought: Beyond the Village

Introduction

So far I have concentrated on describing the agro-pastoral economy of western Rajasthan, emphasising the ways in which it is organised and the way it incorporates risk management. I have also discussed the twin hierarchies of caste and landownership which are an important aspect of the context within which agro-pastoralism operates.

In this chapter I will pursue two themes. Firstly I wish to show in greater detail how economic opportunities are opened or closed by position in either of the caste or landownership hierarchies. This partly involves a discussion of labour relations, but moves to an examination of various types of emigration and the ways in which caste and economic status affect the pattern of emigration. The second theme is the role of the state in famine relief and development.

I have already shown, in Chapter 6, how the options for various strategies of risk management are less available to poorer farmers. This involves the direct benefits of wealth. Production is higher and wealthier households are able to beat the averages and survive during a normal range of good and bad years, while poorer farmers are unable to cope in poor years and may be forced off the land if conditions continue for an abnormal number of bad years. Quite apart from the direct benefits of wealth there are ways in which the *relationships* between the people of various levels of wealth structure the opportunities available to each of them.

Hierarchical Relations

(a) Labour Recruitment and Relations

It is common to divide agrarian occupations into categories such as large farmer, small farmer and agricultural labourer. In fact the separation of various types of farmer from paid labourers is not very useful. Most poorer farmers to some extent work as paid labourers. All agricultural labourers in Hinganiya own some land (or come from households which do so). All except the smallest farmers occasionally need outside labour in peak periods. What is really important is whether farmers pay more out for labour than they receive as labourers. There is a pattern of self-sufficiency, co-inciding with the five landholding categories and described in Chapter 5.

To sum up from Chapter 5: farmers in category 5 and 4 are almost invariably employers, but rarely, if ever, work for pay in others' fields; farmers in category 3 both employ and work as employees, but are net employers; farmers in category 2 sometimes employ others but are net employees; farmers in category 1 work for others, but rarely employ paid labour.

Given that most adult males and unmarried (and, therefore, employable) girls are in categories 1,2 and 3 (because most of the population is in these categories), and given that labour is only short in limited peak periods, it is clear that there is an employers' market. Wages at the time of my fieldwork varied from a reported low of Rs 4 per day to Rs 10 per day (with or without food). The highest figure (Rs 10 per day, plus food) in 1983 was reported by a member of the employer's household and was dismissed as self-aggrandisement by other employers. The lowest figure (Rs 4 with no food) was paid to a group of Jats imported from another village (1983). The landholder had been unable to compete on the local labour market at that particular time with that rate, but was able to obtain workers from elsewhere. Variations in labour demand occur in very short time periods and in adjacent areas. It is, however, somewhat unusual for a landholder to be unable to get local labour. The problem is more often at the other end: how can the labourer maximise his work opportunities?

The answer is that individual lower-caste labourers tend to attach themselves to particular larger or middle range landholders, working with them whenever possible. Working parties on the land of larger landholders tend to form around a core of more or less regular workers (although this is flexible). There is no evidence that these regular workers work for lower pay in return for guarantees of employment. The relationships seem to depend on personal preferences: on one hand it is to a landowner's advantage to be able to obtain reliable labourers whenever he needs them; on the other hand it is to the labourer's advantage to be able to obtain more or less regular work.

Occasionally labourers are employed in semi-permanent arrangements in overseeing roles. In one case where a clear arrangement like this existed the wages were Rs 100 per month. This arrangement was relatively fixed in 1983, but the permanency of employment seemed to have been replaced by a looser patron-client tie in 1985. In essence these arrangements are a form of patronage.

(b) Patron-client Ties, Borrowing and Debt

According to some studies (Mehta 1980) various forms of bonded labour are common in Rajasthan. I have no direct evidence of this for Hinganiya. In several cases where I suspected that it was the basis of what otherwise appeared to be patron-client ties, the patrons were quite generous with wages, food and loans and this is not consistent with the exploitative element of bonded labour. At the same time the line between bonded labour and the obligations involved in patron-client relationships is not always clear. It seems to me that the only way to differentiate is by examining the extent to which there are mutual obligations. To the extent that the obligations are mutual then, in any meaningful sense, we are dealing with patronage. By that definition the situation in Hinganya was patronage.

The clearest case of patronage is the case of the overseer I mentioned. In 1985, although his role as permanent employee to a Rajput landowner had ceased, he worked, as regularly as work opportunities in the drought conditions permitted, for his patron. The patron also arranged a substantial loan (Rs 4000) towards the purchase of a camel and cart to set the Nayak client up in business. The Rajput himself was not particularly well-off (he was a category 3 landholder) and the loan represented a large investment. (In fact I was prevailed upon, under unspecified conditions, to help with a donation.) The arrangement involved sharing the profits on a fifty-fifty basis, with the Rajput providing cash for expenses and the Nayak providing labour.

There were no major money lenders in Hinganiya. Even the richest farmers were poor in comparison to farmers and merchants in larger villages in the wider region. Within the village, loans tended to be short term, often based on patron-client ties and concerned with temporary assistance with cash flow. When people wanted to borrow money they went to a wealthy Chaudary in Kukunda and borrowed money on collateral such as livestock, land or jewellery. I believe that a shopkeeper and a wealthy Rajput in Kur were also money-lenders.[1]

All this sounds awfully egalitarian, within Hinganiya at least: the larger farmers help the poorer ones; interest is not charged on loans within the village, and so on. Sometimes it seemed to me to be too good to be true, and I looked for exploitation, debt-bondage, high interest rates. I found no evidence of them within the village.

There is, I suggest tentatively, an explanation for this. Hinganiya is a small village. It is relatively homogeneous in several respects : there are a

1 There is a farmers cooperative bank. Farmers are able to take out loans, but collateral is needed. This tends to discourage borrowing. Thus the bank is unable to compete with money lenders, particularly as far as small farmers are concerned.

small number of castes; the differences in wealth are large, but even the richest farmers are poor in comparison to others in the region and there is no clearly differentiated system of inequality based on classes with radically different access to the means of production; the male villagers, whatever their caste, had known each other since childhood. Many of the wealthier and middle level farmers felt a genuine desire to help their neighbours. They gained from the clients, but the relationship was essentially a two-sided one.

I don't wish to over state the picture of a happy cooperative village, without conflict. There were tensions between individuals both within and between castes. One of the major in-caste disputes that I observed (between two Rajputs over a land boundary) led to an attempted knife attack by one of the two parties on the other. However, between castes tensions were muted by what I saw as the implicit threat of withdrawal of patron-client ties or opportunities for employment.

A situation in which I was the cause of tensions illustrates the importance of this implied threat. I lived in a Rajput household within a fairly coherent household cluster. The younger brother of the household head was himself head of one of the other households in the cluster. He frequently followed me when I visited Nayak or Meghwal houses, partly to make sure I was not offered tea or anything in breach of caste interdining rules. I believe that the main reason was to prevent me from making gifts or loans to Nayaks or Meghwals. On one occasion, he banned from his house a Nayak, who was my close friend and informant, on the grounds that I was giving him too much. In fact the Nayak was also a client of the head of the household cluster (and often worked with the jealous Rajput himself). The elder brother took no notice of the ban as far as providing employment was concerned, but clearly the fastidiousness of the Nayak in avoiding any hint of breaking caste rules was important here. He said it would be a problem for him if I broke the rules. On one or two occasions when other Nayaks offered me tea, he was clearly worried that the Rajputs would find out. Generally Meghwals and Nayaks made it clear that they kept to interdining rules with me to keep the peace.

Thus, there were underlying tensions. Nevertheless, as long as lower caste people did not break the rules, there was a great deal of good-will.

The main points about differences in hierarchical position are that:

- Those at the bottom of the wealth scale are at much greater disadvantage in bad years.
- There is a strong disincentive for poor people in the lower castes to break caste rules, because they depend fairly heavily on paid labour, and labour supply usually exceeds demand.

- Recruitment of labour is usually through a fairly open system of supply and demand, although some landowners tend to have favoured clients as the core of their workforce.

Migration, Dual Residence, Caste and Kinship

I will now turn to an examination of a major way of reacting to drought and the risk of drought. Emigration, of one kind or another is a common response to drought. This section examines the extent of emigration and will also follow up the argument that caste differences provide some different opportunities in terms of making connections with the world outside the village.

(a) Typology

One of the themes I have been pursuing in this study is the extent to which outward migration is an important response to ecological and economic conditions. There are a number of different types of migration, in terms of the extent to which migrants maintain economic and social ties with people in the village and the permanency of migration. It is possible to construct a typology of types of migrants which is, in fact, a sort of continuum from migration to dual residence.

Type 1

Permanent migration. This type of migration only becomes apparent in retrospect. There are a number of people, who were mentioned in genealogies as being once resident or the descendants of former residents, with no remaining economic (land) interests, maintaining no residence and no longer seen as belonging to the village. It is difficult to study people in this category systematically, because their whereabouts are sometimes unknown and migration may have occurred one or two generations ago. The important point is that there has apparently been some level of migration for several generations.

Type 2

Permanent migration with maintenance of ties. This category consists of permanent migrants (or descendant of permanent migrants), identical to Type 1, except for a registered interest in land. Such people may be resident in a nearby village, thus farming the land themselves, or the land may be farmed by tenants or lineage members.

Type 3

Life-cycle migration. Life-cycle migrants are those who normally live away from the village in connection with employment. They may maintain a residence, are siblings or offspring of existing residents and often hold an interest in land. Life-cycle migrants are not members of a resident household; their wives and children live with them. However, they may frequently visit the village, perhaps even to farm their land. People leave the village to work in three broad types of job: (a) military service (including police and Border Security Force); (b) non-military 'service'; (c) labouring. (Non-military service includes all types of *permanent* employment, but particularly refers to government or semi-government, employment.) Life cycle migrants are regarded as belonging to the village. It is more or less assumed that they will return on retirement, but, in practice, they may ultimately become permanent migrants of one type or another.

Type 4

Dual residence. I refer to people in this category as part-time residents. The category comprises men or boys who are not normally resident in the village because of outside employment, or because they go to school in Jodhpur, but whose wives and children (in the case of married men) or parents and siblings (in the case of unmarried men and boys) are normally resident in the village. In other words part-time residents are members of resident households. Their wives and children may visit them in the city, but themselves remain *normally* resident in the village. Part-time residents differ from life-cycle migrants only in regard to the place of residence of their household of orientation. Some part-time residents are in military or non-military service. Others work as labourers, usually in Jodhpur. In this last group men may return to the village for the duration of the agricultural season. There is, thus, a fairly fine line between seasonally absentee men and the casual migrants of type 5. The difference depends on whether outside labour is a primary and normal source of income.

Type 5

Casual migrants. Those in this category are regarded as full-time residents for the purposes of my census. They perform outside work occasionally, but are normally resident in the village.

Type 6

Crisis migrants. In times of drought some men seek labour outside the village, mostly in Jodhpur. They may, or may not, take their families with them. Obviously there is a strong chance that crisis migrants may become permanent migrants: this can only be determined in retrospect. Many crisis migrants return to the village in a good year. I suspect that the extent to which crisis migration becomes permanent will increase as population grows and land becomes scarcer.

In applying this typology there are some ambiguous cases and the definitional boundaries of the types are not totally mutually exclusive (for example Type 6, the crisis migrants can overlap with Type 4). This would present problems if the typology was to be used for statistical purposes, but the purpose of this typology is descriptive. My aim is to describe some of the different ways in which residence and labour extend beyond the village. The categories are not generally designed for statistical analysis (although Type 4 is used as a statistical category in opposition to 'full-time residents').

An important qualification is that the types are *my* descriptive categories. Villagers apparently do not have a similar typology, although my types do correspond, to some extent, to village perceptions. Villagers do talk about people who 'don't live here anymore'; people whose families live in the village are thought of as being members of resident households, even when they themselves live and work away from the village; and the difference between those who work in migrant labour occasionally and those who regularly do so is recognised.

(b) Dual (Part-time) Residence and Caste

There are differences in the extent to which various castes participate in different types of migration. Not surprisingly, the Nayaks, as predominantly small landholders, are particularly susceptible to drought and are disproportionately represented in the category of crisis migrants. It is quite common for crisis migrants to become permanent migrants. In 1986 there were five Nayak households which had all migrated in search of employment about a year before and remained away largely because of drought conditions. Each maintained an interest in land but none looked like returning. In 1987 three Nayak household heads who were resident in 1986 had either left with their families or had become part-time residents.

In addition to differences in the extent and type of migration between castes there are differences in the pattern of part-time residence between castes. In particular, the type of employment undertaken outside of the village tends to differ on a caste basis.

In Table 9.1, the incidence of employment by part-time residents outside Hinganiya is analysed by caste. It is striking that, with a single exception, all men who are in, or have been in, the military or para-military are Rajputs. I have already explained that this is a product of the values of Rajputs as Kshatriyas. Secondly, all of the other Rajputs on the table are in some sort of 'service', a category which includes all types of permanent employment, but which particularly refers to government or semi-government employment. No Hinganiya Rajputs work in manual labour outside the village.

Table 9.1

Extra-village employment by part-time adult males by caste (Dec 1985-Jan 1986)

Employment Category	Rajputs	Bishnois	Nayaks	Meghwal
Ex-military/para-military	5	1	0	0
Present military/para-military	6	0	0	0
Ex-'service'	0	2	0	0
Current 'service'				
- Tourism	1	0	0	0
- Drivers	2	0	1	0
- Other 'service'	1	1	0	0
Total Service	4	1	1	0
Unspecified or Manual Labour				
- Regular	0	4	2	1
- Occasional*	0	0	6	0

Notes:

1. Except for the inclusion of Occasional labourers (*), figures include only men who are classified as 'part-time residents' as defined.
2. 'Occasional' manual labour refers to those who spend several months each year working away from the village. Those who work on a completely ad hoc basis are excluded.
3. 'Service': permanent position (usually in Government or semi-government agency.
4. There is no column for Jats. The only adult male Jat in Hinganiya is a full-time resident.

The Bishnois have reached into some 'service' occupations, but nowhere near as comprehensively as the Rajputs. Generally, the Nayaks are involved in private employment, mostly as labourers. The single Meghwal is also a labourer.

This table, of course, only tells the story in respect of part-time residents and occasional workers. It does not deal with permanent migrants or life cycle migrants. Unfortunately it is difficult to obtain useful data on a cross-section of either of these types. However, for the limited number of cases for which I have data it is possible to make some generalisations about life cycle migrants/permanent migrants:

All the Rajputs in these categories are in 'service'

- The single Bishnoi (apparently a permanent migrant) is in government service.
- While one Nayak is in 'service' with the water board and one is a truck driver, all others are working as manual labourers.

If we combine the three categories part-time resident, permanent migrant and life cycle migrant a difference between the Bishnois and Nayaks becomes evident. Some resident households in both castes obtain cash income from *members* labouring elsewhere, but the Nayaks are much more inclined to move with wives and children in search of labour. Thus the category part-time resident, taken alone, underepresents the number of Nayaks who are forced to look for work elsewhere. While some reverse migration does occur, crisis migration with wives and children tends to be more likely to become permanent. By and large the Bishnois are able to cope with their landholdings, but the Nayaks are not.

In Chapter 4, I described some features of the various castes which, I argued, affect the options open to people in those castes. I will now briefly discuss some case studies which illustrate the differences between migration and dual residence among the Rajputs and the Nayaks.[2]

Case 1 *Rajput.* *(Figure 9.1)*

This case is that of five related Rajput households, consisting of four brothers and their wives and children. The fifth household is that of Son Singh, the son of Narain Singh, one of the brothers. Son Singh has clearly established himself as an autonomous household head, although he is a part-time resident and in the army. Except for the household of Gaje Singh, the households live in adjacent buildings. Although the households are related (in fact they constitute a minimal lineage) there is not much evidence of economic cooperation between them: they remain fairly independent. Some conflict is evident in the case of Narain Singh and Son Singh. Bhek Singh, another son of Narain Singh, found himself in

2 The names of individuals have been changed in the discussion of these three cases.

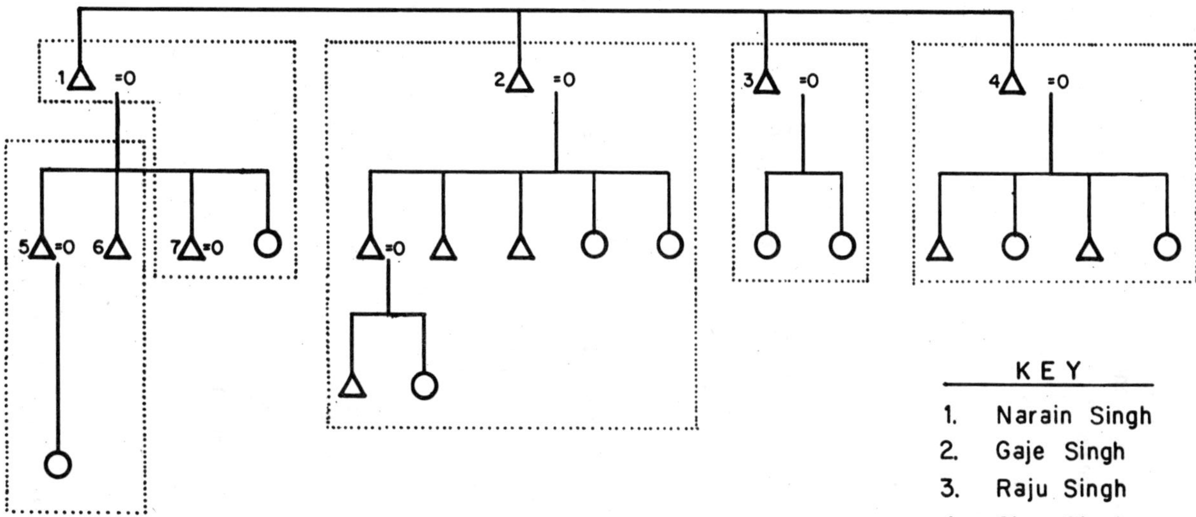

KEY

1. Narain Singh
2. Gaje Singh
3. Raju Singh
4. Sher Singh
5. Son Singh
6. Bhek Singh
7. Ram Singh

Fig. 9.1
Case 1 (Rajput)

Note : 1. Areas enclosed by dotted line indicate separate households.
2. Women married out of cluster not shown.

such conflict with his father that he switched allegiance to Son Singh's household in late 1985.[3]

The significant characteristic of this lineage is the importance of military service among its members. All four brothers were in the army, Border Security Force or police, although they are now retired. Two of Narain Singh's sons (Son Singh and Ram Singh) are now in the army.

In Chapter 4, I suggested that a sub-category of Rajputs with little land may have been the main source of military personnel. This is consistent with the situation in this case. The deceased father of the three brothers was also in military service (in the Maharajah's regiment). Three of the brothers hold only about two hectares of land each, having inherited from their father. Gaje Singh owns much more land than the others (9 ha) because he was adopted by a Rajput who had no son. All of the brothers receive pensions. Narain Singh and Sher Singh have spread economic risks and diversified economic activity, apparently using their pensions as a source of necessary funds: Narain Singh runs a small mill and Sher Singh concentrates on sheep raising.

The decision of Gaje Singh and Ram Singh to join the army assures alternative income while delaying further fragmentation of Narain Singh's land, although, ultimately the two hectares will be divided amongst three sons. In Gaje Singh's case the situation is less crucial, given his larger holdings.

This case demonstrates the way in which some Rajputs have faced the problem of limited landholdings in a way quite traditional to their caste, and in a way which clearly illustrates their incorporation in the nation state.

Case 2 *Rajput.* *(See Figure 9.2)*

This case deals with the members of a cluster of related Rajput households which has taken the alliance option. As in Case 1, landholdings are not large. However, by holding land in trust for his sons and nephews, Bhaktun Singh has prevented the breakup of his holdings into unviable plots. With the exception of Kan Singh, all married males are heads of their own households. Several are completely non-resident: while they visit Hinganiya frequently their wives and children live in Jodhpur.

---

3 Bhek Singh, at least described it that way. Narain Singh may well have denied that Bhek Singh had left at all. In fact, he probably saw it as a case of a child threatening to run away from home. (Bhek Singh was about twenty years old at the time, but was rather simple.) As Bhek Singh was a regular visitor to me, I was reluctant to create additional problems by asking Narain Singh outright about the problem. In 1987 Bhek Singh was back in his father's household, although tensions were still very high.

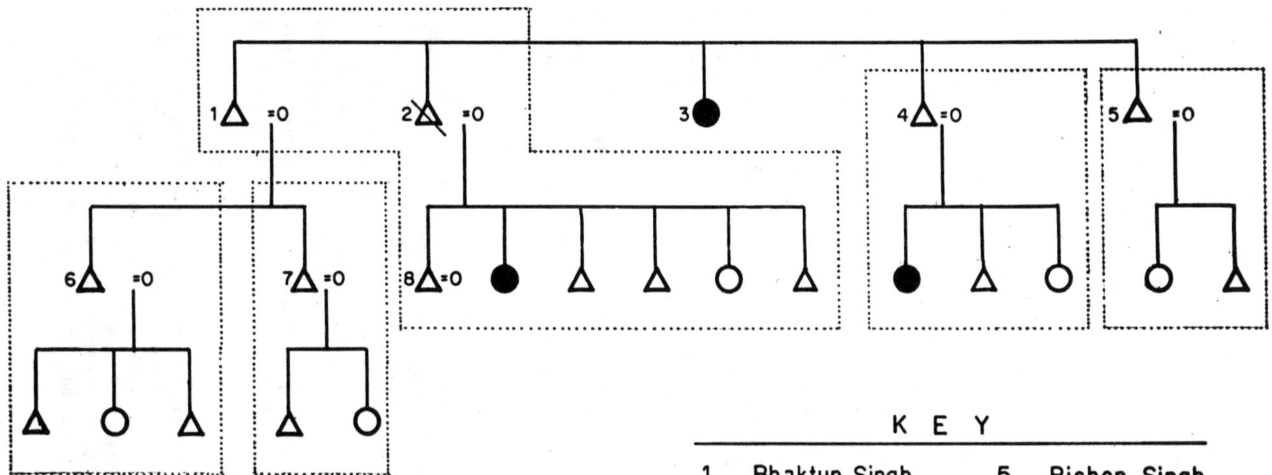

K E Y

1.	Bhaktun Singh	5.	Bishen Singh
2.	Kalo Singh	6.	Umaid Singh
3.	Prem Kanwar	7.	Ranjit Singh
4.	Madur Singh	8.	Kan Sing

● Woman married out of household.

Fig. 9.2
Case 2 (Rajput)

Note: Areas enclosed by dotted lines indicate separate households.

Kalo Singh (Bhaktun Singh's deceased brother) was in the Rajasthan Armed Constabulary (RAC). On retirement from this typically Rajput occupation he became a clerk with Indian Airlines, having learnt to read and write while in the RAC. He encouraged his own children to become educated. Every male member of the second generation has attended or is attending school. (Female children have not been so lucky, although Kalo Singh's youngest daughter attended school for a few years.) Kan Singh was the first (and, up to the time I left the field, the only) person from Hinganiya to complete High School. Now, the pattern of boys going to High School in Jodhpur has become standard within the households in this cluster.

The emphasis on education and subsequent 'service' began with Kalo Singh in traditional military service. But he apparently saw the potential for a new sort of strategy in educating his sons and encouraging the education of his nephews. However, it was a marriage alliance which opened the opportunities, particularly after his death.

Prem Kanwar, the sister in the first generation, was married to a man working at the Umaid Bhawan palace (now as head waiter). The Umaid Bhawan is the Maharajah's residence and much of it is now used as a five-star hotel. The affinal tie was useful in two ways Firstly, the quarters behind the palace became the home for the Rajput boys from Hinganiya while they attended school in Jodhpur. Secondly, presumably through patronage and/or influence, both Umaid Singh and Kan Singh were employed in the palace as room attendants. Kan Singh later transferred to the Government owned Tourist Bungalow.

In this case the affinal tie has been used as the basis for opening economic opportunities. Kan Singh followed the practice of seeking advantageous marriages. In 1984 he married the daughter of a wealthy Rathor Rajput who was also a senior official in the Customs and Excise Department.

Gradually the Jodhpur connection is building up. Bishen Singh, the youngest brother of Bhaktun Singh, has built a house in Jodhpur. (I suspect the costs may have been shared between various members of the cluster, but I do not know the details). While Umaid Singh and his family live in the Umaid Bhawan, the house is almost a colony of the household cluster. Other members stay there when they visit Jodhpur. In fact, when other Rajputs from Hinganiya visit Jodhpur they often stay at this house.

Case 3 *Nayak.* *(See Figure 9.3)*

This case is very different. The first two cases show how Rajputs are able to tap into opportunities which are essentially the legacy of the historical dominance. The Nayaks, on the other hand, were, and remain, at the bottom of both the social and economic orders. Case 3 deals with a cluster of patrilineally related Nayak households.

In this case four Nayak brothers inherited equal shares of their father's land. At this stage only one (Sujha Ram) has married sons. His land has been broken up to some extent. Ultimately his holdings will be divided into five equal shares, one for each of his five sons. Obviously, shares of about five-eighths of an hectare are unviable. At present the two oldest sons, Chunna Ram and Dhana Ram (who have already been given their shares), live in an outer suburb of Jodhpur with their families. Their land is worked on their behalf by Sujha Ram. One of the younger sons also lives in Banar, but remains part of his father's household. His wife lives in Hinganiya and I regard him as a part-time resident.

Two of Sujha Ram's brothers (Puna Ram and Bansi Ram) have also left the village with their families. In both cases the move occurred between my first period of fieldwork, which coincided with a good monsoon season, and the second, which was in the midst of a drought. Both return occasionally to work their fields, My expectation is that they will return whenever good monsoon rains fall. They are crisis migrants.

The process of migration in Case 3 is quite different from that which is apparent in the Rajput cases. In Case 1, income from holdings actually smaller than the 3.13 ha held by each of the four Nayak brothers was supplemented by pensions and drought did not force people off the land. Further, younger Rajputs obtained income from military service (Case 1) or permanent civilain employment (Case 2), which substantially increased the overall capacity of their own and related households to cope with bad agricultural years.

The Rajputs established permanent sources of supplementary/ alternative income by placing members outside the village economy. Further, when Rajputs leave the village they tend to move into permanent employment. The Nayaks, on the other hand, have not been able to establish sources of income as permanent supplements, instead becoming involved in manual labour. Their response to drought tends to revolve around search for lowly paid work when the monsoon fails. When Nayaks leave the village permanently, it is only to join the urban poor.

The argument which I have pursued here, began in Chapter 4 when I described some of the characteristics of the marriage rules and marital strategies of the various castes present on Hinganiya. In this section I have been arguing that migration, the historic response to drought in Rajasthan, still operates as a major response. Crisis migrants moving to urban labour today are moving for the same reasons as the crisis migrants who fled with their livestock in the past. Both intend or intended to return. However certain caste characteristics of Rajputs facilitate access to other economic options for them.

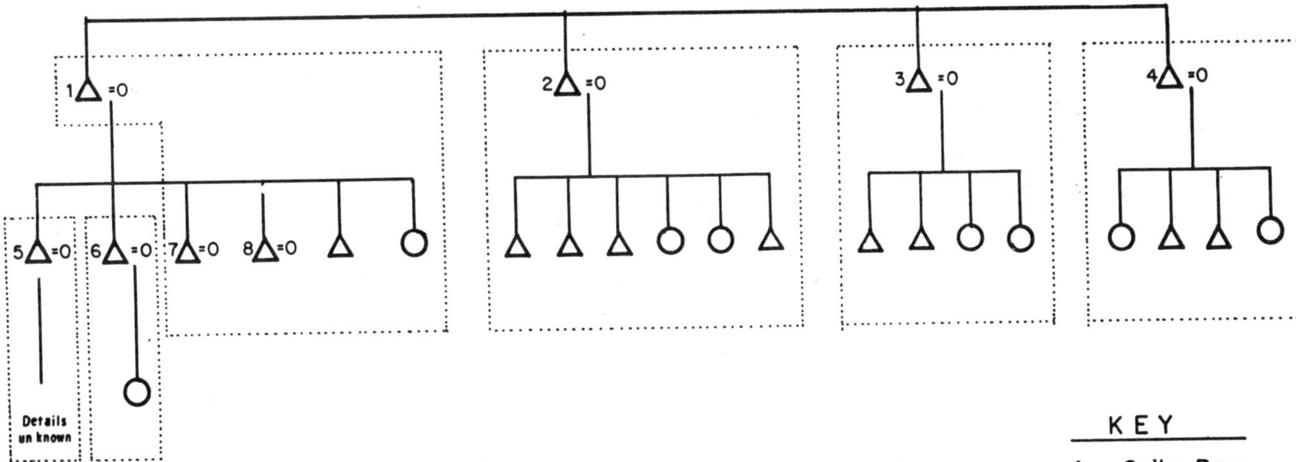

KEY

1. Sujha Ram
2. Puna Ram
3. Bansi Ram
4. Kojha Ram
5. Chunna Ram
6. Dhana Ram

Fig. 9.3
Case 3 (Nayak)

Note: 1. Areas enclosed by dotted lines indicate separate households.
2. Women married out of cluster not shown.

Now, as in the past, the land poor Rajputs are able to beat the limitations of relative landlessness by joining the military services, where they are welcomed and well-paid. Further, using a set of marriage rules which in the past no doubt facilitated military and political alliances, Rajputs now attempt to use affinal ties as a means of opening economic opportunities.

Development, Famine and the Role of the State

So far this study has largely concentrated on a micro-level, although I have talked about migration away from the village and about far reaching affinal ties. Now I will turn to a brief discussion of the role of the state in village economic affairs.

The first point to make is that this is not a case of a peripheral peasant society being newly incorporated into a centralised state. The process of state formation began in Marwar centuries ago and villages provided troops, paid taxes and received limited famine assistance for many years prior to incorporation into modern India.

The development of infrastructure is an important feature of incorporation into modern India. The villages are now served by roads and railways (at least reasonably accessible) which connect them with market centres (Pipar City), regional capitals (Jodhpur) and all of India. There is a market for the sale of surplus millet, milk, wool and meat, at least when surpluses are available. Perhaps more crucially, there is a transport system for the emergency supply of food during famine times. Infrastructure also provides access to water which is piped to the village. While there are seasonal difficulties it is certainly easier to obtain water than it was in the past.

This general development of infra-structure has almost certainly contributed to the ability of farmers to cope with drought conditions. I will turn to a discussion of the role of the state in development and, particularly, in famine relief. (Unless specified the word 'state' is a gloss for both the National and Rajasthan governments.)

Apart from schoolteachers and the police (who occasionally visit villages to break up fights, deliver summonses or make arrests), most of the government officials with whom the villagers are concerned represent the Collectorate (Office of the District Collector). The Collector himself is an officer of the Indian Administrative Service (Central Government), although his subordinates may be seconded from the Rajasthan Administrative Service. The Collector has responsibility for all land revenue matters, for record keeping on crop production, for all development projects and for implementing famine relief where appropriate. He has a judicial role (as District Magistrate) for matters relating to land revenue, land tenure and law and order. The Sub-Divisional Officers (effectively assistant collectors) have responsibility for a specified portion of a District and also have a judicial role (as Sub-Divisional Magistrates). In Jodhpur there were two Sub-Divisional Officers, one responsible for the western half of the District and the other for the east (including Hinganiya). Under the Sub-Divisional Officer are Tehsildars, responsible for a Tehsil (sub-district) and under these are the Patwaris, each responsible for a circle of villages.

In addition to maintaining land records and collecting land revenue, the Patwari is responsible for compiling crop statements. On the basis of these statements the Collector may declare famine in particular villages where there is a net deficit between staple production and what is needed for local consumption. Following such declarations, famine relief policy is developed and action is taken.

Famine relief takes a number of forms, including emergency distribution of water by tankers, emergency construction of wells and tubewells, establishment of fodder supply centres, the provision of rations at fixed prices and work relief projects aimed at providing emergency employment.

The overall cost of these programs is immense. In October 1985 the Rajasthan Government proposed a total relief program of 5,800 million rupees (*Rajasthan Patrika*, 5 January 1986). In Jodhpur District 170 million rupees were approved for relief employment projects. These were to include 165 PWD (Public Works Department) projects, 83 Irrigation relief projects and so on (*Rajasthan Patrika*, 29 September 1985). The projects provided pay for villagers to work on development projects.

The underlying concept of work relief programs is that a developmental project is carried out as emergency employment by villagers. Many of these projects are specifically aimed at building capital works (water storage or irrigation, for example) aimed at reducing risks in future droughts. Thus there is a two-pronged attack which focuses on an immediate crisis as well as on future crisis prevention. For example, in 1983, before the monsoon, there was a large project in Hinganiya to build a pond to hold water for livestock after the wet season.

The form of payment for famine relief schemes in Rajasthan has varied. A food for work scheme was tried at one stage. In pre-monsoon 1983 payment was by cash only. Rates of pay were Rs 7 per day for men and Rs 6 per day for women. In 1985 the policy was different. Payment was on the basis of a combination of cash and food. The relative merits of cash or food relief, or a combination of both, is an important, but difficult, policy question, which also applies to grain rations.

The ration system provides for the provision of wheat, sugar, edible oils, kerosene and rice on a per capita basis at a substantially subsidised rate. Provision of subsidised grain helps solve a basic problem, in that basic calorific requirements can usually be met, but grain alone does not provide adequate nutrition and poorer families in 1985 sometimes did not have enough money to buy the ration. In order to maintain health a more balanced diet is required. Vegetables can only be obtained for cash in areas where there is no irrigation. Because of the drought, vegetable prices are high. Cash is also needed for other things besides food - clothing, medicines etc. In other words, grain at reduced prices does not attack a major problem - lack of available cash.

Sen (1988) points out that there are two types of causes for the failure of a person to be able 'to command food in a market economy' (p. 39). The first is a 'pull failure', in which

> . . .the person loses his or her ability to demand food in the market, e.g., through loss of employment, loss of output, or reduction in real wages. On the other hand, if there is no such change but the person's ability to command food suffers because of supply not responding to the market demand, then there is a case of 'response failure'. (1988:39)

The philosophy behind food rationing is to avoid a 'response failure' by guaranteeing that regular supplies of food will be available at a guaranteed price. However, without emergency income the ability of the poor to 'pull' food from the system is reduced. Avoiding 'pull failure' underlies the policy of providing cash relief. In theory, the 1985 work relief program had the capacity to counteract both 'pull failure' and 'response failure'.

Unfortunately work relief programs did not reach everyone. In the 1985/86 famine the allocation was announced in September, but up to my departure at the end of January 1986 no project had commenced in Hinganya. In August 1987 I saw or heard no evidence of a project having been subsequently approved. There was some criticism of the Sarpanch (a merchant from Kur, who spent much of his time in his shop in Jodhpur) for not pursuing Hinganiya's interests vigorously. In the absence of relief work, a gradual drift of crisis migrants away from the village had commenced before the end of 1985.

Criticism of the Sarpanch raises some interesting issues. According to Chakravarti, writing about a village in Jaipur District

> A successful [local] leader . . . is one who can prevail on administrators and politicians to operate the bureaucracy for the benefit of his followers. (1975: 187)

On this basis the Sarpanch seems not to have been a particularly successful leader. Overall Panchayat activities were very low key. No meeting ever occurred, to my knowledge, when I was in the area. According to the previous Sarpanch, meetings were held barely once or twice a year. I suggest that the relative apathy about formal village politics was related to the relative powerless of the Panchayat. (The Kur Sarpanch, however ineffective in obtaining external aid, took great personal responsibility. In 1987 he was providing, at his own expense, a daily tanker load of drinking water each for Khokhariya and Hinganiya.) A lack of confidence about famine relief projects was common. The Sarpanch of another Panchayat once dismissed the drought relief program as government propaganda.

Criticisms of the effectiveness and reach of famine relief projects has been voiced by more than villagers. An article in a major news magazine alleged in 1987 that much of the relief program had not been implemented (*India Today*, 15 October 1987). A prominent Rajput in Jodhpur told me in 1987 that the Congress Party would probably lose the next Rajasthan state election because it had no effective drought policy.

Despite these criticisms the emergency programs clearly worked reasonably well, given that there was no evidence of large-scale death by starvation. Despite its limitations food rationing met most people's needs for minimum staples. The main result of famine relief is that loss of life due to gross starvation is very rare, because rations are provided before mass starvation becomes a problem. Nevertheless, there is a major shift of the poorer farmers to towns and cities during famines. In these periods they depend on opportunities for paid labour.

Migration to Jodhpur in search of work becomes almost the only alternative for people with no cash resources. Fortunately, Jodhpur is growing rapidly and labouring work in the building industry is fairly readily available at present. As an indication of wages for rural refugee workers (in 1985), one informant said he was earning Rs 300 per month plus food. Another earned Rs 200 per month.

Mass migration of famine refugees to Jodhpur raises new problems, including the poor living conditions faced by workers. While wages available are high in comparison to wages for agricultural labour (up to Rs 10, but available irregularly even in a good year), the cost of living is also high in Jodhpur. The differential may be enough to encourage marginal farmers to stay on in Jodhpur, but migration amounts to moving from their role as rural poor to a new role as urban poor.

In some ways, then, McAlpin's view, that economic development has led to the end of major famine, holds. The state has absorbed much of the risk involved in subsistence farming, and general economic development, particularly in Jodhpur, provides job opportunities. But the situation also demonstrates the great weakness in McAlpin's argument. McAlpin ignored the uneven effects of famine within the rural population; the same uneven distribution of the consequences of famine are evident here.

In terms of entitlement theory, the state has provided a new set of entitlements (to emergency relief) and has reduced the risk of 'response failure' in a crisis by reducing fluctuations in food prices. However, the ability of the poor to command food remains relatively limited.

Chapter 10

Conclusion

The farmers of western Rajasthan are faced with one certainty: the certainty that their livelihood each year is uncertain. My concern in this study has been to look at the way people in one part of the region survive in circumstances of great uncertainty about subsistence in the face of unreliable seasonal rainfall. The study has been conceived primarily as a study of an agrarian system - a system of agricultural production including the ecological, socio-economic and political context.

I have discussed the organisation of production and the annual cycle of production. The object of this analysis was to examine technological and social responses to drought and to the risk of famine. One possible response is intensification of agricultural inputs, either in the form of improved or increased technology (for example, the use of high yield seed varieties, machinery or irrigation) or in the form of increased labour. However, my analysis shows that few technological innovations are economically viable in my study area at present. Certainly few have occurred. Further, there was no evidence that intensified labour inputs are a major factor in the organisation of agro-pastoral production. Household structure does not reflect a high level of labour demand.

The main planned responses by farmers are in terms of risk management. This is a matter of spreading risks by scattering plots, mixing crops and, overwhelmingly, by engaging in a mixed agro-pastoral economy.

However, all this talk of strategies for this and options for that has a great danger. And the danger is this: it may obscure the simple fact that wealth (or *comparative* wealth) is the best defense against the uncertainties of the environment. Richer people have strategies which can allow them to recover economically after a drought. Poorer people are often not in a position to apply these strategies and tend to drop out of the system, by migrating to urban areas.

I have explored the agrarian hierarchy from two points of view. The first relates to the distribution of land. This is decidedly skewed and analysis shows that land reform has left a class of landless (or nearly landless) poor, despite the real benefits which have accrued to the former tenant classes. The landholding aspect of the agrarian hierarchy is essentially predicated on a land equals wealth nexus. However, there is another aspect of agrarian hierarchy which relates to the capacity of the Rajputs to escape this nexus. They do so through continuing in their traditional occupation in military service and by utilising certain structural features of their caste to facilitate the formation of alliances which provide opportunities outside the village. Village Rajputs are sometimes able to tap into the patron-client ties which have survived the dismantling of the Rajput States. This happened in the case of the Rajputs (Case 2, Chapter 9) who used marital alliances to obtain appointments in the hotel in the former Maharajah's palace.

Land reform in the 1950s and 1960s has affected more than the distribution of land between castes and classes. It opened the way to a cycle of land partition which presents a problem to all households. It also has importance in terms of social organisation, particularly in terms of household size. Variations in household size, far from being determined by labour demands, are affected by other factors. Smaller landholders tend to have smaller households mostly because they cannot support large ones; larger landholders may have, but don't necessarily have, large households. Where they do, they often do so because large households enable them to beat the land ceiling laws (in the case of very large households), or because large households defer the partition of land.

A great paradox in the recent history of western Rajasthan is that the increasing population of the present century has occurred at the same time as a decline in human mortality associated with serious drought. General economic development, which provides alternative employment and an increased ability, on the part of the state, to provide for human needs during drought, seem to be the main contributors to the decline in mortality.

For whatever reasons, human population continues to increase. At present land holdings are sufficient to support many of the existing households. But, further population growth will lead to more partition of land and, without massive changes in technical and financial inputs, no significant increase in productivity is likely.[1] Increased migration to urban centres seems to be inevitable. Strategies for delaying the partition of land can only work for a short time.

The agrarian system that I have described is involved in a continual process of change, especially in terms of changes to landholding sizes and the wider political and economic context. The strategies and solutions described are responses to a changing situation at a certain point in time.

1 Any major intensification of agriculture (at least using existing technologies) is likely to have detrimental environmental consequences, and to further raise questions of sustainability.

Conclusion

I have concentrated very heavily on several small villages and on a single small village in particular. The agro-pastoral economy of Hinganiya is not typical of Rajasthan as a whole. It is, however, representative of agro-pastoralism in semi-arid rainfed conditions, which is one of the types of agrarian systems present in western Rajasthan. It is tempting to try to see Hinganiya and the surrounding villages as part of a more general type. The situation described is similar, in many respects, to the 'dry grain agrarian mode' described by Hill (1982).

Hill argues that there is 'a crying need for the systematic categorisation of broad types of rural under-development in the contemporary, tropical, third world - for a respectable typology of agrarian systems'(1982:49). She examines similarities between situations in Hausaland (Nigeria) and Karnataka. She sets out nine 'necessary conditions for the existence of this dry grain mode':

> (1) The population is so dense that nearly all of the available farmland is necessarily manured and cultivated every year - and densities are increasing fast.
> (2) The bulk of the farmland is used for cultivating basic food grains. . . without irrigation.
> (3) The farmland is effectively owned by individuals or households - being inherited by sons on, or before, their father's death.
> (4) Cultivation is undertaken by household members with or without the help of agricultural labourers.
> (5) Cultivators have for long been accustomed to buy and sell farmland for cash.
> (6) However, land scarcity and rising prices have recently led to a much reduced incidence of land-selling.
> (7) Grain yields per acre are very low on any standard. . . .
> (8) Most farm tools and equipment, which are of 'traditional design', are made by local blacksmiths and carpenters.
> (1982:50. Emphasis removed from original)

Hill adds one further factor

> . . .which relates to Hausaland and Karnataka, but might have to be expressed somewhat differently in other regions where this dry grain mode applied.
> (9) In a sense. . . there has been a long-term withdrawal (which is not a large-scale migration) from the countryside. (1982: 50)

The broad picture here is very similar to the one I have described. All conditions, except (5) and (6) apply in Hinganiya. Clearly there is a sense in which broadly similar environmental and political contexts can lead to broadly similar agrarian systems. But the particularities are important. It is the relatively recent shift from a 'feudal' form of landownership and subsequent land reform, that give the agrarian system of western Rajasthan its specific character.

As I understand it one factor underlying Hill's desire to construct a typology of agrarian systems is the wish to demonstrate the diversity of conditions underlying the use of the term 'peasant'. Her intention is to develop a 'large-scale classification', not to assert 'anything so preposterous' as the existence of a single 'dry grain farming mode'. Hill would agree that it is important to balance the need to generalise with the need to particularise.

The comparison of the agrarian system operating in Hinganiya with that operating in Yaavahalli highlights some of the risks which might be involved in taking typology building too far. Hinganiya and Yaavahalli have broadly similar characteristics. But, the existence of relatively accessible underground water in Yaavahalli leads to fundamental differences in the technical and organisational possibilities for agricultural intensification. The combination of such strategic comparison and the type of typology building advocated by Hill (both based on detailed field work) may be one way to achieve a balance between particularising and generalising.

It is an obvious (but not, I think, trivial) point that ecological anthropology (and the social sciences in general) aim to build generalisations which will help people to make sense of the world. However, there is a risk that our typologies and generalisations may obscure important differences. Perhaps the most important generalisation that can be made from this study is that the study of human ecology must, to a great extent, focus on historically and locally specific processes.

Afterword

Reflections on a Return Visit

In July 1994 I spent several weeks in Rajasthan, visiting Hinganiya and travelling further west to Jaisalmer and Barmer. I also visited the now completed Rajasthan Canal. The visit was brief and I had no opportunity to carry out comprehensive research. Nevertheless, what I observed provides a focus for useful reflections.

The early 1994 monsoon had been extremely heavy, causing heavy flooding in parts of Rajasthan. In fact, since my last visit in August 1987, monsoon rainfall had been generally good. This lead to some astonishing changes in Hinganiya.

Judging by the increased number of houses there had been a considerable increase in village population, probably the result of a natural increase combined with the return of crisis migrants. Most strikingly, there were many new *pakka* houses, including several in the Nayak and Meghwal sections of the village. Further, there was quite a lot of new construction activity. One of the Nayaks had become an accomplished mason and was earning around Rs 150 per day building houses. Electricity had been connected to many houses and the village appeared quite prosperous in comparison to earlier visits.

The visibly improved economic situation was clearly the result of a sequence of good monsoons, with excellent crop production. Interestingly, the pattern of caste-related strategies for obtaining non-agricultural income had continued. Several Rajputs who had been at school in 1987 were now enlisted in the various military or paramilitary forces, or working in the tourist industry. Nayaks and Meghwals had continued to seek income as labourers, especially in construction. At least one younger Nayak was working as a bus driver. The Rajput "colony" in Jodhpur continued to be a base for visitors from the village and for the young men working at the Umaid Bhawan Palace Hotel. The Rajputs were placing great importance on the education of young men in Jodhpur.[1]

The combination of good agricultural seasons and continued involvement in non-agricultural activities, had clearly led to a much improved economic situation in comparison to that which existed in 1987. The question which arises is to what extent the next episode of drought would jeopardize the economic gains of the previous ten years. It is difficult to answer this question with any certainty, but it seems likely that the good seasons had allowed most households to build a useful buffer against the inevitable drought. Although I was not in Hinganiya for long enough to quantify my observations, it also seemed very clear that many more men, of all castes, had positioned themselves to take advantage of non agricultural income, largely following strategies traditionally preferred by their caste fellows. All of this seems to reinforce the view that economic development reduces the risk of catastrophic famine.

Western Rajasthan as a whole was, like Hinganiya, astonishingly green in July 1994. Even in the desert tracts near Jaisalmer there were extensive grasslands and (something I had never seen before in the area) large areas of surface water, often amounting to medium sized lakes.

In my original analysis I wondered what effects the completion of the Rajasthan canal would have on the region. I was not able to visit the tail of the canal, near Jaisalmer, because of restrictions on foreigners visiting the area, but I did visit the canal near Phalodi. Clearly agricultural activity and productivity had increased in areas near feeder canals, although it was unclear whether the effects were as great as designers had expected. I wonder personally how much the busy new and expanded settlements had developed as a result of improved agriculture and how much they had developed as a result of the need for workers to build and maintain the canal and the need to provide services for those workers. This is speculative and there is room for a detailed and critical study of the socio-economic impacts of the canal.[2]

The effects of the canal on migration routes were surprisingly limited. Herders at Sam, to the west of Jaisalmer and fairly near the tail of the

1 An example of just how effectively the networking by Rajputs led to economic benefits to the village is exemplified by the involvement of villagers in the production of the film *The Jungle Book*, much of which was filmed in and around Jodhpur. Through tourist industry contacts Hinganiya provided many workers for the production. These were reportedly paid Rs 200 per day.

2 Dr L.P. Bharara, a sociologist at the Central Arid Zone Research Institute, has reported on some impacts of the canal in earlier stages of its construction (Bharara 1985). He believes (pers. comm.) that a comprehensive evaluation is now necessary.

canal, reportedly still take their livestock to Gujarat in bad years. Others, near Barmer, reported that they migrate to Haryana, the Punjab or Gujarat. Others talked of Jaisalmer District. Surprisingly no one interviewed reported taking livestock to the canal zone, although providing fodder was supposedly an objective of canal construction. It is possible that the good recent monsoons (since the completion of the canal) had meant that migration had been very limited, there being no fodder crisis. Consequently, as there had been no really bad years, the option of canal zone grazing had not been tested. It seems, in any case, that the canal zone is not yet seen as a major option by herders. Some herdsmen reported that they had not been 'asked' by the government to take their herds to the zone and there may well be some uncertainty about rights of access to the grazing lands. It is also possible that larger migrations, however onerous, are more attractive because they bring herders in contact with markets for livestock and animal products.

Following this brief return to Rajasthan, I was left with a strong sense of improved economic conditions. The reality of this impression, although unquantified, is unquestionable. What is less certain is just how fragile the changes are. Clearly, the next drought will lead to a downturn, but it remains possible that the period of prosperity will provide a legacy of greater security.

The sustainability, in ecological terms, of rapidly increasing population, remains more problematic. Exploitation of underground water resources is seen as presenting serious difficulties (Goldman 1989). With reference to desertification, the extraordinary growth of grass and other natural vegetation during the 1994 monsoon leads me, however, to question whether soil degradation is as clear a trend as is often claimed. Since my first visit to Rajasthan in 1983, vegetation (both crops and natural vegetation) has varied immensely, but the extent of vegetation in 1994 was far greater than anything I had seem previously. Against this background of great variation over the short term, claims of inevitable long term trends of declining soil condition should, perhaps, be treated with some scepticism.

Appendix

The Twenty-Nine Rules of the Bishnois

The following version of the twenty-nine rules is a composite of the versions translated or quoted by Rose (1911, vol 2:111) for the first two rules and Gupta (1965, quoting Walter, n.d.) for the rest. Rose's account of the last twenty-seven rules differs from the account of Gupta in some respects and is, in any case, quite cryptic. The full set of rules as provided by Rose is version B. Note that I have quoted the wording from both versions verbatim.

(a) Composite Version

1/2 For 30 days after child-birth and five days after a menstrual discharge a woman must not cook food.

3 From the day when a child, whether male or female, begins to eat grain, it should be bathed daily in water.

4 To be faithful always to one woman.

5 Whatever a man possesses therewith always to be content.

6 Always to salute each other five times a day.

7 To pray to the deity every evening.

8 Everyday before partaking of food to put ghee on a fire.

9 Never to speak without consideration.

10 Water used for drinking or bathing to be filtered.

11 To carefully examine all wood for burning to see that insect or other living thing is in it.

12 Never to give way to anger.

13 Never to thieve.

14 Never to speak ill of anyone.

15 Never to tell an untruth.

16 To fast on the 15th of the dark part of each month.

17 Always to call on the name of Vishnu.

18 Never to take life nor as far as it is possible permit others to do so.

19 Never to cut a green tree.

20 To eat only such food as is cooked by the sect.

21 To fix a mark on the ear of every goat and sheep so that its life may be safe and as far as possible to make others do the same.

22 Never to geld a bullock.

23 Not to eat opium.

24 Not to drink spirituous liquor.

25 Not to smoke.

26 Not to take *bhang*.

27 Not to let indigo touch the body.

28 Never to bear enmity to another.

29 So to live as to be always prepared to die.

(b) Rose's version

'For 30 days after child-birth and five after a menstrual discharge a woman must not cook food. Bathe in the morning. Commit not adultery. Be content. Be abstemious and pure. Strain your drinking water. Be careful of your speech. Examine your fuel in case any living creature be burnt with it. Show pity to living creatures. Keep duty present to your mind as the Teacher bade. Do not speak ill of others. Do not tell lies. Never quarrel. Avoid opium, tobacco, bhang and blue clothing. Flee from spirits and flesh. See that your goats are kept alive (not sold to Musalmans, who will kill them for food). Do not plough with bullocks. Keep a fast on the day before the new moon. Do not cut green trees. Sacrifice with fire. Say prayers. Meditate. Perform worship and obtain heaven. . . Baptize your children if you would be called a true Bishnoi.' (Rose 1911, Vol 2:111-112)

Bibliography

(a) Census of India and Census of Marwar

For convenience, all documents published by the Census of India (with the exception of monographs) are cited by the year of the census, not the year of publication, followed by a letter indicating the particular publication according to the following bibliography. A similar approach has been adapted to references from the Census of Marwar.

Census of India

1951. Rajasthan and Ajmer. Part 1A: Report. COI 1951, Vol 10.

1961a. District Census Handbook, Jaisalmer.

1961b. District Census Handbook, Jodhpur.

1971. District Census Handbook, Jodhpur District. COI 1971, Series 18, Parts XA & XB.

1981a. District Census Handbook, Jodhpur. COI 1981, Series 18, Rajasthan, Parts XIII-A &B.

1981b. Census of India 1981: Instructions to Enumerators for Filling up the Household Schedule and Individual Slip. Office of the Registrar General & Census Commissioner for India, Ministry of Home Affairs, New Delhi.

1981c. Primary Census Abstract, General population. COI 1981, Series -1, India Part II B (i).

Census of Marwar

1911. Census of Marwar State, 1911. Part 1: Report. Phiroze R. Kothawala. Jodhpur, 1916.

1931a. Census Marwar State, 1931. Village Directory. Jodhpur, 1934.

1931b. Census Marwar State, 1931. Village Table. Jodhpur, 1932.

1941. Census of Marwar State, 1941. Village Directory. Udey Raj Mathur. Jodhpur, 1944.

(b) General References

Agrawal, Arun. 1993. Mobility and cooperation among nomadic shepherds: the case of the *Raikas*. I. *Human Ecology* 21(3).

Agrawal, Arun. 1994. Mobility and control among nomadic shepherds: the case of the *Raikas*. II. *Human Ecology* 22(2):131-144.

Bibliography

Agarwal, B.D. 1979. *Rajasthan District Gazetteers: Jodhpur.* Jaipur: Directorate of District Gazetteers, Government of Rajasthan.

Aggarwal, Partap C. 1971. *Caste, Religion and Power: An Indian Case Study.* New Delhi: Shri Ram Centre for Industrial Relations.

Alexander, Paul. 1984. Women, labour and fertility: population growth in colonial Java. *Mankind* 14(5):361-372.

Allchin, Bridget; Andrew Goudie and Karunarkara Hegde. 1978. *The Prehistory and Palaeogeography of the Great Indian Desert.* London: Academic Press.

Appadurai, Arjun. 1984. How moral is South Asia's economy? - A review article. *Journal of Asian Studies* 43(3):481-497.

Athreya, Venkatesh B., Gustav Böklin, Göran Djurfeldt and Staffan Lindberg. 1986. Economies of scale or advantages of class? Some results from a south India farm economy study. Review of Agriculture Supplement, *Economic and Political Weekly* 21(13):A2-A14.

Bahadur, K.P. (ed.). 1978. *Caste, Tribes & Culture of Rajputs.* (Revised version of work of A.H. Bingley.) Delhi: Ess Ess Publications.

Baier, Stephen and Paul E. Lovejoy. 1977. The Tuareg of the Central Sudan: gradations in servility at the desert edge (Niger and Nigeria). In Suzanne Miers and Igor Kopytoff (eds) *Slavery in Africa: Historical and Anthropological Perspectives.* Madison: University of Wisconsin Press.

Bapna, S.L. 1976. Slow increase in production of coarse cereals - the case of *bajra*. In S.L. Bapna and B.R. Murty *Bajra Production: Problems and Prospects.* Indian Council of Social Science Research, Studies in Agriculture, 1. Bombay etc: Allied Publishers Private Ltd.

Beteille, Andre. 1972. The study of agrarian systems: an anthropological approach. *Man in India* 52:150-173.

Bhandari, M.M. 1977. Famine-foods of the Rajasthan Desert. In M.L. Roonwal (ed.) *The Natural Resources of Rajasthan,* Vol 1. Jodhpur: University of Jodhpur.

Bharara, L.P. 1980. Socio-economic consequences of drought in an arid tract - a case study. In H.S. Mann (ed.) *Arid Zone Research and Development.* Jodhpur: Scientific Publishers.

Bharara, L.P. 1982. Notes on the experience of drought: perception, recollection and prediction. In Brian Spooner and H.S. Mann (eds) *Desertification and Development: Dryland Ecology in Social Perspective.* London: Academic Press.

Bharara, L.P. 1985Impact of irrigation on the socio-economic changes in arid zone of Rajasthan. In Hoshiar Singh (ed) *Rural Development in India: Evaluation Studies in Policies and Programmes.* Jaipur: Printwell Publishers.

Bharara, L.P. 1993. Indian pastoral communities following livestock migration as a drought adjustment strategy. *J. Anthropological Survey of India* 42:30-54.

Bharucha, F.R. 1955. Afganistan, India and Pakistan. *In Plant Ecology: Reviews of Research.* Arid Zone Research, 6. Paris: UNESCO.

Bhati, N.S. 1979. Historian of the soil - Mohnot Nainsi. In N.S. Bhati (ed.) *Studies in Marwar History.* Jodhpur: Rajasthani Shodh Sansthan Chopasni.

Blunt, E.A.H. 1931. *The Caste System of Northern India.* London: H. Milford, Oxford University Press.

Bose, A.B., S.P. Malhotra and Laj Paul Bharara. 1963. Socio-economic differences in dispersed dwelling and compact settlement types in arid regions. *Man in India* 43:119-130.

Bose, A.B. and P.C. Saxena. 1965. Some characteristics of nuclear households. *Man in India* 45:195-200.

Bose, A.B. and P.C. Saxena. 1966. Opinion leaders in a village in western Rajasthan. *Man in India* 46:121-130.

Boserup, Ester. 1965. *The Conditions of Agricultural Growth: The Economics of Agrarian Change Under Population Pressure.* New York: Aldine Atterton.

Bronson, Bennett. 1972. Farm labour and the evolution of food production. In Brian Spooner (ed.) *Population Growth: Anthropological Implications.* Cambridge and London: M.I.T. Press.

Bryson, Reid A. and David A. Baerreis. 1967. Possibilities of major climatic modification and their implications: Northwest India, a case for study. *Bulletin of American Meteorological Society* 48(2):136-142.

Carstairs, G. Morris. 1957. *The Twice-born: A Study of a Community of High Caste Hindus.* London: Hogarth Press.

Carstairs, G. Morris. 1983. *Death of a Witch: A Village in North India 1950-1981.* London: Hutchinson.

CAZRI. 1983. Outlines of the technologies for reconstruction of the arid zone. *Technical Bulletin* No 7. Jodhpur: Central Arid Zone Research Institute.

Chakravarti, Anand. 1975. *Contradiction and Change: Emerging Patterns of Authority in a Rajasthan Village.* Delhi: Oxford University Press.

Chand, Shyam B. 1947. Settlement Report, Hinganiya. Unpublished report in Collectorate, Jodhpur.

Chauhan, Brij Raj. 1967. *A Rajasthan Village.* New Delhi: Vir Publishing House.

Collector's Office, Jodhpur. n.d. Extract of annexure to report 'Identification of the drought prone areas in the Jodhpur district.' No details provided.

Copland, Ian. 1983. Review of *Subject to Famine* (Michelle Burge McAlpin). *South Asia* 6(1):67-69.

Dahl, Gudrun and Anders Hjort. 1976. *Having Herds. Pastoral Herd Growth and Household Economy.* Stockholm Studies in Social Anthropology, 2.

Dhir, R.P. 1982. The human factor in ecological history. In Brian Spooner and H.S. Mann (eds) *Desertification and Development: Dryland Ecology in Social Perspective.* London: Academic Press.

Doshi, S.L. 1971. *Bhils: Between Societal Self-awareness and Cultural Sythesis.* New Delhi: Sterling Publishers.

D'Souza, Victor S. 1986. Does economic development necessarily lead to a decline in population? Some contrary evidence. *Journal of Sociological Studies* 5:77-94.

Dumont, Louis. 1970. *Homo Hierarchicus.* London: Weidenfield and Nicolson.

Dutt, Romesh. 1902-1904. *The Economic History of India.* (2 Vols). London: Kegan Paul, Trench, Trubner.

Dwyer, Peter D. 1985. Review of 1984 edition of *Pigs for the Ancestors* (Rappaport). *Oceania* 56(2):151-154.

Elder, Joseph W. 1977. Rural landed rights and becoming 'Twice-Born': some interrelations between India's sacred and secular hierarchies. In Robert Eric Frykenberg (ed.) *Land Tenure and Peasant in South Asia.* New Delhi: Orient Longman.

Erdman, Joan L. 1985. *Patrons and Performers in Rajasthan: The Subtle Tradition.* Delhi: Chanakya Publications.

Erskine, K.D. 1909. *The Western Rajputana States Residency and the Bikaner Agency.* Rajputana Gazetteers, Vol III-A. Allahabad.

Evans-Pritchard, E.E. 1940. *The Nuer.* Oxford: Clarendon Press.

Fagan, P.J. 1893. *Gazetteer of the Hisar District 1892.* Lahore.

Fisher, R.J. 1981. Nomadic groups in the caste system. *Man in India* 61(1):55-66.

Fox, James J. 1977. *Harvest of the Palm: Ecological Change in Eastern Indonesia.* Cambridge (Massachusetts) and London: Harvard University Press.

Geertz, Clifford. 1963. *Agricultural Involution: The Process of Ecological Change in Indonesia.* Berkeley: University of California Press.

Geertz, Clifford. 1973. Comments on Benjamin White's 'Demand for Labour and Population Growth in Colonial Java'. *Human Ecology* 1:237-239.

Ghose, Bimal; Surendra Singh and Amal Kar. 1977. Desertification around the Thar - a geomorphological interpretation. *Annals of Arid Zone* 16(3):290-301.

Gold, Ann Grodzins. 1988. *Fruitful Journeys: The Ways of Rajasthani Pilgrims.* Berkeley/Los Angeles/London: University of California Press.

Goldman, Michael. 1989. Cultivating hot peppers and water crisis in India's desert. In Ken Dyer and John Young (eds) *Changing Directions: The Proceedings of the Conference 'Ecopolitics IV', Adelaide University 21-24 September 1989.* Adelaide: Graduate Centre for Environmental Studies, University of Adelaide.

Government of Jodhpur. 1938. *Report on the Administration of the Jodhpur State for the Year 1935-36.* Administrative Reports Vol 48, Jodhpur.

Gupta, C.S. 1965. *Mukam: A Village Survey.* Census of India, 1961, Vol XIV, Rajasthan. Part VI-A, Village Survey No. 4.

Gupta, Giri Raj. 1974. *Marriage, Religion and Society: Patterns of Change in an Indian Village.* Delhi: Vikas.

Haaland, Gunnar. 1991. The ecology of choice and symbol. In Reidar Gronhaug, Gunnar Haaland and Georg Henriksen (eds) *The Ecology of Choice and Symbol: Essays in Honour of Fredrik Barth.* Bergen: Alma Mater Forlag AS.

Harcourt, Max. 1986. India: from stable underdevelopment to turbulent growth. In *Third World Update: Indonesia, The Philippines, India, Nicaragua.* Sydney: School of History, University of New South Wales.

Harris, Marvin. 1979. *Cultural Materialism: The Struggle for a Science of Culture.* New York: Random House.

Hayden, Robert M. 1979. The cultural ecology of service nomads. *Eastern Anthropologist* 32:297-309.

Hill, Polly. 1982. *Dry Grain Farming Families: Hausaland (Nigeria) and Karnataka (India) Compared.* Cambridge: Cambridge University Press.

Hill, Polly. 1984. The poor quality of official socio-economic statistics relating to the rural tropical world: with special reference to South India. *Modern Asian Studies* 18(3):491-514.

Hill, Polly. 1986. *Developmental Economics on Trial: The Anthropological Case for a Prosecution.* Cambridge: Cambridge University Press.

Hitchcock, John T. 1959. The idea of the martial Rajput. In Milton Singer (ed.) *Traditional India: Structure and Change.* Philadelphia: The American Folklore Society.

Jodha, N.S. 1975. Famine and famine policies: some empirical evidence. *Economic and Political Weekly* 10(41):1609-1623.

Jodha, N.S. 1977. Land-tenure problems and policies in the arid regions of Rajasthan. In P.L. Jaiswal (ed.) *Desertification and Its Control.* New Delhi: Indian Council of Agricultural Research.

Jodha, N.S. 1980. The operating mechanism of desertification and choice of interventions. In H.S. Mann (ed.) *Arid Zone Research and Development.* Jodhpur: Scientific Publishers.

Jodha, N.S. 1985. Population growth and the decline of common property resources in Rajasthan, India. *Population and Development Review* 11(2):247-264.

Jodha, N.S. 1987. A case study of the degradation of common property resources in India. In Piers Blaikie and Harold Brookfield (eds) *Land Degradation and Society.* London and New York: Methuen.

Jodha, N.S. and V.S. Vyas. 1969. *Conditions of Stability and Growth in Arid Agriculture.* Vallabh Vidyanagar: Agro-Economic Research Centre, Sardar Patel University.

Kachhawaha, O.P. 1980. A famine in Rajasthan (1868-69). In G.L. Devra (ed.) *Some Aspects of Socio-economic History of Rajasthan.* Jodhpur: Rajasthan Sahitya Mandir.

Kachhawaha, O.P. 1985. *Famines in Rajasthan (1900 AD - 1947 AD).* Jodhpur: Hindi Sahitya Mandir.

Kamal, K.L. 1984. Land reforms in Rajasthan - myth and reality. In Ram Pande (ed.) *Land Reforms and Social Change.* Jaipur: Shodhak.

Kaul, R.N. and D.C.P. Thalen. 1979. South-west Asia. In D.W. Goodall and R.A. Perry (eds) *Arid-land Ecosystems: Structure, Functioning and Management,* Vol 1. International Biological Program, 16. Cambridge: Cambridge University Press.

Keenan, Jeremy. 1977. *The Tuareg: People of Ahaggar.* London: Allen Lane.

Kennedy, John G. and Robert B. Edgerton (eds). 1982. *Culture and Ecology: Eclectic Perspectives.* Washington: American Anthropological Association, Special Publication No. 15.

Khanna, S.N. 1983. Greening the desert. *Illustrated Weekly of India,* May 22.

Köhler-Rollefson, Ilse. 1992. The Raika dromedary breeders of Rajasthan: a pastoral system in crisis. *Nomadic Peoples* 30:74-83.

Kolarkar, A.S.; J.S. Choudhari and R.P. Dhir. 1981. Effects of July 1979 floods on soils of arid Rajasthan: 1. Soil fertility status and other characteristics. *Annals of Arid Zone* 20(2):155-161.

Kolenda, Pauline. 1978. Sibling-set marriage, collateral-set marriage, and deflected alliance among Annana Jats of Jaipur District, Rajasthan. In Sylvia Vatuk (ed.) *American Studies in the Anthropology of India.* New Delhi: Manohar Publications.

Kothawalla, Phiroze R. 1939. *Famine Programme Report Jodhpur Government.* Jodhpur.

Krishnan, A.; Y.S. Rama Krishna and G.G.S.N. Rao. 1980. Is the incidence of droughts increasing in the arid zone of north-west India. In H.S. Mann (ed.) *Arid Zone Research and Development.* Jodhpur: Scientific Publishers.

Le Houerou, H.N. 1970. North Africa: past, present, future. In Harold E. Dregne (ed.) *Arid Lands in Transition.* Washington: American Association for the Advancement of Science.

Lodrick, Deryck O. 1984. A cattle fair in Rajasthan: the Kharwa *Mela. Current Anthropology* 25(2):218-225.

Maclachlan, Morgan D. 1983. *Why They Did Not Starve: Biocultural Adaptation in a South Indian Village.* Philadelphia: Institute for the Study of Human issues.

Maclagan, E.D. 1892. The Punjab and its feudatories. Part 1. *Report on the Census.* Census of India, 1891, Vol XIX.

Malhotra, S.P. 1977. Socio-demographic factors and nomadism in arid zone. In P.L. Jaiswal (ed.) *Desertification and Its Control.* New Delhi: Indian Council of Agricultural Research.

Malhotra, S.P. 1986. *Bishnois* - their role in conservation of desert eco-system. In K.A. Shankarnarayan and Vinod Shankar (eds) *Desert Environment: Conservation and Management.* CAZRI Publication No 26. Jodhpur: Central Arid Zone Research Institute.

Malhotra, S.P. and D.K. Saha. 1985. Population characteristics and its control in arid zone of Rajasthan. Paper presented at seminar on *India's Population Policy: Critical Issues for Future*, 16-18 November, 1985, University of Jodhpur.

Malhotra, S.P. and H.S. Trivedi. 1981. Child population and attitudes towards children in an arid village. *Man in India* 61(4):356-367.

Mann, H.S., S.P. Malhotra and Jagdeesh C. Kalla. 1974. Desert spread: A quantitative analysis in the arid zone of Rajasthan. *Annals of Arid Zone* 13:103-113.

Mauss, Marcel (in collaboration with Henri Beuchat). 1979. *Seasonal Variations of the Eskimo: A Study in Social Morphology.* Translated, with a Foreword, by James J. Fox. London: Routledge and Kegan Paul.

McAlpin, Michelle Burge. 1983. *Subject to Famine: Food Crises and Economic Change in Western India, 1860-1920.* Princeton: Princeton University Press.

McGinnies, W.G. 1979. General description of desert areas. In D.W. Goodall and R.A. Perry (eds) *Arid-land Ecosystems: Structure, Functioning and Management*, Vol 1. International Biological Program, 16. Cambridge: Cambridge University Press.

Mehta, B.C. 1980. *Rural Exploitation in Rajasthan: A Socio-economic Study.* Report of project sponsored by the Indian Council of Social Science Research. Jaipur: Kumarappa Institute of Gram Swaraj. (B.C. Mehta Project Director.)

Mehta, B.C. 1984. Demographic profile of Rajasthan. *Journal of Sociological Studies* (Jodhpur) 3:43-58.

Meigs, P. 1953. World distribution of arid and semi-arid homoclimates. In *Reviews of Research on Arid Zone Hydrology*, 1. Paris: UNESCO.

Misra, Promode Kumar. 1969. Nomadism in India. *Journal of the Indian Anthropological Society* 4:79-87.

Misra, Promode Kumar. 1977. *The Nomadic Gadulia Lohar of Eastern Rajasthan.* Calcutta: Anthropological Survey of India (Memoir No. 41).

Morris, Morris David. 1975. Needed: a new famine policy. *Economic and Political Weekly* 10(5-7):283-294.

Morrison, Jennifer. 1985. The Bishnoi: Rajasthan's guardians of life. *Simply Living* 2(7):43-47.

Murty, B.R. 1976. Technological aspects of increasing bajra production. In S.L. Bapna and B.R. Murty *Bajra Production: Problems and Prospects.* Indian Council of Social Science Research, Studies in Agriculture, 1. Bombay etc: Allied Publishers Private Ltd.

Nainsi, Muhnot. 1968-1974. *Marwar ra Pargana ri Vigat.* (Edited by Narayan Singh Bhati.) Jodhpur: Rajasthan Oriental Research Institute. Three vols: Vol 1 (1968), Vol 2 (1969), Vol 3 (1974).

Orlove, Benjamin S. 1980. Ecological anthropology. *Annual Review of Anthropology* 9:235-73.

Pacey, Arnold (with Adrian Cullis). 1986. *Rainwater Harvesting: The Collection of Rainfall and Run-off in Rural Areas.* London: Intermediate Technology Publications.

Paul, Kim. 1992. Constituting Charan: an ethnographic account of the Maru Charans of Jodhpur. PhD thesis, University of Sydney.

Pisharoty, P.R. 1980. Semi-arid and arid areas of Rajasthan - a physicist's view. In H.S. Mann (ed.) *Arid Zone Research and Development.* Jodhpur: Scientific Publishers.

Prakash, Ishwar. 1964. Taxonomical and ecological account of the mammals of Rajasthan Desert. *Annals of Arid Zone* 2(2):150-161.

Prakash, Ishwar. 1977. *The Amazing Life in the Indian Desert.* CAZRI Monograph No 6. Jodhpur: Central Arid Zone Research Institute.

Purohit, M.L. 1978. Land ownership patterns and desertification in western Rajasthan. *Annals of Arid Zone* 17(1):112-118.

Rappaport, Roy A. 1968. *Pigs for the Ancestors: Ritual in the Ecology of a New Guinea People.* New Haven: Yale University Press.

Resident, Western Rajputana States. 1893. Report from the Resident Western Rajputana States to the First Assistant Agent to the Governor-General Rajputana. Abu 24th April, 1893. Published in *Report on the Relief Operations in the Native States of Marwar, Jaisalmer, Bikanir and Kishengarh in Rajputana During the Scarcity of 1891-1892.* Bombay: Examiner Press (No date of printing).

Richards,Paul. 1986. *Coping with Hunger: Hazard and Experiment in an African Rice-farming System.* The London Research Series in Geography, 11. London, Boston, Sydney: Allen and Unwin.

Robinson, P.J. 1985. The role of forestry in farming systems with particular reference to forest-grazing interactions. PhD Thesis, University of Edinburgh.

Rose, H.A. 1911. *A Glossary of the Tribes and Castes of the Punjab and North-West Frontier Province.* Vol II. Lahore.

Rosin, Robert Thomas. 1968. Changing land tenure and village polity in Rajasthan, India: an interactional perspective. PhD Thesis, University of California, Berkeley (Anthropology). [University Microfilms Ann Arbor, Michigan]

Rosin, Robert Thomas. 1978. Peasant adaptation as process in land reform: a case study. In Sylvia Vatuk (ed.) *American Studies in the Anthropology of India.* New Delhi: Manohar Publications.

Rosin, Robert Thomas. 1981. Land reform in Rajasthan. *Current Anthropology* 22(1):75-76.

Rosin, Robert Thomas. 1993. The tradition of groundwater irrigation in northwestern India. *Human Ecology* 21(1):51-86.

Ruhela, Satya Pal. 1968. *The Gaduliya Lohars of Rajasthan: A Study in the Sociology of Nomadism.* New Delhi: Impex India.

Ruthenberg, Hans. 1980. *Farming Systems in the Tropics.* Third Edition. Oxford: Clarendon Press.

Salzman, Philip Carl. 1986. Shrinking pasture for Rajasthani pastoralists. *Nomadic Peoples* 20:49-61.

Scott, James C. 1976. *The Moral Economy of the Peasant: Rebellion and Subsistence in Southeast Asia.* New Haven and London: Yale University Press.

Sen, Amal Kumar and H.S. Mann. 1977. A geographical appraisal of the expansion and deterioration of the Indian Desert. *Annals of Arid Zone* 16(3):281-289.

Sen, Amartya. 1982. *Poverty and Famines: An Essay on Entitlement and Deprivation.* Oxford: Clarendon Press.

Sen, Amartya. 1988. Hunger and entitlements - research for action. *Frontline* 5(6):32-40 & 5(7):48-53.

Sen, David N. 1982. *Environment and Plant Life in Indian Desert.* Jodhpur: Geobios International.

Shah, P.G. 1959. The Naikas - Naikdas. *Journal of the Gujarat Research Society* 21:123-168;228-263.

Shankarnarayan, K.A.; L.N. Harsh and S. Kathju. 1987. Agroforestry in the arid zones of India. *Agroforestry Systems* 5:69-88.

Sharma, G.D. 1977. Rajput Polity: *A Study of Politics and Administration of the State of Marwar, 1638-1749.* New Delhi: Manohar.

Sharma, K.L. 1970. Changing class stratification in rural Rajasthan. *Man in India* 50:257-268.

Sharma, R.C. 1972. *Settlement Geography of the Indian Desert.* Hauz Khas, New Delhi: Kumar Brothers.

Sherring, M.A. 1974. *Hindu Tribes and Castes,* Vol 1. Delhi: Cosmo Publications.

Singh, Madho. 1943. *Famine Report 1939-40.* Jodhpur.

Singh, Sardar. 1896. *The Lessons I Received and My Pali Tour Diary.* Allahabad: The Pioneer Press.

Singh, Surendra and Bimal Ghose. 1980. Geomorphic significance in the environmental problems of the Rajasthan Desert, India. In H.S. Mann (ed.) *Arid Zone Research and Development.* Jodhpur: Scientific Publishers.

Smith, John D. 1986. Where the plot thickens: epic moments in Pabuji. *South Asian Studies* 2:53-64.

Sopher, David. 1975. Indian pastoral castes and livestock ecologies: a geographic analysis. In L.S. Leshnik and G. Sontheimer (eds) *Pastoralists and Nomads in South Asia.* Wiesbaden: Otto Harrassowitz.

Srinivas, M.N. 1975. Village studies, participant observation and social science research in India. *Economic and Political Weekly* 10(33-35):1387-1397.

Srivastava, Vinay Kumar. 1991. Who are the Raikas/Rabaris? *Man in India* 71(1):279-304.

Tewari, Anil Kumar. 1980. *Human Fertility Behaviour in the Desert Margin.* Jaipur: Books and Periodicals Co.

Thornwaite, C.W. 1948. An approach toward a rational classification of climate. *Geographical Review* 38:55-94.

Timberg, Thomas A. 1978. *The Marwaris: From Traders to Industrialists.* New Delhi: Vikas.

Tod, James. 1984. *Annals and Antiquities of Rajasthan, or the Central and Western Rajpoot States of India.* (2 Vols.) Calcutta: S.K. Lahiri. (First published 1829-1832)

Upadhyaya, Nirmala M. 1973. *The Administration of Jodhpur State (1800-1947 A.D.).* Jodhpur: International Publishers.

Vincze, Lajos. 1980. Peasant animal husbandry: a dialectic model of techno-environmental integration in agro-pastoral societies. *Ethnology* 19:387-403.

Wadia, D.N. 1960. *The Post-Glacial Dessication of Central Asia.* New Delhi: National institute of Sciences of India.

Walter, Major. n.d. *Report on the Political Administration of the Rajputana States, 1875-1876.* Cited in Gupta, 1965. No further details provided.

Wheeler, R.E.M. 1950. *Five Thousand Years of Pakistan.* London: Royal India and Pakistan Society.

White, Benjamin. 1973. Demand for labor and population growth in colonial Java. *Human Ecology* 1:217-236.